'In many nations throughout the world, educational between more local autonomy and centralized m detailed and nuanced way, *Inside the Autonomous S* happens when well-intentioned reforms are subv managerialism. At the same time, Salokangas and Ainscow provide us with clear lessons on what needs to be done to defend substantive autonomy in policy and practice.'

Professor Michael W. Apple, University of Wisconsin, USA, and author of *Can Education Change Society?*

'This book is a must for those thinking seriously about education. It maps the international trend of independent state-funded schooling, while also carefully reflecting on national distinctions. Salokangas and Ainscow dissect the contradictions characterising 'autonomous' schooling policies, illuminating these via the in-depth case of an English secondary school. The insightful result exemplifies how these policy tensions impact practice on the ground, constraining innovation and agency. Building on their analysis of the global and the local, Salokangas and Ainscow offer powerful ideas for sustainable educational change.'

Professor Becky Francis,
UCL Institute of Education, UK.

'*Inside the Autonomous School* follows an English school over an extended period of time to lay bare fundamental tensions in twenty-first century global education policy. In a field of policy littered with hyperbole, they subject superficial exhortations of "autonomy" and "innovation" to a serious empirical examination. That which is described as an innovative drive for greater autonomy is conducted within interlocking boundaries which thwart teachers' attempts towards creative engagement with diverse communities. I have no doubt that education policy-makers will seek out this important book. Hopefully, they will also heed its instruction to reconsider what is to be valued and measured in education, and how to support schools to that end.'

Professor Roger Slee,
University of South Australia, Australia.

INSIDE THE
AUTONOMOUS SCHOOL

Over recent years, education systems across the globe have experimented with the concept of the *autonomous* school. This takes a variety of forms and the schools involved have different titles, such as charter schools in the USA, academies in England, free schools in Sweden and independent public schools in Australia. As this radical trend in policy gains momentum, *Inside the Autonomous School* considers whether the model is achieving its desired aims.

Drawing on evidence from an in-depth, longitudinal study of an academy located in an urban district in England, this book traces the various developments which took place in the school on its journey from 'failing', to achieving an inspection rating of 'outstanding'. The authors present a rich, first-hand account of the impacts that various policies and practices have had on the autonomous school and at the same time, situate their accounts and analyses within a wider national and international context. This leads them to consider what can be done to ensure that school autonomy consistently promotes excellence and equity within education systems.

A fascinating read and invaluable resource for practitioners, researchers and policy makers in the field of education, *Inside the Autonomous School* sheds much needed light on an increasingly established policy which is set to have far-reaching effects.

Maija Salokangas is Assistant Professor in the School of Education at Trinity College Dublin, Ireland.

Mel Ainscow is Professor of Education and Co-director of the Centre for Equity in Education at the University of Manchester, UK.

INSIDE THE AUTONOMOUS SCHOOL

Making Sense of a Global Educational Trend

Maija Salokangas and Mel Ainscow

Routledge
Taylor & Francis Group

LONDON AND NEW YORK

First published 2018
by Routledge
2 Park Square, Milton Park, Abingdon, Oxon OX14 4RN

and by Routledge
711 Third Avenue, New York, NY 10017

Routledge is an imprint of the Taylor & Francis Group, an informa business

British Library Cataloguing-in-Publication Data
A catalogue record for this book is available from the British Library

Library of Congress Cataloging-in-Publication Data
A catalog record for this book has been requested

ISBN: 978-1-138-21540-5 (hbk)
ISBN: 978-1-138-21541-2 (pbk)
ISBN: 978-1-315-44408-6 (ebk)

Typeset in Bembo
by Keystroke, Neville Lodge, Tettenhall, Wolverhampton

CONTENTS

FIGURES

FOREWORD

Through the decades, education has been characterised by conflicts over who should control our schools. During the recent past, education systems across the globe have experimented with *autonomous* schools, where traditional education bureaucracies have been flattened and decision making devolved to local school communities: England has its academies (independent state-funded schools); there are charter schools in the United States; independent public schools in Australia; and free schools in Sweden. Policy goals of autonomous schools are strikingly similar across national contexts. The theory of action argues that if control over the budget, personnel and the education program are vested in the local community – teachers, school leaders and parents who are closest to students – then decisions will better address students' needs and their performance will rise.

At the same time, countries around the world have been engaged in *standards-based reform*, which enforces the authority of centralised governments to determine uniform learning goals for local schools. Many countries now operate public schools under a single national curriculum; the United States' version, the Common Core State Standards, reflects the country's limited federal role in education. While attention has been paid separately to the implementation of these two seemingly contradictory reforms, this volume is one of the few that paints a picture of how an autonomous school fares in an education system operating under a centralised curriculum.

Maija Salokangas from Trinity College in Dublin, Ireland and her colleague Mel Ainscow from Manchester University in England, take on the subject of autonomous schools and offer a longitudinal case study of Parkside Academy, an under-performing English secondary school, in a low-income, high-minority neighbourhood. One author's involvement was as a participant observer working as an occasional consultant. The other author carried out ethnographic research in the school over a one-year period, from September 2011–2012. The evidence the authors present is a rich account from the inside, through the eyes of teachers and school leaders, as the school matures into a successful, high-performing academy. By the end of the story, centralisation has won out over decentralisation and Parkside loses its grip on success.

At the start of the book, the authors lay the foundation for the story of Parkside by introducing the concept of autonomous schools from an international perspective – what do autonomous schools look like around the globe? A unique feature of this book is its frequent crisscrossing among local, national and global contexts. As the story unfolds, the autonomy initially enjoyed by Parkside as an independent state-funded school is usurped by the centralised government which mandates a national curriculum, along with student performance assessments. Closer to home, the charitable trust which sponsors Parkside responds to pressures from the national government by clamping down on Parkside's autonomy; the alignment between what the central government mandated and what the sponsor advocated became one and the same. Lesson plans, typically the purview of classroom teachers, were heavily influenced by the sponsor's interpretation of the central government's national curriculum.

As a scholar, my academic interests are grounded in alternative ways of governing public schools, including site-based managed (SBM) schools and charter schools in the USA. My work focuses on questions about autonomy – which areas of decision making ought to have relatively high or relatively low levels of autonomy? The issue of accountability – for what and to whom – is also a major emphasis in my work. In *Inside the Autonomous School*, Ainscow and Salokangas set out to contribute new knowledge about the conditions under which these two levers – autonomy and accountability – can and cannot work in concert to improve school performance.

One of the book's most important contributions is its detailed account of policies and practices in action. There is limited evidence regarding what is happening within autonomous schools in relation to decision making and accountability, and the extent to which the reforms are leading to improved student outcomes.

The story of the rise and fall of Parkside rests on the goals set for the school, both locally and nationally. Key among England's goals related to governance and accountability is the unique role of sponsoring organisations or patrons of autonomous schools or academy chains. No such entity exists in the US and while sponsors may be religious organisations, businesses or voluntary organisations, US charter schools fancy themselves as democratic organisations that empower parents with high levels of autonomy and accountability. Indeed, over 30% of charter school laws mention parent involvement as a goal.

In view of governance arrangements in England, Parkside's evolution was largely steered by its sponsor and was closely aligned with the standards set forth in the national curriculum. What is learned from the story of Parkside was that forces external to this autonomous school, namely the charitable trust (academy chain) and the national government, exerted the most control over accountability. As Salokangas and Ainscow explain, decisions about what school leaders and teachers should know and be able to do and what was taught were decided by others outside of the local community and what the school did and did not do was the result of these external pressures and demands and not necessarily the result of the local community's preferences.

In the US, the Common Core State Standards and its accompanying assessments also have eaten away at localism. However, the extreme centralisation exhibited in England's autonomous schools seems to have been mitigated to some extent. Pedagogy (how teachers teach and how students learn) and professional development continue to be largely under the purview of the US charter schools. One explanation for this outcome may lie in the role of parents.

In the US, we typically see a large role for parents within autonomous schools. Parent involvement or engagement is often mentioned in school mission statements and many charters are founded by parents and feature strong parent involvement in decision making. While both England and the US argue that parental choice influences the marketplace of schools in decentralised systems, little evidence of this is provided in the book. Did Parkside parents complain that teachers did not differentiate instruction according to students' needs? Did dissatisfied parents leave Parkside and switch to other schools? We learn little about how parents viewed the evolution of Parkside and its single-minded goal of raising test scores to improve inspection ratings. Had Parkside operated differently and included parents in decision making, the fate of the academy might have been different. As the authors conclude, 'on reflection, we recognise that it is major limitation of our work that their [parents'] voices are not heard in this book'.

The research presented in this volume is clearly written, colourful and comprehensible. *Inside the Autonomous School* serves a broad audience – practitioners and the general public – that follows education issues. It also offers valuable guidance for policy makers interested in the appropriate balance between mandates – reforms controlled centrally where uniformity is the goal – and other education reforms designed locally for local constituents, but does not presume to recommend what decisions should be made and for whom. I know I will find this book an invaluable resource as an academic pondering the question of how autonomous schools can maintain their localism and autonomy while situated in a centralised education system.

> Priscilla Wohlstetter Ph.D.
> Distinguished Research Professor
> Teachers College
> Columbia University
> New York, USA

PREFACE

The story is told of an education administrator who said he was looking for a 'one-handed researcher'. When questioned he explained that his experience was that researchers tended to respond to his requests for advice by saying, 'well, on the one hand, but on the other hand'.

In writing this book we have tried to offer a balanced view, although our own position is barely concealed. It seems to us that this is inevitable when focusing on an agenda that is so vital to people's lives. In this respect, our two perspectives and very different life experiences – a Finnish teacher turned academic, with experiences of schools in different countries, and a British practitioner, also turned academic, with extensive international experience – have proved to be important resources as we have debated the implications of our interpretations of the evidence we have accumulated.

At the heart of the book is our account of developments in one school over a period of more than ten years. In this sense, the book follows a well-established tradition of in-depth studies of individual cases. However, it is important to stress that the book is not about the school. Rather, it is about a radical policy trend that is gaining momentum at a remarkable pace across the world.

Looking at what this policy trend means to those most closely involved helps to throw light on the social and political complexities that shape its thinking as it plays out in particular ways in particular contexts. It also helps us to appreciate how the efforts of committed individuals are influenced, limited and, sometimes, distorted by these complexities.

Bearing all of this in mind, we want to pay tribute to the many men and women who dedicate their lives to helping children and young people from disadvantaged backgrounds to have better life chances. For us, such teachers are the most important policy makers upon which educational reforms should be based. Our hope is that those who read this book will recognise the importance of this argument. In this way, we argue for the creation of contexts in which teachers have the space, freedom and encouragement to work together, and with other stakeholders, to find better ways of educating the citizens of tomorrow.

The nature of the analysis we provide means that we have benefitted from the views of many people we cannot name, some of who may disagree with certain of the interpretations we make of their experiences. We hope that our respect for their efforts comes through as readers engage with the text.

There are, however, some advisers and supporters whose names we do want to mention. In particular, we must thank our colleagues Alan Dyson, Jaakko Kauko and Wieland Wermke, who read an earlier draft of the book and offered detailed comments and suggestions that proved to be influential. Other colleagues at Trinity College Dublin, the University of Manchester and in our wider network, have also been important influences, particularly (but in no particular order) Laura Seppälä, Ruth McGinity, James Duggan, Steven Courtney, Lou Harvey, Dom Egan, Harriet Rowley, Dani White, Eljee Javier, Ines Alves, James McAllister, Chris Chapman, Dave Hall, Helen Gunter, Kirstin Kerr, Sue Goldrick, Olwen McNamara, Andy Howes, Mel West, Ron Glatter, Dennis Beach, Michael Apple, Andrew Loxley, Paula Flynn and Gerry Harvey.

We would also like to thank our friends and family for endless support and encouragement. Maija's Finnish and Irish family, especially husband Ciaran O'Neill, have been there every step of the way. Mel has been fortunate to have the constant support, encouragement and challenge of Kiki Messiou.

Thanks, too, to Anna Clarkson at Routledge for her support and guidance on the production of the book. And, of course, we are especially grateful to Professor Priscilla Wohlstetter for providing such a stimulating foreword that locates our account within wider international developments.

Maija Salokangas and Mel Ainscow
March 2017

1

A GLOBAL TREND

As countries throughout the world seek to improve their national education systems there is an increasing emphasis on the idea of school autonomy. This takes a variety of forms and the schools involved have different titles, such as charter schools, academies, free schools and independent public schools. Implicit in these new types of schools is an assumption that greater autonomy will allow space for the development of organisational arrangements, practices and forms of management and leadership that will be more effective in promoting the learning of all of their students. Although the idea may sound simple, in this book we argue it is more problematic than the policy rhetoric may lead us to believe, and that a lack of clarity prevails in terms of what autonomy actually means in relation to these schools.

In thinking about this lack of clarity, the work of Caldwell (2016) is helpful. He suggests that 'autonomy', in the full sense of the word, is misleading, since a school in a system of public education can never be fully autonomous. Therefore, it is better to refer to a relatively high or relatively low level of autonomy, whilst being careful to specify the functions over which schools have secured more authority and responsibility. This suggests that a closer look is needed at those schools that are said to have become more autonomous, which is the purpose of this book.

Setting the agenda

We refer to the idea of publicly funded autonomous schools as being a global trend deliberately, as it has become apparent that the idea has gained momentum worldwide over the past two decades. Well-established autonomous school systems include the American charter schools, Swedish free schools and English academies. Independent public schools in Australia are a more recent example, and proposals have been put forward for establishing autonomous schools in systems as varied as Ireland, New Zealand, Norway and Spain.

This global policy trend is a matter of considerable debate and there are varied views as to the extent to which it is leading to the desired outcomes. In particular, there is a concern that the development of education systems based on autonomy, coupled with increased competition between schools and high-stakes accountability, will further disadvantage learners from low-income and minority families. Meanwhile, there is limited evidence regarding what is actually happening within these schools in relation to decision making about policies and practice, and the extent to which this is leading to improved educational outcomes and increased innovation. This lack of evidence arises, in part at least, because these developments are relatively recent. It is also the case that researchers have found it difficult to get access to the schools in ways that would allow them to dig deeper into what goes on because of the intensive political pressures that are often associated with their existence.

This book begins the process of filling this vacuum, using evidence from our longitudinal study of one independent state-funded school, a sponsored academy we call 'Parkside' that serves an urban community in England. Taking advantage of a unique opportunity to experience life in this school from the inside, we examine how it evolved from being seen as failing to become one judged as outstanding by the national inspection agency. In so doing, we focus specifically on the themes of autonomy and innovation.

As the school was seen as something of a 'flagship' of one of the larger academy groups (known as 'chains' or, more recently, multi-academy trusts) operating in England, a significant focus of our interest was on its relationship with the sponsoring organisation. Linking our analysis to research carried out in other parts of the world, we consider the potential and risks associated with this policy reform. As such, throughout the book we traverse between local, national and global developments. In so doing, we demonstrate what these developments look like for people implementing and negotiating them at the grass roots.

The analysis we present in the book is guided by the following questions:

- What does autonomy mean for those involved in independent state-funded schools?
- To what extent have these schools delivered on their promises?
- What does this mean for thinking and practice in the field?

With this overall agenda in mind, this introductory chapter sets the scene for our account of developments at Parkside Academy (it should be noted that this is not the real name of the school), locating this in relation to international evidence regarding what have been called, generically, 'independent state schools' or, sometimes, 'independent state-funded schools' (Meyland-Smith & Evans, 2009). We start, however, by examining the thinking behind this policy move.

Structural reforms

The autonomous school systems this book draws from are the American charter schools, English academies and Australian independent public schools. As such, we do not offer a comprehensive account of all school autonomy initiatives globally (as there are many more). Rather, we consider carefully selected systems which, together, offer an illustrative example of how international developments are used to justify national policy developments. Another reason for including these systems in this discussion is that they have all emerged in the English-speaking world: charter schools in the USA, in the early 1990s; English academies during the early 2000s; and the Australian independent public schools in the early 2010s. The fact that important documentation concerning these systems, including policy statements and research reports, are accessible in the English language also influenced our decision to focus on these examples.

In what follows, we provide a brief introduction to each of these different education systems. We will return to report the evolution of each system in greater detail in Chapter 8, where we discuss the extent to which they have delivered on their promises. In describing these systems, we take a chronological approach, starting from American charter schools. We then move on to academies in England and, finally, to independent public schools in Australia.

United States

Charter schools emerged during the early 1990s, with Minnesota being the first state passing a charter school law in 1991. Proposed originally in the late 1980s by Albert Shanker, the then president of the American Federation of Teachers, charter schools are arguably one of the earliest forms of independent state-funded schools (Kahlenberg & Potter, 2014). Shanker's idea was that charter schools would be publicly funded but independently managed. They would be given a charter for a set time to try out new approaches, which would only be renewed if they succeeded. The emphasis was to be on giving teachers a greater voice in school policy in order to find ways of improving the achievement of all students, particularly those from disadvantaged backgrounds. At the same time, the goal was to reduce segregation within the education system.

The schools are authorised to open once they have received a charter, which is a statutorily defined performance contract. The length of time for which charters are granted varies, but most are for three to five years. Although the charter school laws differ from state to state, resulting in a heterogeneous system, what underpins the policy is that these schools enjoy increased autonomy in comparison to district schools, are state-funded and can be managed by a variety of organisations, businesses, philanthropists or parental groups (Goldring & Mavrogordato, 2011).

A key defining feature of charter schools is the increased freedoms they are allowed in comparison to traditional public schools, including a degree of autonomy over student admissions, hiring teachers and their pay and conditions, as well as curriculum and teaching methods (Malloy & Wohlstetter, 2003; Buckley & Schneider, 2007). Charter schools are made accountable through the monitoring of student achievement, and there are frequent renewal processes of the charter (ibid). In justifying these reforms, it has been argued that autonomy, coupled with public accountability, will create fertile conditions for educational innovation and change (Wohlstetter et al., 1995; Lubienski, 2003).

Since their inception, charter schools have spread across United States and, to a much lesser degree, in parts of Canada. For the academic year 2014–2015, the National Alliance for Public Charter Schools (2016) listed 6,633 charter schools in their records, educating almost 2.7 million American students overall. They are aimed at addressing the achievement gap by improving educational outcomes for children in disadvantaged communities. In practice, charter schools serve a greater proportion of urban disadvantaged communities than more traditional district schools, educating more low-income, Black and Hispanic children than most traditional district schools (U.S. Department of Education, National Center for Education Statistics 2006). After almost three decades of their existence, the Management Organisations (MOs) running several charters have become powerful actors, educating over 1.1 million students. As a result, charter schools have spread across the country, and have become a distinctive branch of schools within the American educational system.

England

A major strand in the move towards school autonomy in England has been the rapid expansion of the academies programme. This involves schools being funded directly by national government, rather than through a local authority.[1] The foundations for academies were laid well before the programme was launched, during the period of the Thatcher governments from 1979 to 1997, with the creation of what were called grant-maintained schools. Some of the other key policy changes of that era that had long-term consequences included: the introduction of a free market approach to education by increasing parental choice and school diversity; the introduction of public league tables of schools' 'performance' in tests; local management of schools, including changes in funding allocations to a per-pupil basis; and the introduction of the national curriculum (West & Bailey, 2013).

Academies were launched in the year 2001 with the aim of replacing inner-city secondary schools that were defined as requiring special measures as a result of being inspected. What was distinctive about the early academies was that, although they were state-funded, they became autonomous from local authority control, and were given greater freedom regarding the national curriculum and national agreements on teachers' pay and conditions. Instead of local authority governance, these schools are self-governing non-profit charitable trusts, the terms of which are set out in an individual funding agreement. Like all other state-funded schools in England, they are subject to regular inspection.

The academies programme has undergone considerable changes and growth since its inception, such that it has now become a system-wide structural reform, which has caused seismic shifts in the English education landscape. Since the election of the Conservative-led coalition government in 2010, followed by the Conservative government in 2015, it has moved from targeting urban secondary schools seen as 'failing', to a system-wide structural change. Writing about this reform, Eyles and Machin (2015) comment:

> The academies programme that has been undertaken in English education is turning out to be one of the most radical and encompassing programmes of school reform that has been seen in the recent past in advanced countries.
>
> *(p. 1)*

An independent commission set up to review these developments pointed out that the original aim of academies was 'to address entrenched failure in schools with low performance, most particularly, schools located in the most disadvantaged parts of the country' (Husbands et al., 2013, p. 4). Since then, the focus has changed towards increasing the autonomy of all schools and setting up new academies throughout the country. More recently, the government announced that the policy goal was to require that all schools are academies by 2022, although this was subsequently withdrawn following political protests (Ladd & Fiske, 2016). Meanwhile, all new schools that open must now take the form of free schools, using the academies legislation as their legal framework.

Since 2010, government policies have also encouraged relatively successful schools to convert to academy status, as well as further emphasising the idea of forcing schools in difficulty to become members of an academy chain. Together, these responses have accelerated the pace of change, leading to the years 2010–2013 being referred to as the 'Wild West' of academy growth (Ladd & Fiske, 2016). Consequently, the number of schools that have become academies during the past six years is such that, by July 2016, 60% of secondary schools and 18% primary schools were operating under academy status, with about two-thirds of them being converter rather than sponsored academies (DfE, 2016). Considering that the number of academies up and running in the year 2010 was only 272, the rise to 5,774 by the summer of 2016, in addition to 1,176 schools in the pipeline waiting for conversion, indicates that the pace of change has been fierce.

These developments are set within policy context in which the dominant model has become schools linking together in multi-academy trusts, or academy chains, with oversight coming from national rather than local government (Mansell, 2016). This has also brought with it new players, as noted in a report the House of Commons Education Select Committee, which states:

> Academy sponsorship has encouraged and facilitated the contribution of individuals not previously involved in education provision and laid down a challenge to maintained schools to improve or face replacement by the insurgent academy model.
>
> *(House of Commons Education Committee, 2015, p. 3)*

In July 2016, 455 trusts that oversee the management of more than three academies were listed on the DfE website (2016). Although most of these are smaller groups, there are 46 trusts that oversee the management of ten or more academies, six of them running over 40 academies, the largest being the Academies Enterprise Trust, with 66 schools. The best known include United Learning, with 41 academies, Ark, with 29, and the Harris Federation, with 28. There are 17 trusts that have been established by universities, involving a total of 38 schools, an approach that the government is keen to encourage.

As a result of this expanding academies programme, as well as other contributing policies, the education system in England has become increasingly diverse. Furthermore, the introduction of various other types of schools that operate under the academy legislation – such as free schools, studio schools and university technical colleges – has contributed to the complexity of the scene. Indeed, in a mapping exercise of schools, based on legal status, curricular specialism, student selection, types of academy and school groupings, Courtney (2015) identifies as many as 70 or more types of school are currently operating in the English system. All of which suggests that, autonomous schools are well on the way to becoming *the* system of English state education

So, where American charter schools have come to be distinctive system *within* a system, the academies project has turned into a structural change that is reforming the administration and governance of the English education system as a whole.

Australia

The independent public schools (IPS) initiative in Australia is a more recent example of moves towards an autonomous school system. Although it started in the state of Western Australia, it is now influencing developments in some of the other Australian states and territories. However, it is still a relatively small feature of the educational landscape.

All of this is taking place in a country where equity is a long-standing and seemingly intractable challenge (Harris et al., 2017). This relates, in part at least, to the way that the education system has developed into three parallel sectors – independent, Catholic and government – all of which receive some state funding. The evidence is that this has led to the privileging of the independent and Catholic sectors, leaving government schools to deal with the majority of students from the more disadvantaged sections of the community (Kenway, 2013). This being the case, it is hardly surprising that the performance of government schools in the high-stakes national testing regime tends to draw attention to them as a source of concern. Meanwhile, it is the higher performing government schools that have gone down the independent, public school route.

In thinking about the Australian context, it is important to bear in mind the differences between the various states and territories. So, for example, while the administration of schools in the state of Victoria has followed principles of self-management since the early 1990s, more centralised administrative systems were maintained across other states and territories. Over the past decade, however, new more autonomous approaches to school management have been trialled across three states: Western Australia, New South Wales and Queensland (Gobby, 2013).

Caldwell (2016) provides a helpful history of these developments, pointing out that giving schools a greater say regarding how they achieve their goals is a well-established tradition in Australia that goes back to the 1980s. Referring to this trend as the 'self-managing school', he sees it as involving the decentralisation of a significant amount of authority and responsibility to schools. This means that they can make decisions related to the allocation of resources, albeit within a centrally determined framework of goals, policies, standards and accountabilities.

According to Caldwell, the independent public schools that have emerged in recent years – with Western Australia being the first jurisdiction to adopt the term – are a continuation of this history. He notes, too, that this formulation has since been embraced by federal government, which has set an expectation that one-quarter of the nation's public schools will become 'independent'. However, he argues, that, for him, the balance of centralisation and decentralisation is best captured in the concepts of 'school-based management', or 'school self-management'. This seems to imply an approach that is less radical than the American and English developments, an impression confirmed by experiences in the state of Queensland (see Harris et al., 2017).

The initiative in Western Australia was announced in 2009 and is closely aligned to other independent school reforms, particularly the American charter schools and English academies, as well as the New Zealand 'Tomorrow's Schools' initiative (Trimmer, 2013; Gobby, 2013). The policy goals are to improve student outcomes and achieve greater efficiency in school operations through reducing unnecessary bureaucracy, and allowing schools greater autonomy. By 2016 already 445 schools in Western Australia had undergone the transition to become IPS, educating 70% of public school students (Department of Education, Western Australia, 2016). As evident in relation to other countries, critics have claimed that rather than based on a considered review of international evidence, the IPS reform has been an ideological political project in which limited evidence has been used to push the reform through (Reid, 2016; Dinham, 2015).

We return to these systems later, in Chapter 8, where we discuss the effects they have caused since their inception. Meanwhile, we go on to consider the way that this global policy trend has gained so much momentum.

Learning from others

As mentioned earlier, the idea of making schools autonomous in various countries has not emerged in isolation. Rather, the idea has travelled across the world, influencing national education policies. As such, the evolution of the autonomous school movement is a striking example of how, nowadays, national education policies are shaped by global trends (Lawn & Grek, 2012; Steiner-Khamsi & Waldow, 2012). However, drawing from work conducted on 'policy flows' (Dale, 1999), we acknowledge that there are multiple means for policy transfer. Nevertheless, even though autonomous schools have taken somewhat different forms in different national contexts, instead of direct policy borrowing, it seems clear that certain international examples have been used to legitimise national reforms.

It is also important to recognise that research on educational governance has shown how global 'travelling policies' adapt to national, regional and local 'embedded policies' (Ozga & Jones, 2006). As a result, global policy trends tend to take different forms in different national and local contexts. In explaining this phenomenon, researchers of educational policy talk about 'path dependency' (e.g. Simola et al., 2013). This refers to the national and more local historical, political and cultural contexts, which, to some extent, determine how global reforms are interpreted and enacted. Indeed, earlier research has shown that schools themselves have an active role in shaping reforms, as they adapt and enact them to their ways of working (Tyack & Cuban, 1995).

Charter schools in the USA have been particularly influential in offering practical examples for policymakers in other countries to draw on. In this way, the justification of national policies through international examples has become a particular feature of the autonomous school movement globally. For example, in England the American charter schools, as well as the Swedish free schools, have been consistently referred to in order to justify reforms (The Conservative Party, 2007, 2010; Shepherd, 2010; Cameron, 2011; Wiborg, 2010a). In particular, the former English Secretary of State for Education, Michael Gove, worked closely with actors involved in American charter schools, promoting their success for English audiences (Fischer, 2012). Swedish reforms have also been repeatedly referenced by the supporters of the English academy reforms, especially prior to the coalition government that was formed in 2010 (Salokangas et al., 2016; West, 2014; Wiborg, 2015). Similarly, the Australian reforms have drawn from charter schools and academies, as well as policies for increasing school autonomy in New Zealand (Caldwell, 2016).

Drawing surface level policy comparisons between different education systems is problematic for a variety of reasons. Take the Swedish and English comparisons as an example. First of all, the conditions from which Swedish free schools emerged were influenced by what is a well-established socially democratic welfare state tradition. Within what is largely a homogeneous education system, equity and equal access to opportunities for education, as well as economic and social justice, were considered fundamental principles guiding education policy (Marklund, 1989; Sainsbury, 1996). Considering the long and strong traditions of selection within the English education system − not least the existence of private fee-paying schools, which have also influenced the academies movement (Glatter, 2012) − the difference between the bases on which these two systems work is considerable. Nevertheless, regardless of these contextual differences in which the Swedish voucher reforms and the English academy schools emerged, English policy makers have consistently drawn comparisons between the two developments.

The ways in which advocates of the movement have referenced international examples of other autonomous school has been called into question. So, for example, in her account of the treatment of the Swedish free school system within English policy discourses, Rönnberg (2015) provides a convincing account concerning how selectively the supporters of the movement have used evidence available to support their cause.

Charter schools have also been used consistently as positive examples by some policy makers and other advocates of academies (The Conservative Party, 2010; Husbands et al., 2013). For example, this is how the former English Secretary of State for Education, Michael Gove, referred to developments in North America:

> . . . . from autonomous schools in Alberta, Canada, to the Charter Schools of New York and Chicago, freedom is proving an unstoppable driver of success.
> *(Gove, 2012)*

Critical observations have also been made in relation to the Australian discourses, as charter schools and academies have been raised on a pedestal, despite the body of evidence available that would paint a much more mixed picture (Jha & Buckingham, 2015). In this context, supporters of the movement have been seen to draw from isolated cases of success, in order to simplify the positive effects of autonomous schools elsewhere, and, even worse, ignore unfitting evidence.

A remedy?

As autonomous schools have emerged in different national contexts, similar arguments underpin their introduction. For example, Wiborg's (2015) and West's (2014) comparative accounts of English academies and Swedish free schools show that, despite considerable differences in the political and social contexts in which these types of schools have emerged, the policy goals have been strikingly similar. In particular, the idea that autonomous schools are in a better position to address the needs of the students they teach is a familiar one across the different systems. Similarly, it has been argued that enhancing the autonomy of teachers and school-level management will create conditions in which schools may experiment with educational practice to best address their students' needs and, in so doing, raise attainment. In line with Wiborg (2015) and West (2014), then, we believe that there are considerable similarities in the arguments supporting autonomous schools in different countries. Using the analogy of autonomous schools as a 'remedy', we will explain what we mean.

In all the countries mentioned earlier, autonomous schools have been introduced as a remedy for certain ills that are perceived to be evident in publicly funded schools. In general terms, these ills are seen by the advocates of autonomous schools as being related to the considerable achievement gap that exists between students of different economic and cultural backgrounds. This is a global concern, as noted in a report from the OECD (2012), which states that, across its member countries, almost one in five students does not reach a basic minimum level of skills to function in today's societies. It is also noted that students from low socio-economic backgrounds are twice as likely to be low performers, implying that personal or social circumstances are obstacles to achieving their educational potential.

In responding to these challenges there is growing interest internationally in the use of strategies that place an emphasis on the power of market forces (Lubienski, 2003). For example, the early academies in England operated in challenging urban areas, the vision being that these schools would inject new energy into the system, deliver rapid improvement in terms of attainment, and challenge other schools to work harder in competing for students. The early charter schools in America were designed to have a similar impact, whilst at the same time addressing the problem of residential neighbourhood segregation in order to create schools that bring together children from different backgrounds (Kahlenberg & Potter, 2014).

Another ill in public education systems that autonomous schools are meant to address is the considerable bureaucracy associated with public administrations. Indeed, advocates of the movement in different countries have deemed public administration inefficient for the purposes of school management (Adonis, 2012; Caldwell, 2005; Geske et al., 1997; Malloy & Wohlstetter, 2003). Local authorities, municipalities and school districts are argued to be expensive, slow and inefficient in addressing the needs of schools and their students, and it is argued that something needs to be done to address these inefficiencies.

In all these contexts, it seems that making schools autonomous has been seen as the remedy to help cure the ills of the education system. The logic is that, if certain steps are taken in relation to administrative and governance arrangements, schools will be in a better position to educate all of their students, whatever their personal characteristics and home circumstances. In summary, the steps taken to achieve this overall goal are as follows:

- **Making schools more autonomous.** The logic is that giving schools more freedom will put them in a better position to address the needs of their students. In this way, it is assumed, more decisions can be made locally, by the people involved in the schools, rather than by administrators at the district, local authority or municipality level. The matters over which schools became more autonomous varies from one country to another but include, for example, increased decision-making capacity over student admissions, curriculum, classroom practices, finance and regulations concerning staff recruitment and contracts.
- **Bringing new 'actors' into the management, administration and governance of schools.** The criteria concerning who these actors may be has varied from country to country. They have included organisations and individuals who have not traditionally been involved in the management of publicly funded education, such as: private, semi-private and charitable organisations; parent groups; religious organisations; and wealthy philanthropists. These new actors, it is argued, will bring fresh ideas that will inject new energy and more efficient ways of working into public education. One of the central debates concerning these new actors in school management has been whether or not they will be permitted to make profit from running autonomous schools. Such for-profit 'edubusinesses' (Erixon-Arreman & Holm, 2011) have grown

to be big players in the management of charter schools and free schools, but at the time of writing, are not permitted to run academies for profit in England.

- **Introducing (or maintaining) heavily regulated quality assurance systems.** Here, the aim has been to make the schools' performance transparent for wider audiences. For example, charter school accountability is ensured through charter renewal processes, based on 'results-driven, marketplace-oriented accountability system to furnish parents, policy makers, and taxpayers and others with information about the school's quality and effectiveness' (Manno et al., 2000, p. 476). In England, students at autonomous schools sit the same national tests as those in other state schools, and the academies are subject to similar school inspections as others. The results of both the testing and the inspections are made publicly available. Such narrowly defined measures of effectiveness are used for accountability purposes, not only in autonomous schools, but widely in the education systems where autonomous schools operate (Schildkamp et al., 2012; Lingard & Lewis, 2016).

The *intended outcomes* of these reforms are ambitious, in that autonomous schools are assumed to hold huge potential to address the fundamental problems facing public education. In summary, they are:

- **Educational and managerial innovations.** The autonomy given to these schools is seen as enabling those involved to explore new ways of working. It is assumed that such changes are not possible in more tightly controlled, traditional public schools, which are bound by the heavy bureaucracy and inefficient management that is seen to be associated with public administration. It is, therefore, anticipated that management arrangements will become more efficient, as public administration have little, if any, involvement in schools. Related to this, the dissemination of new, more effective methods of working across the system is seen as part of the rationale. For example, the early vision for charter schools was to create 'laboratories' which would produce educational innovations that could contribute to wider system level improvements. Enhancing levels of teacher voice and empowerment, was seen as being crucial in creating the contexts in which experimentation will occur (Kahlenberg & Potter, 2014). Similar arguments were also used for the early English academies, which were seen as trailblazers for educational improvement, sharing practice and, as such, contributing to improvement across the system (Adonis, 2012).
- **Improvements in student attainment.** This will be achieved, it is argued, because practitioners working in these schools are in better position to address the particular needs of their students, due to their increased freedom to make decisions about their educational practices. In the USA and England, specifically, at the early stages of the reforms this argument was mainly focused on students from economically disadvantaged and minority backgrounds, as the early charter schools and academies, were usually placed in poorer urban locations.

- **Greater diversity of provision and, as a result, increased parental choice.** This has been a further major justification for the autonomous school movement (West, 2014; Manno et al., 2000). In addition, independent state schools have been presented as offering attractive alternatives to more traditional (perhaps 'failing') public schools, as the general trend has been that these schools have more freedom to experiment with curriculum and teaching methods. The new autonomous schools were, therefore, seen as a chance to start afresh, especially in areas where there may have been legacies of underperforming and non-attractive local schools. In addition, some advocates have argued that increasing diversity of local provision will improve overall standards by intensifying competition between schools. In fact, choice reforms have usually been initiated in competitive educations systems, where schools are set up to compete on their student intake and results. In such policy contexts, high-stakes testing systems are intended to inform decision making, whilst at the same time driving improvement efforts (Au, 2009). The supporters of such logic argue that competition has positive system-wide effects, as it encourages schools to improve their school's results in order to attract more students.

Staying with our analogy regarding ills, whilst these are seen as the desired outcomes, it has to be remembered that remedies can also cause side effects. What we mean by this is that, although a reform is introduced in order to address particular issues within an education system, once implemented, it may also produce outcomes in addition to, or, perhaps, opposed to those that are intended. Indeed, this is a theme we pick up in later chapters.

There are also questions to be raised regarding the appropriateness of the original diagnosis. Bearing all of this in mind, in this book we explore the extent to which autonomous schools are delivering on their ambitious promises, whilst also keeping an eye open for other, unintended effects they may have on education systems.

Making sense of school autonomy

Questions regarding school autonomy have been raised since the emergence of independent state schools in a number of countries. Although it has been a central feature of the international independent state school movement, the concept has been used rather loosely by the advocates of these reforms. For example, terms such as local autonomy, school autonomy, teacher autonomy and freedom from bureaucracy have all been used interchangeably to justify such policy moves.

In thinking about all of this, we take schools to be complex social systems in which various actors, such as students, teachers, school leaders and support personnel, operate with a range of agendas. Therefore, when examining school autonomy, it is, we believe, essential to acknowledge these varied actors. In terms of our own research, we have found Gewirtz and Cribb's (2009) work particularly useful, as they recognise the complex nature of schools as organisations. In thinking about who is autonomous, they offer the following rational:

. . . . if we want to evaluate the effects on autonomy of new modes of regulation consequent upon policy change, we need to consider a range of agents and be sensitive to the differential impact of policies on different agents, including the way in which one agent's autonomy can foster or inhibit the autonomy of other agents.

(2009, p. 170)

More specifically, their work encourages us to focus on individuals and/or groups who have autonomy, the matters over which they have autonomy, and the ways in which autonomy may be exercised. International research focusing on school autonomy has also highlighted that autonomy is multidimensional (Ingersoll, 1996; Wilches, 2007; Frostenson, 2015), as well as context dependent (Mølstad, 2015; Wermke & Salokangas, in press) and dynamic by nature (Finnigan, 2007).

Debates concerning school autonomy and control are by no means new, and stretch far beyond education. One of the key debates in the field relates to the suitability (or unsuitability) of top-down bureaucratic forms of control in school organisations (Ingersoll, 2003; Bidwell, 1965; Lortie, 1969). Arguments for bureaucratic control in schools state that, since they are public entities dealing with a mass clientele of children, rigorous measures should be in place to ensure that they operate as efficiently as possible, do what they are expected to, and deliver expected outcomes.

Such a view emphasises the importance of standardisation, transparency and efficient control mechanisms, and is preferable from an administrative and managerial point of view. However, the counterargument states that the core work taking place in schools – teaching and learning – does not lend itself to such 'machine-like' view of systems. The argument goes that teachers need a degree of flexibility in their work, as they educate groups of children and young people with varied characteristics and interests. According to this view, teachers, as opposed to administrators, are considered to be in the best position to determine what students need.

At this stage, it is also important to introduce another key concept that has been a fundamental building block for the independent state school movement: that of innovation. This idea is tightly embedded in neoliberal policy rhetoric more generally (Hodgson, 2012), with its emphasis on transferring control of economic factors from the public to the private sector. Meanwhile, the idea that these new schools will create innovations that can feed into the wider system has also been appealing and has also been used to justify the movement.

However, as with autonomy, the concept of innovation tends to be rather inexplicitly defined in the rhetoric of those advocating independent state schools. Yet again, international research offers conceptualisations which help us to make sense of these developments. First of all, we find useful the ways in which Lubienski (2003) conceptualises American charter school innovation to be two-dimensional, encompassing *educational/pedagogical* and *administrative/managerial innovations*. It seems to us that this formulation is applicable to any autonomous school initiative, since the policy rhetoric tends to suggest innovations may be educational (e.g. curriculum or teaching methods) and/or administrative (e.g. contractual or budgetary) in nature.

Second, the definition Preston et al. (2012) give for charter school innovation is also helpful, as they consider this to involve forms of practice which are only possible within such schools, and not in any other type of public sector school. This is how they put it:

> In defining innovation, we submit that educational practices cannot be deemed innovative in an absolute sense, but innovations must be considered in terms of their relative prevalence in a local and state context. A charter school is innovative in its use of a practice if the traditional public schools in its local school district are not using that practice.
>
> *(p. 318)*

This is an important definition that, in our view, is also applicable to other national contexts, as the argument usually is that autonomous nature of independent state schools leads to innovative practices that would not be possible in the constrained environment of the maintained sector.

This has been a brief introduction to the conceptual thinking tools that we have utilised to make sense of developments in autonomous schools. Chapter 7 goes into more detail in discussing how this thinking about autonomy and innovation has assisted us in writing this book. Meanwhile, with the help of this international research literature, in the chapters that follow we explore how greater autonomy affects people involved in these schools, through an in-depth longitudinal study of one of the first English academy schools. This leads us to discuss the extent to which this particular school, and independent state schools more widely, have been able to deliver on their intended outcomes.

Conclusion

In this introductory chapter we have described international developments in relation to the idea of independent state-funded schools, looking specifically at three countries in the English-speaking world where this idea has, to varying degrees, become a feature of national policy. This has drawn attention to a series of arguments for greater school autonomy made by various advocates. We have argued, too, that independent state schools have been introduced as a remedy to address issues faced by education systems, with ambitious expectation that they will deliver certain outcomes.

Using these arguments as an organising framework, this book draws on our close-up study of one English school, which we call 'Parkside Academy', over a period of ten years or so. Relating our analysis to international research, we go on to examine in detail the factors that shape the trends that are occurring. In so doing, we focus particular attention on the extent to which these moves are leading to innovation, particularly in respect to the agenda of equity, which is a major policy challenge across the world.

The following chapters offer a close examination of developments at Parkside. Chapters 2 and 3 begin this process by providing a chronological account of key developments in the school over a ten-year period. Chapter 2 casts light on some key developments in the predecessor school, and in the locality that led to the decision to turn Parkside into an academy. This discussion is contextualised in the English academies policy, leading us to provide a detailed account of national developments at the time. Chapter 3 provides a history of Parkside's first years as an academy, tracing developments that led it to be recognised by inspectors as an outstanding school.

The next three chapters take a more thematic approach. Chapter 4 is dedicated to pedagogical practices in Parkside, and, as such, offers a detailed description of what teaching and learning looked like in the school. We also look at how this was developed and monitored. Chapter 5 turns the attention to governance arrangements and the relationship the academy had with its sponsoring organisation. Chapter 6 retains the focus on management and governance, by describing a series of events which took place in Parkside during the process of appointing a new principal.

In Chapter 7 we reflect and analyse the developments in Parkside in relation to the aspirations of those who have advocated the idea of independent state schools. As such, the chapter offers us an opportunity to discuss the extent to which the school was able to be the remedy it was expected to be. In our analysis, we draw on English and international literature – particularly conceptualisations of autonomy and innovation – that help us in making sense of the developments at Parkside.

Chapter 8 leaves Parkside Academy behind, zooming out to examine global developments in the independent state school movement. First of all, the chapter discusses the key development in the English academies policy since our involvement in Parkside ended. From England, the discussion moves on to developments in American charter schools and the Australian independent public schools. Throughout these discussions, we analyse the extent to which these schools have delivered on their ambitious aspirations, as well as looking at their unintended outcomes. Finally, in Chapter 9 we take a step back and draw conclusions on what we have learnt in order to suggest ways forward.

Note

1 There are 152 local authorities in England. Traditionally they have been responsible for schools in their areas.

2

INDEPENDENT STATE-FUNDED SCHOOLS IN ENGLAND

So far, we have described the growth of the idea of school autonomy as a global trend. In so doing we have explained that a fundamental presumption is that increased autonomy will enable those involved with schools to innovate in educational and managerial practices. As we have explained, this assumption has underpinned the independent state-funded school movement in varied national contexts, where concepts of autonomy and innovation have remained at the core of the policy discourse.

We now turn our attention more specifically to developments in England, a country where school autonomy has been on the agenda for over 20 years, such that it is now central to national education policies. It is also the context for the account we provide of one of the first English independent state schools set up at the start of the century. These pioneer schools were known as city academies, although the word 'city' was subsequently dropped as the policy expanded.

The chapter presents the early history of the school, explaining how it replaced one that was deemed to be failing. The story of what happened is largely a positive one in the sense that it led to significant improvements in respect to student achievements as determined by scores in national examinations and evaluated by inspections. Before describing these developments, however, we begin by explaining a little more about the policy context in which they occurred.

The English policy context

Despite a history of attempts to improve its education system over many years, England faces a continuing challenge regarding the issue of equity. This was noted in a 2007 OECD study, which reported that the impact of socio-economic circumstances on young people's attainment was more marked in the United Kingdom than in any other of the 52 countries considered.[1] The implication is that home background is still the best predictor of the success of its students.

Although statistics identify broad patterns in relation to this challenge, different factors often interact to compound the links between social disadvantage and education in England. For example, children with low attainment tend to come from poorer families. These families often live in deprived urban areas, where there are high levels of ill-health, poor housing and overcrowding, unemployment and a whole host of other factors associated with poor educational outcomes. We also know that is not just levels of poverty in these areas which impact schooling – neighbourhood dynamics are also important (Kerr et al., 2014; Lupton, 2003). For example, in some areas of inner city social housing, and in neighbourhoods with many Asian heritage owner-occupiers, examination results are consistently better than would be anticipated based on indices of poverty. By contrast, some of the areas with the worst performance are those where predominantly white pupils live on large, city-overspill, public housing estates and in coastal towns around the country. Such neighbourhoods, although struggling educationally, are often not identified as being acutely poor or disadvantaged.

A variety of studies also suggest that underachievement cannot simply be explained by children and young people's backgrounds. They argue that the type of school they attend, the mix of students in the school, where the school is located, and their experiences of teaching and learning in the school, are also important (Clifton & Cook, 2013; Duncan & Murnane, 2011).

Annual reports from the national inspection agency, Ofsted,[2] have consistently signalled that schools in deprived areas are more likely to be judged inadequate than those in more affluent areas. More recently, the Chief Inspector reported that many low achieving pupils from poor backgrounds are an 'invisible minority' in schools rated good or outstanding in quite affluent areas (Ofsted, 2013). This is in line with the view that school and non-school factors may well combine to lower the attainment of children and young people who are already disadvantaged by their backgrounds.

Policy responses

Recent years have seen intensive efforts by successive governments to address these concerns. This has been part of an intensification of political interest in education, especially regarding standards and the management of the state system (Whitty, 2010). During the period of successive Labour governments (1997 to 2010) this led to a series of highly centralised national strategies to strengthen practices of teaching and leadership. At the same time, competition between schools was seen to be one of the keys to 'driving up standards', whilst at the same time further reducing the control of local authorities over provision.[3]

In addition, the government made various attempts to improve schools that were seen to be a particular cause for concern. One particularly high-profile approach that was tried was that of 'Fresh Start'. Modelled on ideas imported from the USA, this approach placed particular emphasis on the role of the headteacher as the key, leading to the use in the media of the term 'superhead'.

In England, Fresh Start was presented as 'an option' for local education authorities to use in tackling school failure. Blackstone (2000) argues that it offered a 'radical approach to securing school improvement for failing schools showing insufficient evidence of recovery'. The scheme, under which the worst performing schools, as identified by Ofsted, were re-launched under a new name, a new headteacher, without staff who were unsuccessful in reapplying for their old jobs, and with extra cash, was, however, dogged by controversy, including the resignation of the first four superheads to be appointed.

More recently, the emphasis on competition has been intensified as increasing numbers of state schools have been encouraged – and, in some instances, required – to become academies. As we have explained, these changes are intended to liberate schools from the bureaucracy of local government influence and establish a form of marketplace. In this way, it is intended that families will have greater choice as to which school their youngsters will attend (Adonis, 2012).

In this uncertain and confusing policy context, progress is monitored through national tests, the results of which are available to parents in order to assist them in choosing schools (Muijs & Chapman, 2009). In addition, schools are regularly inspected, the outcomes of which are published in a report, which is a public document. If a school is judged as failing (or likely to fail) to provide an acceptable standard of education, it is made subject to 'special measures' and may be required to become a sponsored academy.

Underachievement and low levels of attainment amongst students, a high proportion of unsatisfactory teaching and ineffective leadership, are seen as the most consistent features of failing schools (Nicolaidou & Ainscow, 2006). However, there are those who feel that the system is more likely to identify schools in challenging circumstances as 'failing', while schools in more affluent areas are given the benefit of the doubt (Benn, 2012). In addition, Ofsted inspections have been judged by some to have had a harmful effect on schools (Tomlinson, 2005). On the other hand, research by Allen and Burgess (2012) contradicts this view, suggesting that 'failing' an inspection leads to far greater student progress within a school than passing an inspection.

As explained in Chapter 1, since the election of the Conservative-led coalition government in 2010, followed by the Conservative government in 2015, school autonomy has become much more central to education policy in England. This builds on developments that began some 25 years or so ago that have been taken forward by governments of different political persuasion. Academies are the most significant part of these reforms, with these schools being funded directly by national government, rather than through a local authority.

An English academy

The original aim of the academies programme was 'to address entrenched failure in schools with low performance, most particularly, schools located in the most disadvantaged parts of the country' (Husbands et al., 2013, p. 4). In this chapter – and in the four that follow – we examine what all of this has meant to stakeholders at a local level: students, classroom teachers, school leaders and community representatives. We do this through an analysis of developments in one English secondary school, which we call 'Parkside Academy', during the early years of its existence. In so doing, we keep in mind the conceptualisations of autonomy and innovation that have emerged from our analysis of international research, and the debates that these have created in policy and research circles.

Our study of developments at Parkside Academy was carried out over period of some ten years or so, up to 2012. This led to an account that was developed as a result of one of the author's involvement as a participant observer over this period (Mel), working as an occasional consultant. During that time, data were also generated in the school in relation to a number of more formal research studies. More in-depth evidence was collected through systematic ethnographic research carried out by the other author (Maija), who spent the academic year September 2011–July 2012 in the school, examining documents, observing practices and decision making, and carrying out interviews (more details of the methodology for this research are provided in the Appendix). In these ways, a considerable body of evidence drawn from local actors – teachers, support staff, school leaders, governors and sponsor representatives – was generated. As a result, we are able to provide a rich account of practices, leadership and governance in the school.

We see our work as following the established tradition of British researchers who have carried out ethnographic research within individual school communities (Hammersley, 2013), whilst also recognising that circumstances did not always allow us to be as systematic as those who carried out earlier studies. Nevertheless, we have been careful to check the credibility of the evidence we have collected and, indeed, our interpretations of this information with key stakeholders. On top of this, our research is distinctive in the way it is able to trace the story of the school over a period of more than ten years. Nevertheless, we are conscious that our account remains a partial one.

The data we utilise include informal notes about developments in the school and evidence from a series of research projects over the ten years. In addition, we draw on conversations and formal interview data, plus participant observation data from classrooms, school assemblies, staff meetings, governing body meetings and staff training days. Sponsor and school-level policy documentation was also consulted. Drawing on this evidence, in what follows we begin our account of developments at Parkside Academy, starting with a description of its context. All names have been changed to avoid identifying individuals or places, and we have deliberately avoided the use of demographic details, specific dates and other publicly available information that could allow identification of the school. The methodology is explained in more detail in the Appendix.

A new academy

Parkside Academy opened in the early 2000s. Initially it was located in the building of its predecessor school, 'Oak Drive High' (not the real name), and then moved into purpose-built accommodation some 24 months later. Its principal was appointed before the new school opened, giving her time to assess the situation and formulate what were to be radical changes in the way it would operate. For example, one of us was present when the Principal announced to the staff that teachers, as well as students, would be expected to follow a dress code once the new school opened. The Principal also made a decision to distance the school from the local authority of which it had previously been part. Indeed, various decisions were made to draw boundaries between the Academy and the authority; for example, through choosing different service providers from the ones the predecessor school had contracted from; and, more importantly, by reducing communication with the representatives of the local authority to a bare minimum.

The school is now located in a splendid new building, beside a leafy park, in a densely populated urban district we will refer to as Green End. On arrival, the visitor is greeted with a large sign indicating the name of the school, a photo of children playing musical instruments, the name of the Principal and the sponsor's logo and strapline. The car park through which the visitor approaches the Academy is neatly landscaped, with bushes and trees that provide a pleasant welcome. The building itself is impressive, one of its distinctive features being large floor-to-ceiling windows, which allow natural light to flow into the rooms and corridors. Approaching the visitors' entrance, there is a shiny placard on the wall stating that its foundation stone was laid by a former Minister of State for School Standards.

The first thing the visitor notices when stepping into the building through the visitors' entrance is a large sponsor logo woven on the carpet of the registration office, surrounded by matching coloured carpet and chairs. It is worth mentioning at this stage, that before registering as a visitor to the Academy, three different references to the sponsor – we call it the 'Education for Future Trust' (EfFT) – are encountered.

Visiting the school, the generally calm behaviour of students is evident, as is their ethnic and cultural diversity. The high standards to which the Academy is equipped are also noticeable. It is striking, too, how clean and tidy the corridors are, with no obvious graffiti to be seen. The interior design, including the chairs and carpets, match the corporate colours of the sponsor, as do the colours of student uniforms.

The management suite, which is separated from the main corridor by a locked door, is located on the first floor, directly above the school reception area. It consists of the Principal's office, plus a meeting room and two small offices for administrative staff. From this office there is an excellent view of all those entering and leaving the building.

The context

As we have explained, the early academies programme was aimed at inner city secondary schools seen to be 'failing'. The argument supporting this policy was that closing down a failing school, operating in challenging circumstances and with a history of underperformance, and replacing it with an academy would cut the cycle of underperformance. This was explained in the 2001 green paper, 'Schools:

Building on Success – Raising Standards, Promoting Diversity, Achieving Results'
(DfEE, 2001):

> City Academies offer a radical option to help raise achievement in areas of
> historic underperformance. . . . City Academies are all-ability schools with
> the capacity to transform the education of children in areas of disadvantage
> and need. They will raise standards by innovative approaches to management,
> governance, teaching and the curriculum, offering a broad and balanced
> curriculum with a specialist focus in one area.

As with all of the first wave of academies that opened in the early 2000s, Parkside
replaced a secondary school with a bad reputation. The Green End area is associated
with a troubled history of financial and social disadvantage. An Ofsted inspection
report in the late 1990s described the communities the school served as being
predominantly areas of extreme social disadvantage, with concentrations of very
poor housing and very high levels of unemployment.

Green End, which is within the wider catchment area of, first, Oak Drive High
and, later, Parkside Academy, is associated with a history of severe financial and
social disadvantage, as well as cultural diversity. In terms of the diverse multicultural
nature of the area, according to Census 2001, just over 50% of the ward's population
consisted of ethnic minority groups. Of these groups, African-Caribbean and Black
African are the largest groups, others including Indian, Pakistani and Chinese.

The African-Caribbean community mainly settled in the district during the
1950s–1960s, as Green End was a reception area for arriving immigrants. In addition
to the African-Caribbean community there are other immigrant and ethnic minority
groups, such as Somali asylum seekers, who have added to the ethnic and cultural
diversity of the area. Although there are many large employers nearby, they tend to
employ relatively few people from the Green End district.

The area has been reported to lack social cohesion, with tensions – and, at times,
open conflicts – between resident groups. There were race-riots in the early 1980s,
of which a social worker in the area commented: 'The disturbances have to be set
aside the background of young people in the area being denied hope. The local
schools' expectations of them were pretty low.' While those with long connections
to the area feel that it is now safer, more cohesive and more prosperous than in the
1970s and 1980s, there remain concerns about incidents of gun crime and gang
violence

Having said that, it is important not to fall into the trap of assuming that
everything about the area is a problem. One of us was part of a team of researchers
that carried out an analysis of the area during the early years of Parkside's existence
(Ainscow et al., 2007). This pointed to the many assets and resources that can be
built on. So, for example, we found that there are many within the community that
have a high regard for what schools have to offer. Indeed, some families have gone
through enormous difficulties to bring their children to a part of the world that they
see as offering many opportunities to achieve a better life.

Echoing such attitudes, the area has a strong network of community run supplementary (i.e. informal out-of-hours) schools, each of which have been established by, and cater for, a distinct ethnic group. At the time of the earlier study, there were around 50 such schools serving the area. These were monitored by the local authority and fulfilled a variety of functions which mainstream schools either could not, or did not serve. These included: teaching community languages, religion and culture (including dance and art); and extra support for maths and science taught in learners' mother tongue. Some supplementary schools had also established English language classes for adults, and helped the government's Sure Start initiative to establish links with parents of preschool children in the area. Interestingly, some of these activities were, at that time, taking place in the Parkside building.

Fair access to an appropriate education is seen to be a key equity issue in relation to secondary education in the Green End area. Amongst the secondary schools serving learners from the area, apart from Parkside, there are a faith school and three single sex schools. In addition, there are three independent selective grammar schools, where families are required to pay fees, within a short bus journey. This diversity of provision is rather typical of the pattern across the country, although the details vary from place to place.

During the period when Parkside was opened, local authority officers reported an established 'hierarchy of desirability' based on attainment, with the faith school at the top and the Academy at the bottom. Data at that time also revealed distinct patterns in school populations, with the faith school catering predominantly for white and Afro-Caribbean learners; the separate girls' and boys' schools, white and Asian learners; while Parkside had a much more ethnically diverse population. One parent explained these patterns as resulting from particular groups of parents choosing to send their children to schools where, in the light of growing inter-ethnic tensions within the district, 'they thought they would be safe'.

Government policies to increase parental choice and, with this, diversity in educational provision, were reported to be doing little to change the nature of educational provision in the area, nor was it equitable in terms of access. The view was expressed that 'all schools in the area select', and that this was particularly the case with the higher attaining schools, which attracted more applicants than places.

Meanwhile, some parents were seen to be better able to manoeuvre the admissions system than others, leading to a lack of choice for ill-informed families – who are also often the most vulnerable families. It was suggested that these families often assume that their child will go to the nearest school and do not complete admissions procedures, meaning that the local authority is unable to act to facilitate access to schooling.

Parents were also reported to make school choices based on factors such as whether they liked the uniform and local hearsay, with schools' reputations and their actual performance not necessarily matching. Some parents were known to express a negative preference, making comments such as, 'I want my child to go anywhere other than the Academy', with the consequence that their child ended up going to the only schools left open to them as alternatives. In terms of their academic profiles and levels of deprivation, these schools were, at the time, on a par with the Academy, and children who attended them had to travel significant distances to get to school, and were therefore unlikely to have many peers from their local neighbourhood alongside them in the classroom.

As a result of these historical factors, it is reasonable to assume that, when it was set up, Parkside Academy had a more 'challenging' intake than other secondary schools serving the area. Certainly, its student population was drawn almost exclusively from the immediate locality, and tended to include those whose parents did not look to exercise a choice through local authority admissions procedures, and those children who did not get places at other 'more desirable' schools. Compared to the other schools in the area, the Academy's intake was, therefore, skewed towards those experiencing the highest levels of deprivation.

Competition between the secondary schools in the area to attract 'good' students, and to be seen as academically successful (and thus 'desirable'), rather than leading to diversification of educational provision, had, it seemed, led to schools having very similar approaches – strict, formal, teaching from the front of the class. One local authority officer commented: 'Effectively, it's an attempt to emulate grammar schools for all, but is this what the community needs?' The resulting lack of diversity among the schools' approaches to learning was seen as a factor perpetuating the exclusion of certain groups, and the unwillingness of some learners/families to engage with schooling.

The school population

An Ofsted inspection report of Oak Drive High in the late 1990s gives a flavour of its then student profile, noting that it closely reflected the ethnic mix of the local community. More specifically, it explains that roughly one-third of the students were European, just over one-third are African and African-Caribbean, and just under one-third Asian.

These observations by inspectors were very much in line with the descriptions members of staff who had worked in the school during the Oak Drive High days gave regarding the school's student population. For example, one teacher said:

> This school is very much about serving the local community. You can see it when you walk around the corridors and pop your head into classrooms and talk with the kids we teach. It is very much a local school serving the families who live here. And that was always the case, the students are very similar here now as they were during the Oak Drive High days: they are the younger brothers, sisters and neighbours of our former students, as well as new arrivals to the neighbourhood and the country.

As this teacher points out, lots of the students attending Oak Drive High School were new arrivals to the country, many of them having little or no English, and some with limited previous experiences of formal education upon arrival. As the archive of student data was not available for our research, we again rely on earlier Ofsted inspection reports on Oak Drive, which provide an indication to some of the challenges the school faced in relation to student attainment. One of these reports explained that a range of baseline assessments showed that the school population was heavily skewed towards lower attaining pupils. In particular, almost all students had reading levels below that for children of their age nationally, and about two-thirds two or more years behind in their reading. Results of nationally standardised tests showed that about three-quarters of pupils had scores below average and a quarter were very low scoring or did not achieve a score at all. Attainment on entry to the school in all national curriculum subjects, including the core subjects of English, mathematics and science, was, according to the inspectors, 'either low or very low'. Around 80% of pupils were designated as having special educational needs, most of which related to what was referred to as social, emotional and behavioural difficulties.

In addition to diversity in attainment and cultural background, the majority of students came from low-income families. This is a reflection of the surrounding community of Green End, which, as we have explained, is financially disadvantaged and has consistently had amongst the highest unemployment figures in the country. For example, in the year 2001 Census, the unemployment rate for Green End reached 14.8%, which was almost triple as high as the local authority average of 5% and significantly higher to the national average of 3.2%.

As there are no student data available to us from Oak Drive High, it is beyond our reach to examine features of the student population in great detail. However, an Ofsted inspection report from the late 1990s gives a flavour of the level of disadvantage that the students came from, with about 65% of students being eligible for free school meals, which was, at that time, very high compared to national average. The report goes on to say that there was a high concentration of homeless family units around the school, a number of travelling families and a large number of refugees, especially Somalian. There was also a high proportion of family breakdown and a resultant demand on young people to act as carers. About 50% of pupils came from one parent families, foster homes or are living with other family members. A black male youth unemployment figure of 80% was given for Green End. According to the inspectors, the community was picked out in distorted public perceptions and negative media coverage and stereotyping had been particularly damaging.

In addition to its multicultural population and financial disadvantage, the reputation of the district we have called Green End, locally and nationally, is largely a negative one, associated with antisocial behaviour, such as the riots in the 1980s, prostitution and drugs. More recently, gang related crimes and gun crimes have been associated with the area, all of which have seriously damaged its reputation. Significantly, a Google search for the area offers the following options: 'Green End crime', 'Green End gangs' and 'Green End bloods'. And the first three Google search results for Green End include a Wikipedia entry and two national newspaper articles related to gang violence in the area. One of the teachers summed up the situation as follows:

Let's face it, it's no secret what the reputation of Green End and the school is like. When you tell people you meet the first time where you work in you get the odd look and they say things like 'really, what's it like, is it really that bad?' You know. . . . And to be honest, that was my reaction as well. I had quite mixed feelings about applying for the job because of the reputation of the area and the school.

It is worth stressing, too, that the student population is particularly challenging in terms of the sheer number for whom English is not their home language, students with statements of special educational need, as well as those from families suffering from social and financial disadvantage.

As we indicated earlier, Oak High had also suffered from a poor reputation, partly reflecting the area it was located in, which had an impact on student admissions. A senior member of staff who had worked in the school since the 1980s elaborates issues related to student admission:

The thing is, it was always a difficult school. And at the time every authority needed an Oak Drive High. You know, because at the time there were no pupil referral units, we just didn't have them before. So before those, the children who were excluded from other schools were sent to Oak Drive. So we collected this mishmash of permanently excluded students in Oak Drive and the students from the local area who couldn't find any other place to go. You know, that's what it was like. . . . One of the difficulties we've always had, have been the perceptions of the school, which were always very harsh.

A failing school?

In addition to operating in a context tormented by a complexity of challenges – or possibly as a result of it – Oak Drive High was regarded as seriously underperforming, with a long record of low attainment. So, for example, student performance in the GCSE examinations[4] during the last decade of Oak Drive High was poor, with only 4–13% of students usually gaining five A*–C (all subjects). The final results from the Oak Drive High in the year before the opening of the new academy were 13% of five A*–C grades (all subjects). This meant the majority of students left the school without any recognisable qualifications.

To bring the attainment of Oak Drive students into context, the standards of Oak Drive were far below the local average: in the school's final year the figure for five A*–C grades in the local authority was 33% and the national average the same year, 52%. In the school performance league tables published by the BBC, in which altogether 3,571 schools were listed according to their student performance in GCSEs, Oak Drive High was within the lowest 70 of all English schools.

One of us recalls visiting Oak Drive a couple of years before it closed. At that time, student numbers were extremely low, and falling, as more aspirational families sought places in other local schools. On other indicators, such as student attendance and exclusions, the school was clearly a cause for great concern. This sense of a school that was 'out of control' was immediately apparent in the way that the deputy headteacher carried a large bunch of keys that enabled him to open and close areas of the building in order to minimise unauthorised movement during lesson times.

Despite these unfortunate circumstances and, indeed, the widely recognised reputation of the school, Oak Drive never actually went into special measures.[5] Quite the opposite, in the late 1990s Ofsted inspectors presented the school in a positive light as having 'many very positive features' and 'making good progress in improving pupils' educational standards'. They went on to say that the school serves its pupils, their families and community well, noting that 'learning takes place in a safe, caring and positive ethos within an excellent new building'. It was, the inspectors concluded, truly a school that was 'justifiably the pride of its community'.

The fact that Oak Drive was not placed in special measures was something members of staff who had been involved in the school were rather keen to explain to us. Indeed, there was a strong sense of pride clearly present amongst these teachers who had witnessed the evolution of the school from within. Reflecting on what happened, they argued that the motives driving the local authority towards the decision to convert the school into an academy were financial and political in nature, some even suggesting the conversion was pushed by the government. This is how an assistant principal of Parkside explained it:

> Yes, basically, because of all the issues with numbers, we were carrying a £1.5 million budget deficit the council decided that could not carry on, it had to close. But there was more to that. If you look at the area, you have got the Holy Mary's secondary, which is a religious school, you have got Orange Grove, which is an all-girls school. So there's no mixed gender non-religious school in the locality and that's why they didn't want to shut us down forever. This is why they tried to use the academy system to bring in the extra money to be able to bring the school down and start a fresh. The first attempt failed because the government realised the council was playing silly games. You know, their partner was the science park, of which the council is 50% owners. So the government realised that. Then they wanted to shut the school and then open it again. No chance. So they said no. So we went for two years looking for a sponsor and eventually Education for Future Trust came along.

An alternative account was offered by a member of the Oak Drive governing body, who explained his version of the story that led up to the opening of Parkside Academy. At the time that the decision was being considered, he recalled, 8% students in the school had only achieved five A*–C grades; the projected Year 7 intake was about 50 students; and the school had a budget deficit. As a result, the local authority had proposed that the school should be 'twinned' with another school in the district with a strong record. However, this idea was, he explained, blocked by a local politician. The decision to close the school and replace it was therefore taken.

This brief history points to the complexity of the factors that impinged on the educational experiences of students who attended Oak Drive High School and, indeed, on the efforts of its staff to engender positive outcomes. It is a story that, in our experience, is not uncommon in those schools that serve the most disadvantaged communities within a highly competitive system of education – schools that seem to have 'the odds stacked against them' (Ainscow et al., 2012).

So, alongside of its track record of poor performance in national examinations, Oak Drive arguably fit well with the stated intentions of the city academies policy. The undeniable fact of the significant budget deficit the school had generated undoubtedly encouraged the decision to close down the school. However, whether the school would have actually qualified as failing is still somewhat debatable, as the Ofsted interpretation of the school was relatively positive.

Curtis et al. (2008) note the difficulties associated with the definition of a 'failing school' and the problematic nature of labelling schools in such a way, as similar debates have been recorded from other early academies. However, regardless of the debate around whether Oak Drive would have qualified as failing, the closure of the school and its re-establishment as an academy provided the school community with an opportunity to start afresh. This new beginning led to the arrival of new people – such as school management staff and the sponsor – who brought with them different attitudes and new approaches to governance and management. The next section provides a brief introduction to the sponsor, and its vision about what the new academy was to become. We also give an initial flavour of its style of operation.

The sponsor

One of the key features of the early City Academies programme was the involvement of an external sponsor. Although research has begun to address the broader national implications of the independent state-funded school movement in England, current understandings regarding local implications of what are known as 'chains' of sponsored academies, or, more recently, academy 'trusts', remain limited. As our own work was located in an academy attached to a chain, which we will call the 'Education for Future Trust' (EfFT), it begins to address this gap in knowledge.

Those entitled to sponsor an academy during the early years of the programme were business, church or voluntary organisations (Adonis, 2012). The sponsoring organisation which took over the governance of Parkside Academy represents the latter group: it is a charitable trust.

The general perception staff had of the sponsor during the early days of Parkside Academy could be described as being relatively distant, but genuinely interested and very supportive. The Chief Executive of the organisation at the time became known as a distant but caring and compassionate patron, recognised for an ability to raise funds and his true interest to improve the education of young people in need, as noted by some staff members:

> Maybe this is just my perception, but I think when [the Chief Executive] was in charge it was very much like a charity, he was like a beneficiary for the charity, raised a lot of money.

> When [the Chief Executive] was still around, he was a lovely man who really cared about education and of these kids, and I think he genuinely wanted good things for these children.

The perceptions staff had of other members of the early EfFT organisation were rather similar to how they perceived the Chief Executive: that is to say, they were generally seen as generous 'good-doers', who were genuinely interested in improving the life changes of the Green End youth. A local governor shared his experiences from the early interactions with representatives of EfFT:

> I remember when they were still in the old building, which wasn't that old, they had a topping out event – it's when you have these hard hats and you have champagne. And it was a lovely summer's day and I looked around and thought here we are in the middle of Green End, and they are all white faces, quite a lot of them looking like posh people. One was even wearing an MCC tie. I thought, what we've got here is middle class people doing good, and to some extent that's still there. And all the senior people I've occasionally met [from EfFT] are genuinely people who want to do good for the poor.

As suggested by these comments, EfFT fits rather well with the typical profile of many of the early academy sponsors. According to Adonis (2012), who was a government minister during that period, they were usually wealthy charismatic philanthropists, motivated by their will to 'pay something back' to society and, as such, keen to improve the educational experiences of young people.

According to participant accounts, the early involvement of EfFT in the day-to-day life of the Academy was not extensive, and it was left largely to the senior staff to oversee the daily management of the school. It seems that, at that stage, the sponsor representatives stayed in the background, governing from a distance, whilst the Principal and the new management team began the process of transforming Oak Drive High into Parkside Academy.

It is worth adding that there was also a 'local governing body', made up of school and community representatives. The exact role of this group remained ambiguous during the time of our involvement, particularly in relation to the extent to which it had responsibility for decision making regarding policies and use of resources. The nature of this ambiguity is examined in subsequent chapters.

Conclusion

In this chapter we have described the introduction in England by the then Labour government of the programme of city academies in the first few years of the twentieth century. These new schools followed the trend of international developments, in that they were 'freed' from the control of their local authorities. In this way, the stated intention was that this would provide greater space for innovation in order to find ways of breaking the link between poverty and low educational achievement. There was also an assumption that their progress would act as a stimulus for system-wide improvement.

Keeping these aspirations in mind, we have begun the process of analysing developments in one of these schools, which we call Parkside Academy. This school, which replaced one that had been seen to fail, was part of one of the new chains that emerged at that time. Located in an urban district serving a community that had a population that was ethnically mixed and characterised by economic disadvantage, the school fitted the circumstances that the new academies were intended to serve.

In the chapters that follow, we describe how the school was reshaped into a context characterised by greater optimism, a far safer working climate and much higher expectations. And, as we will explain, this was reflected in the school's massively improved results in national examinations and in an inspection report that defined the school as being outstanding. At the same time, we use evidence gained from our privileged access to the school in order to explore to what extent those involved were able to make or influence decisions.

In analysing what happened over a period of ten years, in what follows we throw light on the social and, at times, political complexities of policy implementation. In so doing, we keep in mind the idea that within education systems, policy is made at all levels, not least that of the classroom. Probing this complexity, we seek to explore the potential of greater school autonomy for the development of more equitable education systems, whilst also illuminating the barriers that need to be overcome in order to mobilise this potential and pinpointing the risks involved.

Notes

1 It should be noted that the four countries that make up the United Kingdom (England, Northern Ireland, Scotland and Wales) each have their own educational policies.
2 Ofsted (the Office for Standards in Education) is the national agency that inspects English schools. Inspection reports are published so that parents have these as part of the evidence they use in choosing schools.
3 There are 152 English local authorities. They are democratically accountable for providing a range of services for their local communities, including education.
4 The General Certificate of Education (GCSE) is a national examination taken by almost all English students around the age of 16. The results are aggregated in order to draw comparisons between the performance of schools as part of the national accountability system. At the time of our involvement, A* to C grades in five subjects was seen as the gold standard. However, the bar was subsequently raised, with an insistence that the five subjects must include English and mathematics.
5 A school is placed into this category following an inspection that finds that it has failed to provide an acceptable standard of teaching, has poor facilities or otherwise fails to meet the minimum standards for education set by the government.

3

A PHOENIX RISING FROM THE ASHES

Having described the setting up of Parkside Academy, one of the early independent state-funded schools in England, in this chapter we begin the process of describing what happened during the first ten years of its existence. As we explained in the previous chapter, the story of those years is a mainly positive one, as the school came to be seen as one of the early successes of the new policy.

As we will explain, in the light of this success, some of those involved developed their own narrative about what had brought about progress. This 'official' version of the school's story was presented in the form of a PowerPoint presentation, to be used with visitors and at external events. Later, this same narrative formed the basis of a school drama production, an account of which we provide towards the end of the chapter. At the same time, we point to areas of concern, as the purposes of the school autonomy agenda and the efforts of the staff to make it a success are seen to be influenced by other policy initiatives.

Early days

The new Principal of Parkside Academy (we will call her Elaine, which is not her real name) had had considerable experience in various roles within the education system, including a period spent working for the government. Most significantly, she had successfully 'turned around' a previous urban school in which she had worked.[1] Members of staff and other stakeholders consistently described an exceptionally strong leader, determined to bring about changes to the school and delivering the vision the sponsor had for the Academy. For example, a senior teacher who was there throughout this period explained:

> [The Principal] was appointed ten months before the school opened. She got the senior leadership team she was bringing in, I think they were appointed

in March and we opened in September. So, during that time they were setting up the new rules, the uniforms, there was a lot of contracts that needed to be signed in terms of who was going to provide the services, because you know that's one thing, the academy was not bound to accept what the local authority offered. So we were entitled to change the cleaners, the catering, we were not paying for the education psychologist. All the services the local council offered the academy pulled away from. There was a lot of negotiations going on, and that's what the new management was doing. So for the first 18 months we had very little to do with the local authority, which caused a certain amount of aggravation.

According to staff members who had been involved since the Oak Drive High days, the Principal had a crucial role in redefining local relationships. To give a flavour of what this involved, a local governor of the Academy, who also had a role as a councillor in the local council, describes the ways in which local relationships were redefined:

> This particular academy – and maybe it's true in all the EfFT schools – stress very much the independence of their model, rather than what I would like to see independence within a strong mode of co-operation with other schools and local authorities. And this has led to the governance structure in which decisions are taken away from the authority. And to me it's a disappointment. This academy was the first one to be created [in the locality] and learning from this we [the local authority] have tried to make all the remaining academies much more strongly linked in to the community than this one is. And all the other sponsors have much stronger local links, either they are companies or institutions with local links. This academy was a bit isolated in relation to the community itself.

According to those who had been involved since the early days of the Academy, the isolation this governor talks about was to a great extent the choice of the new Principal. Her rather radical approaches to local relations were reported to have caused some tensions, as noted by another local governor:

> When the Academy was set up, there was an enormous tension between Elaine, particularly, and the local authority. The story was that during the first week of the Academy, the then director of education and one of his colleagues dropped in and she told them to leave. She was creating the lines really.

At the same time, headteachers have no option other than to be outward facing, working with and supporting their local communities. The nature of the intensive pressures this can create in tough urban districts of the sort served by Parkside Academy was vividly illustrated early on in the life of the new school when one of its students was involved in a tragic event. Media coverage was massive, with the local newspaper reiterating that the area in which the school was located had become a byword for gun violence and gang warfare, since the bloody feuds over cocaine and heroin trafficking between infamous street gangs that had gripped the area in the 1990s. Inevitably this meant that the Parkside Principal was placed on the frontline, dealing with the distress this event created within the school, not least amongst the students, whilst, at the same time, acting as its public face across the local community.

Relationships beyond the school gates were not the only area in which the Principal was required to take action. She was determined to take a new direction within the Academy, leading her to propose significant changes in its way of working. So, for example, some of the staff who had worked in the Academy since the Oak Drive High days described changes in the management and leadership style. For example, an assistant principal commented:

> The previous head teacher had been much more *laissez faire*, which was one of the reasons why the predecessor school was in difficulties. So the leadership style changed quite dramatically. It became instructional, you did what you were told: 'Because I am telling you this is the way it's going to be'. And some people didn't like that. . . . We were one of the first academies to open and there was that anti-academy feeling, we have been under spotlight since we opened. So as a result, some of the demands placed on the staff were heavier than in other schools, so we've had a high staff turnover.

Going on to comment on the style of the new Principal, he added:

> When it came time for you to go, you know, you went. I remember joking it's worrying if she asked you to come and meet her on Friday before half term. Because that's what happened to some people, staff who were struggling were encouraged to move on. . . . The three Cs: compliance, consistency and control, was about creating a calm quiet system that was, you know, staff doing what they were told, the [Principal's] way: just do it, don't argue, or don't argue, don't question, just do as you are told, and I want it done at all times.

As this assistant principal implies, not all members of staff embraced the radical changes in leadership and management style introduced by the new Principal and, as a result, a sense of disapproval was apparently present in the early years. Here another member of staff who also witnessed the transition period explains some of the frustrations staff had:

> . . . since then we have had no ownership of our own jobs. They started treating us like we're not professionals really and we get told what to do rather than them letting us getting on with our jobs. Obviously if people are taking the mick and not doing their job properly, then yes, do something, but if teachers are doing their jobs properly, don't be a control freak. A lot of it used

to be micro management like: 'Right, I want to know what you're doing with every hour of the day'.

As suggested by these quotes, there was a general agreement amongst those who had worked previously in Oak Drive High and witnessed the transition, that the new Principal adopted a more directive leadership style.

More neutral descriptions of the Principal's style of leadership included adjectives such as 'forward looking', 'strict' and 'precise', and depending on how positively or negatively her style was perceived, words such as 'hard working', 'tireless' and 'formidable' were used. What is not in doubt is that, from the very beginning, she was determined to deliver on the new strapline of the Academy: 'High expectations, no excuses', with both students and staff alike. In this respect, she was responding directly to the then government's education policy agenda, in which notions of firm leadership were heavily emphasised. Academy heads were, it was argued, to be: 'powerful and effective leaders' (DfES, 2002, p.1), a description with which the Parkside Principal seemed to fit well.

The new building

The early sponsored academies were all entitled to new facilities, and in this respect Parkside Academy was no exception. It began its operations in the old building of Oak Drive High, while the new facilities were built. The Oak Drive building had, in fact, undergone an extensive refurbishment in the mid-1990s, less than ten years prior it to becoming an academy. An Ofsted inspection report, shortly after this work was completed, described the renovated school building in quite a positive light, noting that the school had excellent amenities, including good access via lifts and ramps for disabled pupils. It was also noted that rooms were sufficient in number for each full-time teacher to have his or her own room base for teaching, and these were generally arranged in departmental suites.

Teaching staff who had been involved in the school since the Oak Drive days also described the old school building quite positively:

> Actually there was nothing really wrong with the old building. It was fine. Needed a bit of paint but that's it really. The arts department was much better actually than what we have in the Academy, we had a studio which we don't have here for example.
>
> The building we were in before this one, just there (points out of the window) was ok, it was old but there wasn't really anything wrong with it. This is why some people though it a little bit unnecessary and strange to build a completely new building, even though the old facilities were fine.

Nevertheless, the new building for Parkside Academy was finished two years after it opened and the school moved in, an event that was reported in the local media. The shiny new accommodation, which cost over £25 million, was well equipped and up to date, with the latest technology, such as smart-boards in all the classrooms. It was located in close proximity to the site of Oak Drive High School, on the fringes of the Green End community. The old building was later demolished and replaced by blocks of apartments.

Measuring progress

From the outset, the Principal of Parkside was adamant that the most important thing was to serve local children, and that her commitment to this goal was unshakeable. However, not everyone saw things in this way. Some community representatives we spoke to criticised the school for not being linked in to local networks. Meanwhile, others doubted the Academy's avowed commitment to local children, fearing that, as it became more academically successful, it would stop being 'a local school'. Some in the local community also argued that the school was quietly excluding less desirable students, although we found no evidence of this happening. What was clear was that the establishment of an academy outside local governance systems and, yet, accountable for meeting centrally imposed centrally imposed targets, had generated suspicions locally that were likely to make collaborative approaches more difficult.

Meanwhile, the key objective for Parkside was undoubtedly to raise levels of attainment, since the predecessor school had been performing so poorly in comparison to other schools in the locality. The Principal was persistent in emphasising this at every opportunity, particularly during meetings of staff. Part of her regular input around this agenda was to repeat the statement, 'We are not social workers, we are here to teach'. Having said that, we observed how she herself put enormous amounts of time and energy in supporting students and parents experiencing difficulties. She also held regular gatherings, where groups of parents joined her over a breakfast in school to discuss how they could support the teachers' efforts by helping their sons and daughters to study at home.

During the first two years of the new school, the GCSE examination results did not improve significantly. As a result, like many others at that time, Parkside was 'named and shamed' in the national media for not being able to raise standards sufficiently. It is worth keeping in mind, here, that the Academy, like its predecessor school, was still serving a challenging population of students, many of them in need of additional support, as reported by inspectors during this period. The report explained that, while the school admitted students of all abilities, many had low scores in national tests at primary school, and had achieved standards well below the average for their age. Mention was made, too, of the high proportion of students categorised as having special educational needs. It was also noted that far more students than is typical would join or leave the school at times other than at the start of Year 7, including a significant number whose families had sought refuge or asylum in this country.

However, after those first two years, the Parkside results began to rise steadily, reaching 63% of students achieving five A★–C grades after five years, and 94% after ten years. This rise in educational outcomes was impressive, and helped to redefine the status of the academy in the locality. In fact, it climbed from the bottom (33rd) place in the Local Authority's secondary school league table, to 20th place. In this sense, the raised attainments provided tangible support for those who advocated sponsored academies.

The rise in standards was not only visible through educational outcomes, but was also recognised by Ofsted inspectors. In an inspection report published a couple of years after the school opened, the overall effectiveness of the academy was rated 'satisfactory, with several good features'. Four years later the inspection describes a very different school, rating it 'outstanding' and, in so doing, crediting much of the success to exceptional leadership.

Being one of the early academies, and by all existing measures (inspections and examination results) a successful one, the developments at Parkside were followed with great interest in both the local and national media. As the standards began to rise, the senior leadership team, particularly the Principal, began to share 'the story' in a range of contexts, including conferences. As a result, staff and students became used to welcoming visitors on a weekly, or, at times, daily basis.

Developing the 'official' story

The mounting focus of attention on the success of Parkside led the Principal and some of her senior team, to develop a PowerPoint presentation that told of the progress made since the moment that it replaced Oak Drive High School. We both heard this account on a number of occasions, usually when visitors came to the school to learn from its experiences, as well as at various events elsewhere.

The presentation reflected the Principal's view that the new academies should be seen as having a pathfinder function, assisting other schools facing challenging circumstances. And, of course, this was in line with those in the USA who had argued that charter schools should be seen as laboratories, experimenting with new ways of breaking links between economic disadvantage and poor educational outcomes, and acting as a stimulus for the system as a whole.

The presentation was entitled: 'Parkside Academy – An Education for Future Trust Sponsored Academy: The Journey So Far . . .' It is worth spending time summarising its key messages, since these captured what came to be viewed as the 'official' story of the Academy.

The first slide of the presentation stated the background of the school:

> . . . . the LEA (Local Education Authority) decided Oak Drive High School would either have to close, or become an academy. Why? It was dysfunctional:
>
> - A huge deficit – low numbers
> - Attendance – year 11 = 50%
> - Behaviour – Appalling
> - Expectations – couldn't go lower

The next slides went on to develop this rather depressing image of the predecessor school. One, which was headed, 'Look how it ended up', presented the notably low exam results of Oak Drive High School students for the decade prior to the opening of the Academy. There were also a few photographs showing images from the old school building in which students' desks and walls were covered in graffiti.

From this rather glum past, the presentation moved on to outline the success story of the school since it turned into an academy. The steady rise of results and several other performance indicators describing the improvement were shown, illustrated with photos of smiling students in smart uniforms engaged in various activities. The overall message of the presentation was that the predecessor school was in a miserable condition, failing its students and the wider community. The Academy was described to have significantly increased the life chances of the young people it serves, using phrases such as: 'The Phoenix rising from the ashes of Oak Drive High School'.

Over-egging the pudding?

So far we have explained the contexts in which Parkside Academy operated. This contextual examination has set the scene for a much deeper analysis, one that will focus on how notions of autonomy were experienced at Parkside over a ten-year period.

At this stage, it is important to recognise that our investigation reveal complexities and tensions in how different actors understand the history of Parkside. Nevertheless, there are certain facts all interviewees and documentary data agree upon. In summary, the predecessor school, Oak Drive High, operated in challenging circumstances in an economically deprived location and had a track record of poor performance. Whether the school actually qualified as a 'failing school' seems more debatable, as it was not placed in special measures following inspections, which, during the early days, was part of the criteria for schools to become sponsored academies (Curtis et al., 2008). However, as we have noted, the financial troubles of the school provided a strong push for its closure and replacement with an academy.

The evidence we have presented so far suggests that staff involved since the Oak Drive High days have, to some extent, a differing narrative of the past events than the one given by the leadership of the Academy. Here a veteran member of staff reveals some of the tensions in these different narratives:

> You know the PowerPoint [summarised earlier in this chapter], and there has been a lot of other similar things too. I just had to sit there, swallow and bite my lip and just keep quiet, because that's the way people wanted to play 'the story'. And it's silly because, you know, this story would have been good enough in itself without having to overegg the pudding. . . . There's one slide that particularly irritates me, the one with photos of the paintings on the wall [referred to earlier in this chapter]. I didn't agree with the method of that arts

therapist, that's what the room was used for. So it was one specific room used for something I was questioning the validity of, and this surely was not the way the whole school was. It doesn't matter the fact that the school was in poor state: parents didn't engage, numbers were dropping, achievement levels were low, that you can argue, but it gets told that it was worse than it really was.

Like this teacher, the general consensus amongst the few members of staff who had transferred from Oak Drive High and stayed in Parkside Academy was that the new management team had a tendency to exaggerate the severity of the state the predecessor school was in. The condition of the school building provides a tangible example of how this was done and the ways in which it was introduced to what is called here 'the official history' of the Academy.

The story to which this teacher refers was delivered by different members of the senior leadership team to the numerous guests visiting the school as the official narrative of the school. Two of the leaders we heard giving this presentation were relatively new additions to the staff: one had joined the academy five years previously and the other six years after Oak Drive High School was closed. Eventually, the essence of its content became the basis of a school production.

The musical

The production, which was called 'The Green End Musical', was a piece of drama developed to illustrate the school's journey of improvement. It seems that, at some point during its production, the Principal decided that it could also be used as a tribute to the contribution of the retiring Chief Executive of EfFT.

The musical took place in the 2011 summer term, and was clearly successful in the way it offered students splendid opportunities to participate in what was an impressive production. We must stress that it was by no means representative of the extracurricular activities provided in the Academy. Rather it was a quite extraordinary event in the life of the school, one that further illustrates issues around power dynamics and teachers' professional autonomy. In particular, it raised questions for us about the powers the senior leaders of the Academy and EfFT appeared to have over the teaching staff, and the ways in which this power was used at times to steer their practices.

The task of producing the musical was assigned to an assistant principal. At this stage (as we explain in Chapter 6), she was helping out in one of the other EfFT academies that been experiencing difficulties, although during the months prior to the production she visited Parkside on Fridays to direct rehearsals.

The assistant principal had been approached some 12 months earlier to write and produce the musical by the Principal. At the time of its production she was acting as Deputy Chief Executive of EfFT on a part-time basis, whilst also continuing to be Principal at Parkside. Eventually, it was decided that it should become a retirement tribute for the Chief Executive Officer (CEO). We were told by a number of staff that it was then, to some extent, micromanaged by the

Principal, who expressed her opinions on the script, as well as during the production process.

The musical was by far the most high-profile drama production that took place during our involvement in the Academy and a professional theatre stage from a local university was hired for the purposes of the performance. There were five shows, for which students, their parents and anybody interested could buy tickets, in addition to a VIP event for an invited guest audience consisting mainly of representatives of the EfFT.

The plot of the musical described the story of the Academy, from the failing Oak Drive High to its emergence as the now successful Parkside. The predecessor school was portrayed as a dull and unfortunate environment for students and staff alike, in which they had little if any hope of succeeding. The prelude set the scene:

> The CEO is being shown round a school by a student and the Principal.
> STUDENT: *This is the main hall . . .*
> Image flashes up [from inside the old school building with graffiti on the wall]
> STUDENT: *. . . and this is the counselling room . . .*
> Image flashes up [A picture of graffiti on the wall: the same one as in the PowerPoint presentation described above, and later referred to as an unfair representation by the veteran teacher quoted earlier]
> THE CEO: *The counselling room?*
> STUDENT: *There's a lot of people here who need more help than just lessons, sir.*
> THE CEO: *Tell me about your ambitions, young lady, what would you like to do when you leave school?*
> STUDENT: *I want to be a doctor, sir.*
> THE CEO: *I see . . .*
> Pause, he looks back at the images on the screen, thinking.
> THE PRINCIPAL: *Well?*
> THE CEO: *I must help her.*

The EfFT and its retiring CEO were portrayed as stepping in to save the school from, what can only be described as its inevitable doom. The CEO was presented as the visionary and fundraiser, and the Principal as the foot soldier, who, through hard work and with 'tough love', made his visions a reality and led the school to success.

The following note, written by one of us at the time, summarises the presentation of the CEO's character and the final scene of the musical in which he had a central symbolic role:

> The musical was the 'story of the school' in which [the CEO] was presented as an angelic saviour, offering his helping hand to save the struggling school. The boy playing his part appeared on stage every now and then, talking on a mobile phone, sorting out funding for various things, such as the basketball grounds, etc. At the end of the musical, the second last scene, all student and

staff characters stand on the stage solving a fight between students, which had escalated in a local park and ended up making headlines in the local newspapers. This was considered a devastating incident violating the reputation of the new Academy. The scene ends as the 'trouble-maker-but-from-deep-down-a-good-lad' starts singing: 'Like a bridge over troubled water', to which all others join. The problem gets solved as, one by one, the young people and adults on stage join together holding each others' hands, forming one big circle with one spot in the middle left empty. Then [the CEO] enters the stage, walks to the empty spot, grasps the yet unheld hands, making the circle complete.

The musical was, at times, uncomfortable for an outsider to watch, as the perspective from which the story was told and the central message it sought to deliver were made apparent to the audience. This message was mainly articulated by the character of the Principal, whose guidance, it must be remembered, was reported to have been influential on the emphasis placed within the production. What was left for the staff and students to work on was the presentation of the message through music, acting and choreography.

The overriding impression the production left was that the talent of the young actors and musicians on stage was used for what could be called a branding exercise and, as such, a retelling of the history of the school. The fact that the musical was a commissioned piece – influenced by the Principal – raises questions in relation to the professional autonomy and respect of the staff. It lends itself to an interpretation that the motive behind Green End Musical were something other than simply a passion for drama and theatre education. It is possible, of course, that there are other interpretations.

At the time of the musical, the members of staff involved were, understandably, reluctant to engage in a conversation regarding its production. Indeed, three of those who had been closely involved indicated that they would rather not discuss the production at all. However, about 12 months later, one senior colleague described some of the feelings and thinking of the staff who had been involved:

> INT: *This is a bit off the radar now, but were you involved in the musical last year?*
> *Yes!* (laughs)
> INT: *Could you tell me about that?*
> *I don't know what that was!* (laughs) *What do you want me to tell you? (keeps on laughing) I sold myself to the EfFT, and to how amazing it is . . . How this man is so amazing and how this woman is so amazing.* (keeps laughing)
> INT: *Where did the idea come from?*
> *I think* [the Principal] *had the idea, and then* [the assessment lead] *wrote the musical . . . I just used some tools. I think the difficult thing last year was how to get staff to participate. Because they didn't believe in it and they ddidn't buy into it. And they just did it as a favour to me and Ms Heart. That's where that came from!* (laughs)

INT: *didn't buy into it. And they just did it as a favour to me and Ms Heart. That's where that came from!*

These comments provide a sense of the awkward manner in which the production was perceived by some of the Parkside staff involved. The remarks also draw attention to the loyalty they felt towards certain of their colleagues and to the students, rather than to the representatives of the EfFT. Our own somewhat critical analysis of the musical leads us to locate the production as part of a stream of branding exercises, actively executed to promote the success of Parkside to the wider community, the media and, we assume, to those politicians who were encouraging the policy moves associated with academies.

As noted earlier, during the period following the successful Ofsted inspection, we had often observed senior members of staff retelling a polished version of the school's history to visitors, as well as in events elsewhere. Like the musical, this type of activity seemed to underpin the school's external relations, suggesting there was an unwritten, or at least unpublished, marketing strategy. Certainly, the Principal appeared to be very preoccupied with public image and there were numerous strategies in place to stay in control of how the Academy was perceived elsewhere. At the same time, we sensed that EfFT was increasingly concerned about the ways in which the growing community of academies and academy sponsors nationally perceived Parkside. In this context, our interpretation was that the musical provided a tangible example of the process of 'academy-isation' in action.

Conclusion

The 'official' story of the success of Parkside was, indeed, impressive, even if sometimes exaggerated in its claims. At the same time, it is essential to stress that a school that had previously lost its way had genuinely been reshaped into a context characterised by greater optimism, a far safer working climate and much higher expectations. And, as we have explained, this was reflected in the school's massively improved results in national examinations and in an inspection report that defined the school as being outstanding. It is also important to report that we have subsequently heard reports from former students who talk with pride regarding their experience at the school, not least the impact that the Principal has had on their post-school life chances. In all these respects, what was achieved at Parkside was remarkable by any standards.

Thinking about this account, a member of the governing body argued that the crisis situation that was inherited from the previous school demanded a period that was characterised by 'top-down' measures – 'a drive for consistency'. He explained that, with this in mind, the Principal has been relentless in 'sharing a vision but backing it up with hard demands'. The big question now, he argued, is can this approach be changed to one of 'self-driven demands'?

The management and leadership structures that were put in place seemed to offer considerable potential for making such a move. Commenting on this as the school began to make progress, a middle manager noted that she and her colleagues felt that they had been given more space. She explained: 'There was frustration in the past. People wanted to innovate but there were no methods through which you could get your own ideas across'.

In these senses, Parkside is an encouraging example of how the policy of giving schools that are struggling a new start and greater freedom, under different management and governance arrangement, can act as a catalyst for change. As we go on to explain more about the development of the school, it is therefore vital to distil lessons from what happened.

In attempting to draw lessons, it is important to remember that schools are complex social institutions, with as many stories and versions of stories as there are people to tell them. In this respect Parkside Academy is no different. As researchers, we were lucky to gain privileged access to the school over a relatively long period. This provided us with remarkable opportunities to get close to this social complexity by discussing what happened during those years with teachers, students, middle leaders, governors, teaching assistants and other support staff, as well as senior leaders and employees of the sponsor. As a result of these discussions, as well as time spent in classrooms, corridors, the schoolyard and meeting areas, as we have shown in this chapter, nuances and details of the story began to unravel.

We believe that, as researchers, it is our duty to bring these stories together in order to cast light on the complexities and tensions in perceptions of this fascinating school. We choose to do this in order to contribute constructively to thinking in the field. In so doing, we continue to be respectful of the remarkable progress made in the school. We are also keen to acknowledge the massive commitment and efforts of those involved. Bearing this in mind, in the chapters that follow, we provide more detailed accounts of the development of Parkside Academy, filling some of the gaps left in the Principal's PowerPoint presentation.

Note

1 'Turn around' is a phrase frequently used in the field to imply significant improvement of a school seen as failing.

4

RESULTS, RESULTS, RESULTS

The previous chapter provided a history of Parkside Academy over a period of more than ten years. In so doing, it threw light on the contexts in which the school operated, giving a flavour of its style of leadership and its governance arrangements. This has portrayed the milieu in which the school's ways of working evolved. In this chapter we move on to focus more closely on practices in the Academy and how they were developed.

Much of this material was collected during the school year 2011–2012, by which time Parkside was seen to be a highly successful school. This helps us to identify some of the key strategies that appeared to have facilitated its progress. The overarching feature of these strategies was a sense of compliance, as school-wide strategies were introduced by senior leaders and systematically monitored in order to ensure they were implemented. Focused mainly on the improvement on examination results, these strategies were seen to limit the freedom of teachers to make decisions regarding the planning of the curriculum, classroom practices and forms of assessment. We show how this approach was regulated through the overall management style used in the school, under the direction of its sponsor.

Despite this emphasis on standardised practices, our account also shows that there were spaces for creativity in practice. To illustrate this point, the chapter concludes with an account of the efforts of one department in the school to explore the use of collaborative professional development as a way of promoting experimentation in classroom practice in order to find better ways of responding to learner diversity. This initiative led the school to participate in a European Union funded project, involving schools in three countries. It gives strong indications of the untapped potential within the school that could be mobilised to improve its capacity to educate all of its students, provided that the conditions are created for this to happen.

Planning the curriculum

The overall responsibility for the Parkside curriculum rested with one of the assistant principals, who liaised with all heads of departments, ensuring departmental curricula were in line with Academy policy, as well as EfFT guidance. In practical terms, this role was distributed to the various subject departments, where the main responsibility for leading and managing lay with the heads of department. The extent to which individual teachers engaged with this curricular work differed between departments, but in those departments that we looked at in detail, teachers were encouraged to contribute to some of the decision making.

In terms of the EfFT's approach to curriculum planning, in 2010 the organisation invested in a full-time member of staff to take on a chain-wide lead role. She was promoted to this role from her post as Parkside's assistant principal, in which her remit had been for the curriculum during the period the school came to be rated 'outstanding' by the Ofsted inspectors. She described her role in the organisation and her involvement with the academies in the group as follows:

> So, the role I do now, in summary, is to support academies to the right curriculum, because at the moment a lot of them don't offer an appropriate curriculum, or the management of the organisation isn't sufficient for the schools to get the best grades. And I think this is for several reasons, for example, some curriculum planners in academies don't see the bigger picture so they might have particular groups of kids who are allowed to do such and such course, but they might not think of the consequences of such arrangements and see that with such an arrangement students would not be able to achieve more than grade D to G, and those students would not meet their A to C target. So there's things like that. Sometimes students are doing a wrong combination of courses, so you might have students in courses that discount each other, say two technology subjects, which, for the school only count as one. . . . Also there's a lot of national changes going on at the moment that some academies don't keep up with as much as they should so I have to source that sort of information for them as well.

Since the sponsor's guidelines regarding the curriculum were rather broad, individual academies attached to the chain had significant freedom to develop their own approach as they saw fit. However, as this senior leader highlights, this was deeply embedded in the preoccupation of EfFT to support academies in providing a curriculum that most effectively raised student attainment. And, at that time, it was apparent that some of the schools were seen to be falling short in relation to this goal.

This concern with what national policy defines as 'standards' was also present in conversations with the Parkside staff, many of who quite forcefully articulated that the focus of their curriculum must stay on this agenda, and that the curriculum must best prepare students for examinations. Therefore, even though one of the key features framing academies policy is their autonomy from the national curriculum (DfE, 2010; Academies Act, 2010), and even with only a light involvement of the EfFT, there was very little evidence that Parkside staff had experimented with the curriculum. Some did report minor alternative approaches in Key Stage 3 (students 11 to 14 years of age), but as far as KS4 (14 to 16) and KS5 (16 to 19) were concerned (i.e. the stages nearest to the high-stakes examinations), the national curriculum was rigorously followed.[1] For example:

> We teach national curriculum, it has all these different focuses within the grids, so focus 1–8, for reading and writing. So what I brought this year is that we all teach towards those grids, so that we can follow that, yes, they are making progress, but so that they are making progress against the national curriculum standards.

And:

> What has happened with the league tables and all that pressure, pushing the grades up and picking more BTECs[2] is that, I was hoping they [SLT and EfFT] would have the freedom to run more courses and a wider range of courses but still they haven't really, they still stick to the national curriculum and there isn't anything that new. We've taken the EDEXEL, so we just follow that scheme. It would be just ridiculous to do something that wasn't thought out well in advance.

These comments highlight the extent to which the national curriculum was taken for granted, and help to explain why staff were more secure with this rather than experimenting with alternatives. Indeed, there was a general consensus amongst the staff that contesting the national curriculum would be risky, and, as it is seen as preparing students for examinations, it would be foolish to experiment with it.

According to the experiences of the EfFT curriculum lead, other academies in the chain had chosen a similar approach. As a result, little innovation was taking place in relation to curriculum development:

> Although the academies have the flexibility to do what they want, I think because we are still judged against performance tables with other schools, I don't think schools do as much as they could. And I think some of them don't because they don't have the curriculum leaders who are bold enough to do it. So, say there might be alternatives to the courses here and there but they are not recognised in the performance tables . . . in Year 7 a lot of academies tend to do their own curriculum which tends to be based on project based provision but on KS4 and KS5 I don't say they [EfFT academies] explore. This has also got to do with the nature of the EfFT, you know they take on board failing schools, that's why they got to be able to perform rapid

improvements and, unfortunately, they are measured on results, so to some extent you have still got to play the game.

This explanation illustrates the constraints that appeared to bound the autonomy of EfFT academies over the curriculum. Although they were legally autonomous as far the national curriculum is concerned, their performance was measured against the same national performance indicators as other schools, which, based on the evidence from Parkside Academy, significantly limits the actual autonomy of staff to innovate with the curriculum. This performance-oriented culture is further discussed later in this chapter, in relation to assessment.

In terms of day-to-day lesson planning, there were certain Academy-level policies that guided staff in all departments. An example of this was the 'Lesson Plan Sheet' that was expected to be used for every lesson. This focused on basic elements of a lesson: learning objectives, learning outcomes, methods and differentiation. Teachers with experiences from working in other EfFT academies mentioned that similar procedures were also in place there, too, as noted by one teacher:

> The lesson plan proformas differ from academy to academy but again they expect differentiation, progress, the general things that have to be there.

Although this quite general basis for lesson plans was used across the Academy and the expectation was that each class taught in the school would be planned using it, during extended visits within the departments we observed how some teachers took liberties in its use. There was, however, a general consensus amongst the staff that the planning sheet is used when formally observed by senior leaders of the school, or during an Ofsted inspection.

Another example of a policy guiding teachers' day-to-day lesson planning related to the structure of lessons, leading to what could be seen as something of a 'house style'. So, for example, the majority of lessons began with a short warm-up exercise, as explained by one teacher:

> We begin the class always with a short game or some other kind of quick warm-up. It's good to wake up the students and get them going. We often go for games and fun things like that, we are encouraged to do that, I know some teachers do it, some don't, but I think it's not a bad way to start a lesson.

In general, Academy-level policies framing teachers' lesson planning were few, and as suggested by this teacher, staff tended to apply the ones in place rather selectively. Instead of guidance and instruction over lesson planning, a collaborative ethos amongst teachers would be a better way to describe the approach used in the Academy. Indeed, we witnessed many examples of joint lesson planning and the sharing of practice on a daily basis, and it became obvious that many teachers made an effort to foster collaborative ways of working. For example, a head of department commented:

I try to make everything in my power to facilitate collaboration in this department, from developing material banks to, say one of the things I did, last year, everybody in Year 7, 8 and 9 was taught different thing, so one class would be reading a different book than another, so teachers were developing separate schemes of work in isolation. However, with Year 7 this year, what I've done is, I've redesigned what is going to be thought and I've bought whole year sets of books, to encourage teachers to plan and teach together. So it's been a massive pot of my budget, as I've bought 150 copies of *Percy Jackson*, 150 copies of *War Horse* to get teachers to plan together. Obviously they have to differentiate it, but I think it's just a much better collaborative approach.

This collaborative thinking appeared to underpin much of the lesson planning across the school. So, for example, teachers uploaded teaching material to shared material banks, and conversations on corridors and in the staff room regarding methods and teaching material took place frequently. Whilst lesson planning as a daily practice was not heavily influenced by the Academy or EfFT policy, on the occasions of formal observations staff tended to pay more attention to the few existing school-level policies framing lesson planning, making sure the planning sheets were filled out accordingly and that the required lesson structure was in place.

In terms of longer term planning, the Academy-level and EfFT-level instructions were rather loose, and teaching staff and heads of departments especially, appeared to be largely autonomous in determining the actual content of the curriculum. Also, wider themes that EfFT and the Academy emphasised in their policy documentation, such as the Christian ethos, or the specialism in Business and Enterprise, appeared to have little impact on curricular decisions. Rather, the main drivers for curriculum-related decision making were external, particularly pressures to improve student performance in national examinations. The exam-focused culture and its implications for the planning and practice of teaching are further discussed later in this chapter in relation to assessment. Prior to that, however, the next section examines influences on classroom practice.

Teaching methods

The physical environment in which teaching at Parkside took place provided a framework for its practices. We observed, in particular, how the architecture of the school, the layout of classrooms and the available material for teachers and students to use all impacted on what was taught and how.

The environment is such that beside each classroom door there is a window, providing a view to the classroom from the corridor, even when the doors are closed. Therefore, it is possible to develop a rapid sense of the material environment of classrooms across the Academy. As noted in the previous chapter, the school was well equipped, with interactive white boards in all classrooms, as well as other latest technology in the school library and technology areas. Consequently, there was no shortage of computers for student use, and a department of four ICT technicians worked full time, making sure that the available technology was working. The Academy had not only invested in technology providing excellent facilities for teaching and learning, but also in training the staff, who actively put the technology to use.

There were some observations regarding the material environment of teaching and learning that we discussed with staff in more detail during extended visits in departments. Here the intention was to seek clarification as to departmental as well as school-wide policies. One area of policy related to the layout of classrooms, as, in most, tables and chairs were organised in a similar manner, usually grouping four students together. This was the arrangement in most rooms, excluding those with permanent fittings, such as science laboratories, or rooms with limited space. Members of staff clarified it was an all-Academy policy, introduced by the senior team in order to encourage group work amongst students. A member of staff commented on the benefits of the approach:

> I think it's ok that the desks are the same everywhere. There's a lot of teachers touring around so at least they are in the same order in every class.

However, there were exceptions. For example, a teacher who had decided to organise the classroom in a different manner argued the reasons for using their own judgment regarding the layout of the class rather than following the initiative:

> There was an all-school initiative about the desks in classes, to keep them in groups, and it works for some people, but with some of my classes it just distracts some of my students, so I've kept the desks separately. And nobody has said anything. It doesn't mean that I wouldn't do group work with them, not at all, I just don't want the desks to be like that all the time.

Another obvious school-wide influence was the way in which material used for teaching was organised across the Academy. Apart from pens, planners, and the occasional homework sheets that students carried, all other teaching material was stored in classrooms, or elsewhere in the department area. To focus on one aspect more closely, students' workbooks provide possibly the most interesting example of how school policies directly frame teachers' pedagogical decision making. These workbooks were identical in each subject, the only variable being the size of the book, some being A4 and others A5 in size. On the cover of each book was a sticker with the EfFT logo and a similar set of 'traffic lights' as could be seen on the walls of most classes. These indicated the 'level' at which the student was currently working and the level they were working towards.

It was not only the appearance of the books that was strikingly similar across the Academy, but also the ways in which these books were used. Here a head of department describes the school's policies regarding the usage of workbooks:

> We have quite strict guidelines about what students should be doing and how books should be marked. So, I know this sounds ridiculous, but students

should be writing in blue and black ink, and every student should have a date in the title, underlined, in each lesson.

Expectations regarding the use of workbooks were similar across the Academy and were rigorously followed in all departments. As a result, the presentation and form of the work students produced was strikingly similar, both in the different subject areas and across the year groups. In order to prevent unwanted graffiti, students were not allowed to draw in their workbooks, resulting in what struck us as rather monotonous and dull pages across all the year groups.

The workbook guidelines are an example of a school-wide policy directly constraining teacher's pedagogical autonomy regarding teaching methods and material. Rather than encouraging teachers to experiment with alternative approaches in pedagogy, this appeared to be limiting their decision making. Given the evident diversity of learners in every class, this seemed perverse in the way it limits possibilities for experimentation with different approaches.

Another set of rigorously followed school-level guidelines was the homework policy. In all departments, students were given homework fortnightly on a specific homework sheet. The responsibility for this in each Key Stage was assigned to a member of staff in the department. One of the teachers responsible for homework clarified the process:

> I do it for Key Stage 3, I'm responsible for that. So they [the Academy SLT] have a policy that every few weeks students have an extended homework, which is from 3–4 hours of work, depending on what they have learnt and passed two weeks. So I put together a work sheet for Year 7s and 8s. Then they get them marked and they get sent back to me. This is the homework policy throughout the school.

The impact this policy had on teachers' professional autonomy were rather significant in the sense that individual teachers were not able to contribute to the content, nor the procedures of their students' homework. However, this departmentally coordinated approach was not contested by members of staff and teachers across the school seemed to have a rather neutral take on it.

Arguably the most significant factor limiting teachers' pedagogical autonomy, however, was the school's performance management policy. Central to this was a strict routine of lesson observations. This came to the surface during initial discussions with heads of departments regarding observations for our research, in which we discussed possibilities for classroom data collection. They advised that the word 'observation' might be best avoided, using 'visits' instead.

According to Parkside's policy, every teacher is subject to a formal observation, which is conducted by their head of department and one of the assistant principals three times a year. The observation follows criteria used by inspectors and, as one senior member of staff put it, 'serves the role of a mock Ofsted inspection'. Here one of the teachers explains these formal observations practices and expresses some of the perceptions of the teaching staff:

We have an inspection every term. . . . They give you three-day notice for a two-day window. Those two days they can come on any lesson they want to. So you have to be fully prepared for those two days, any lesson they can come. So, it's hard to get used to. . . . So it's either, unsatisfactory, satisfactory, good or outstanding. They do it to the Ofsted criteria and progress is the main factor. If the lesson doesn't show any progression it's a limited factor and you get an unsatisfactory straight away, even if the lesson was wonderful, even if the kids behaved wonderfully well and did all the work they were asked to do and they were all happy about it, that's still an unsatisfactory, we have to show progression in the lesson, that's for sure. Books need to be marked accordingly. Kids should be able to talk about their grades they are on and how do they progress. Strategies should be there, like the red, amber and green cards, and the assessment should be there. Then there should be something for all learning styles: kinesthetic, visual, auditive. If we are unsatisfactory or satisfactory, they will come and observe us again after. And we have training every Thursday from 3 to 4 – people who are unsatisfactory or satisfactory, you have to attend.

In addition to these formal termly observations, other forms of monitoring of teaching practice took place. For example, 'learning walks' were a less formal form of lesson observation, serving a slightly different purpose than the formal observations. A head of department explains how and why learning walks were carried out in their department:

I do learning walks as well. I do them every week. I make sure that I go to every single classroom, and check that the teachers are ok with the behaviour, but also that the students are learning, and that there are learning objectives in place and lessons are being planned and stuff like that.

These learning walks were carried out in a similar manner in all departments. They were generally described – by both teachers and heads of departments alike – as informal visits, giving both parties a chance to discuss whatever seems to be the burning issue at the time. In addition to learning walks, teaching staff were used to having members of senior staff dropping into their classroom for various reasons, such as monitoring student behaviour or informal visits with external visitors.

The evidence we have presented so far has highlighted issues regarding the nature and extent of limitations imposed upon teachers' pedagogical decision making regarding classroom activities. We have explained how tangible policy constraints, such as instruction regarding the layout of the classroom, as well as workbook policy, had a direct impact, appeared to narrow teachers' capacity to utilise a variety of teaching methods. However, as we have seen, there was evidence of levels of agency, as some teachers decided to swim against the stream and opt out from the Academy policy. These were exceptional cases: confident teachers with a track record of approved successful practice, and, even more importantly, mainly carried out in day-to-day practice, not during formal observations.

As to less tangible constraints, it was clear that the rigorous observation procedures at Parkside had a direct impact on teachers' choice of methods and activities. However, apart from the observations, teachers were not directly guided to use a specific method in relation to specific content. Nonetheless, the frequent observations clearly influenced teachers' practices, and they were a reoccurring topic of conversations amongst teachers. When asked about a certain method or way of working, teachers would often reflect back to feedback received following observations in ways that implied that this could not be overlooked. Indeed, it was clearly the case that teaching practices were framed and steered by the lesson observation procedures and that their key purpose was to ensure that the departmental and school-level guidance was implemented in the classrooms. The impact of observations is revisited in a later section in relation to student assessment.

Despite these arrangements, teachers we talked to were conscious of their theoretical liberty to experiment with aspects of practice. However, their overhanging fear of failure in respect to the high-stakes examinations prevented them from creative pedagogical approaches and risk-taking. This standards-driven culture and academy-level assessment policy regulated teachers' pedagogical decision making heavily, not only framing teachers' assessment practice, but steering also their pedagogical decisions. This became apparent through the ways in which planning and teaching were designed and conducted to most efficiently prepare students for national exams.

Pressures to improve

As we have seen, intensive top-down systems to raise the performance of both students and staff undoubtedly paid off, in the sense that Parkside saw rapid improvements in its examination results. Their introduction points to the strategic dilemmas faced by senior staff working in very challenging circumstances and with the added pressures of being seen as part of a politically controversial effort to reform education. More specifically, they reveal the challenges facing academy principals as they try to establish a common sense of purpose across a whole school community. So, for example, at one point the Principal justified why she had imposed tight procedures to track student and staff performance. These were, she explained, to ensure that the values to which she was committed were reflected in the way the school worked.

Some staff spoke positively about the overall strength of these management arrangements in terms of supporting them in carrying out their classroom tasks. For example, a head of department talked about the obvious presence the Principal had around the school, commenting, 'She likes to keep her finger on the pulse'. A young teacher said that she appreciated it recently when a senior colleague told her to make sure she 'has a weekend'. The Principal offered an interesting commentary on the complexity of this issue, when she commented, 'I've banned staff from coming in at weekends. Now they say that you are making my life more difficult'.

Talking to staff, the sense of pressure to raise standards rapidly was a common theme. Commenting on this, one experienced teacher argued: 'We put ourselves under pressure'. Another teacher, in her third year at the school, talked about the very long hours she and some of her colleagues put in, noting she has 'good days and bad days'. Despite the strong systems in place, she explained, behaviour still remained a challenge, particularly with 'middle groups'. She went on: 'Friday afternoons I struggle and the end of the day can also be hard'. On the other hand, she explained that she never felt in any way intimidated by students and that there was very little violence in the school. It is worth adding here that staff commented that some difficulties arose because some students did not want to leave the school at the end of a day. A teacher commented: 'The children look forward to school. They just don't like the holidays.'

It is worth noting here, too, that many staff appreciated the way consistency in implementing systems helped create a much more positive working atmosphere across the school. So, for example, a teacher who described seeing how things had changed over the first five years of the new school felt that the management systems were 'very supportive', not least because when problems occurred they were dealt with quickly. Another member of staff explained: 'These kids need routines, so there is a logic. The logic is routine, routine, routine'. On the other hand, she added, none of this encouraged 'risk-taking', something that is surely needed if schools are to find ways of reaching hard to reach groups of learners.

It is clear, then, that the progress made at Parkside during its early years – turning what was a challenging and potentially dangerous environment into a context that became safe and supportive of learning – was quite remarkable. This research also suggests that this first step – creating the initial momentum and the self-belief among staff and students alike that goes with it – is difficult. In such contexts, focusing on teaching and on learning are both important, and once a school is into a cycle of improvement, both are kept under regular evaluation and review.

The big doubt regarding all of this, however, relates to sustainability. Our observations at Parkside suggest that the teachers involved – many of whom were young, energetic and committed individuals – eventually ran out of steam. As one young teacher said, 'everything here is for the students'. Responding to the positive response to this statement, she added, 'nothing is for the staff'.

In addition, what was seen as 'strong' management was perceived by some staff as being threatening. So, for example, one teacher commented: 'Staff feel they are told to do things. . . . At this school it is more about what you are not doing, rather than what you are doing'. He went on to explain that, sometimes, as part of quality assurance measures, senior staff would arrive unannounced in the classroom: 'They walk in the classroom. I always feel they are looking out for what I'm doing wrong'. Apparently, during such visits lesson plans were checked. Later, feedback was sent by email and usually offered suggestions for improvement.

Another young and obviously very committed teacher argued that the preoccupation with imposing systems and procedures was aimed at a small number of staff who 'don't plan'. She felt that this was unfair on colleagues such as her. She added, 'There are very committed people here who feel they are not coping'. Another teacher commented, 'There's not much fun here. Sometimes it feels more like a business rather than a school'.

Assessing student progress

The ways in which Parkside staff evaluate the learning of their students was heavily framed by a combination of EfFT, school and department level policies and guidance. As a result, teachers were even more restricted in their assessment practices than in relation to curriculum planning and teaching related decision making. The sponsor's assessment policy was rather general, outlining some criteria and methods for student assessment, with an intention to inform assessment policy and practice in all its academies. These expectations were outlined as follows:

- Schools/academies must publish an assessment recording and reporting policy.
- Schools/academies must publish an examinations policy. The policy should include an explanation of how assessment links to curriculum and an examination entry policy.
- Schools/academies must incorporate regular assessment points for all students throughout the school year.
- Schools/academies must have mechanisms in place for measuring progress using QCA points or NC levels.
- Teachers must use assessment to inform planning and to track and record the progress and achievement of students.
- Teachers must record a range of assessment evidence for each student.
- Assessment practice must be differentiated so that all students may demonstrate what they know, understand and can do.
- Schools and academies must send parents at least one written report every year.

Assessment, Recording and Reporting Policy, August 2009
(withdrawn from the Academy staff shared area 5 May 2012)

The actual ways in which these expected criteria were to be achieved was not defined in the policy, leaving individual schools with a degree of flexibility. To support schools in taking the policy forward, EfFT had created an 'assessment lead'. This is how the person involved described this role:

So all the chain wide roles are: Ann in curriculum, Colleen in Business and Enterprise and Keith in data and assessment, but in a different meaning of assessment as me. Mine is more classroom based teacher assessment and Keith on assessment on data.

The assessment lead worked closely with several academies across the chain, as well as continuing to hold a senior leader status in Parkside. Due to her other senior leader responsibilities in the school (described later, in Chapter 5), her influence was greater in areas of the school other than assessment, leaving most assessment responsibilities to the assistant principal overseeing teaching and learning.

The person in this role was responsible for ensuring that the Parkside approach was in line with EfFT policy and implemented consistently in each department. Members of the SLT were quite directive in this respect, providing detailed instructions on several aspects of formative and summative student assessment. So, for example, a visible presence across the school to aid formative assessment was the 'traffic lights' system, mentioned earlier. Most classrooms had a poster on the wall, with a picture of a red, amber and a green light. Some classrooms also had little cards with similar colour codes. Here a member of staff explains how the traffic light system was expected to be used in student self-evaluation:

> So, green is for yes I understand it completely; amber is I'm kind of there; and red is I'm completely lost. So, kind of checking have they understood the first part so that we can move to the next part. Which is progress from grade C to Grade B. So they have these little cards and they show how well they understood what they had just learnt.

Although the material was available in classrooms for teachers to use, it turned out that not all staff were supportive of the approach and some had adopted alternative methods. Here another member of staff highlights issues related to this student self-evaluation method, as well as broader issues to do with Academy-wide policies:

> There's initiatives are coming left right and centre in this Academy. For example, they told us to use the traffic light cards, so that every student has them cards in their books or on the table. But who would want to use them? Who wants to say I don't know something in front of other students? And as if teachers wouldn't pick up on what the students don't know. Believe it or not, I actually failed an observation [carried out by senior staff] because I didn't use those cards. Seriously! Then after a while the Ofsted came and told us that the cards are rubbish. You know what happened the next day? We were told: don't use the cards; don't use the cards.

These comments regarding the rapidity of pace in which initiatives were introduced and changed reflected the rather frantic nature of leadership activity in the Academy.

The teaching staff considered the SLT to be a constant presence around the school. This was partly because there were so many senior leaders: ten altogether, all of them working on their own remits. As a result, changes were being introduced on a frequent basis, resulting in a degree of confusion, especially amongst more junior staff.

However, some policies related to matters of assessment were more consistently followed and, therefore, more deeply rooted in day-to-day practice. An example of such would be the workbook marking policy, as noted by the following teachers:

> Teachers are meant to mark their books [student workbooks] every three weeks and have evidence of detailed marking. This is not just our department but across the school.

And:

> In our department we do the 'star, wish and a question' in students' work books once every three weeks. So the person in charge in our curriculum area checks the books but sometimes SLT come in and check them so that we are using the same assessment criteria across the Academy.

The frequency of workbook marking was set by the SLT, carried out by teachers and monitored by the heads of department and senior staff. However, the ways in which the student books were to be marked was determined at the department level, in an effort to secure similar practice across each curriculum area. Generally, teaching staff – particularly those in the English and maths departments – were relatively positive about this arrangement. The only issue arising was in relation to the differing nature of curriculum areas, as marking tended to be more time consuming in English than in maths. Therefore, frequency of marking added more to English teachers' than maths teachers' workload.

The departments in which staff raised most concerns in relation to methods of assessment were arts and technology, as explained by one of the specialist teachers involved:

> There's a lot of issues around assessment and student capabilities in our curriculum area [arts and technology]. As it stands, much of assessment is based on students' academic abilities, written and articulation, and the practical work is just a part of it, which is a real challenge for many students. Say an example of a girl with hearing impairment as well as being visual impaired is getting a D for her work, which was a massive achievement for her, but they [SLT] are only interested in how she could get a C, even though it was a huge achievement for her and possibly through much harder work than other, more capable students.

The teacher refers here to two different issues concerning assessment in her subject. Firstly, she highlights the practical nature of some subjects – such as the arts, home economics, textile work, woodwork – and the challenges of assessing these subjects through written as well as practical work. She went on to explain that teaching staff in these departments are expected to assess students on a similar frequency as staff in other subjects, but as the nature of the work differs, the assessment criteria must emphasise both the written and practical work students produce. So, for example, with textile work, prior to getting involved with the practical side of production, students were expected to produce a written portfolio, including: a written description on the planning process, a detailed work plan and often also a marketing plan for the product they are about to produce. These portfolios were significant pieces of work, including several pages of text, images and material samples taking weeks for students to produce.

A few teachers raised concerns about the unfairness of such methods of assessment, arguing that students who might be talented, motivated and hard working in their practical work, may, at times, find the literacy side challenging, resulting at times in lower grades, as well as reduced motivation. The concern of some teachers was that the expected criteria meant that they were not able to develop assessment strategies appropriate for their subjects.

The second issue referred to by the arts and technology teacher was one that was also raised in other departments. It concerned the emphasis the Academy put on students' examination results. As we have noted, the pressure on staff to raise standards was ever present and was the single most determining factor framing teachers' practice. This is illustrated by the following observation:

> The most defining feature of the school experience for the Year 10 and Year 11 students is the never-ending revision for exams. They do one mock exam a week, up until their actual exams. And as the teachers explained, that's all they do after Christmas – lesson after lesson they work on the previous year's exam papers.

So, pressure to improve examination results steered the professional practice of staff to a remarkable extent, as teachers, heads of departments as well as senior leaders, in all curriculum areas emphasised the importance of raising student achievement. Indeed, the pressure to raise standards was mentioned during all staff interviews as the main driver for teachers' and heads of departments' professional practice. For example, one teacher commented:

> Results, results and results. That's all they [SLT] care about.

And a head of department argued:

> There's a lot of pressure for results in Year 11. That's the main thing that keeps me up at night. . . . It is constantly coming down from above. So, almost weekly, I get from above: have we converted any more results, have we got any more A★ to Cs. And the problem is, no. Because English is modular, and the final exam is on April the 29th, and we won't know what most people have got until then. But the Academy wants to know how many are we going to get. And we can't say for definite. That's the main pressure.

There was also a shared consensus amongst many staff that the underlying pressure on results was 'coming down from above', as this head of department put it, and was considered constant and at times unnecessarily harsh. There was also a common view that the SLT imposed unrealistic expectations regarding exam results, creating an overly stressful work environment for teaching staff, and, as such, limiting their professional autonomy. Here a teacher expresses a perspective on what he saw as Parkside's Academy's result-driven culture:

> The difference between this Academy and a more traditional school in my experience is that this is run like a business. The more kids we get in the more money we get, and that seems to be all that matters. And how we get more kids in is through success in exams. So the SLT have these completely unrealistic expectations about kids' progress. Like, say if you compare to business, if you make a 10,000 profit one year, it is unreasonable to expect 40 million profit the next year, and this is what the expectations here are like.

Although this teacher's perception emphasises the role of senior leaders in creating the results-driven culture at Parkside, discussions with senior members of staff clarified their somewhat differing perception regarding the source of expectations. Raising standards was a central objective and a driving force for EfFT since the Academy was established, but changes in the organisation management led to a cultural shift, further strengthening the emphasis on standards. Looking back at what had happened, one senior teacher commented:

> When xxxxx was the CEO [of EfFT] there was more emphasis on enrichment. He was a lovely man who really cared about these kids and there was more room for other things. Now we have the new person in charge who has more political experience and he is mainly interested in success. So any attempt to give an overall ethos to the group of schools went out of the window when he came. With the Labour government and the immediate success of the Academies Programme, EfFT being a big player on the field, we are now told: Get results!

This assistant principal locates Parkside in a bigger picture by offering wider political as well as organisational motives and explanations for the results-driven culture underpinning the day-to-day life of the school. As suggested by the teachers we quoted earlier, staff across the Academy were under significant pressure to raise standards and improve student outcomes, but the pressure was not solely shaping their thinking and practice, but that of more senior staff as well. We have seen, too, this pressure to improve results influenced and steered practices to a great extent, not only in relation to student assessment, but also in terms of planning of the curriculum and the style of teaching.

The intensity of these pressures – on both the teachers and senior members of staff – was vividly illustrated by the story told by the Principal the morning after a previous evening's staff meeting. She explained how she had used a series of graphs to demonstrate the progress she was expecting in examination results in the coming year. By her own admission, this was expecting a massive improvement from the previous year. Each member of staff held two cards, one green and the other red. She asked everybody at the meeting to wave the card that best described what they thought was possible. In response to those colleagues holding up red cards she commented that it looked like some people would be looking for a new job soon.

Reflecting on what had happened later that same evening, the Principal recalled thinking that there might be some resignations the next day. Interestingly, one very committed teacher later commented privately that the event had made her wonder if she should start searching the job adverts.

Untapped potential

So far, this chapter has illustrated the many ways in which practitioners at Parkside were limited in relation to their influence over curriculum planning, teaching practices and forms of assessment. It has also shown that, despite or possibly because of the pressures this involved, staff tended to work collaboratively. Our concerns about all of this relate to the extent to which such pressures can be sustained and the way in which they may limit experimentation, something that seems to us to be particularly important in a school that addresses so much diversity and uncertainty within its student population.

During the period following the inspection that saw Parkside being designated as outstanding, there was an initiative in the English department that threw light on how greater experimentation with new ways of working might be encouraged, building on the forms of collaboration that already existed within the school. Starting as a small-scale action research project in one department, it eventually became part of an international study involving schools in three countries.

This initial project explored ways of developing teaching practices within the English department, which, at the time, was seen to perform particularly well. Focused on making lessons more inclusive, it involved action research with all the staff in the English department, supported by researchers from a local university, who also took responsibility for evaluating and reporting the findings of the project. In this way it was intended to develop a staff development model that could subsequently be used school-wide and, possibly, shared with other schools in the chain.

The project made use of evidence from international research regarding strategies for fostering forms of teaching that are effective in engaging all members of a class (Villegas-Reimers, 2003). This suggests that developments of practice, particularly amongst more experienced teachers, are unlikely to occur without some exposure to what teaching actually looks like when it is being done differently, and exposure to someone who can help teachers understand the difference between what they are doing and what they aspire to do. This research also suggests that at the heart of the processes in schools where changes in practice do occur is the development of a common language with which colleagues can talk to one another and, indeed, to themselves about detailed aspects of their practice. Without such a language teachers find it very difficult to experiment with new possibilities. It is through shared experiences that colleagues can help one another to articulate what they currently do and define what they might like to do. It is also the means whereby taken-for-granted assumptions about particular groups of students can be subjected to mutual critique.

This raises questions about how best to introduce such an approach to professional development. In the Parkside English department, the approach chosen was that of 'lesson study', a systematic procedure for the development of teaching that is well established in Japan and some other Asian countries (Lewis et al., 2006). The core activity is collaboration on a shared area of focus that is generated through discussion. The content of this focus is the planned lesson, which is then used as the basis of gathering data on the quality of experience that students receive. These lessons are called 'research lessons' and are used to examine the teachers' practices and the responsiveness of the students to the planned activities.

Drawing on these ideas, over a 12-month period, staff in the English department worked in trios to trial the lesson study approach. Members of each group worked together to design a lesson plan, which was then implemented in turn by each teacher. Observations and post-lesson meetings were arranged to facilitate a reflective discussion and plan for possible changes of the research lesson between each trial. It should be noted here that the main focus was on the lesson and the responses of students, not the teacher. In this sense, the forms of observation used were very different to the approach with which Parkside staff were familiar.

In planning a joint lesson, the teachers identified students within each of their classes who they saw as being particularly vulnerable. They felt that by thinking about the lesson with these individuals in mind they might create new and different ways of facilitating the learning of all of their students. So for example, one teacher talked about a student who had an understanding of language but would not speak, even when invited. Another teacher focused on one of his students who had severe dyslexia. The third teacher considered a student newly arrived to the country. This led the teachers to discuss how they might plan their lessons differently; for example, they talked about getting the students to write on the whiteboard, and getting students to rehearse verbally what they wanted to say, rather than writing arguments down.

Encouraged by the good experience of this small-scale pilot, in 2011 the Academy agreed to take part in a three-year project involving schools in three European countries. During the first year of the project, activities were carried out by a small group of Parkside teachers. First of all, they conducted detailed surveys in order to gather student views on teaching and learning in the school. With this in mind, they distributed questionnaires to sample groups of students across the school. In these questionnaires, all students were encouraged to respond openly in detailing their views on teaching, learning and school life more generally. The survey questions themselves were designed in such a way as to take account of different learning styles, asking students to draw diagrams, write notes and answer in detail. Further information was collected through a series of focus group interviews with Year 9 students, carried out by researchers from the university.

The teachers felt that the views of student had influenced their thinking about practice. For example, one teacher commented:

> I guess the one thing that you learn is that if you're getting the students' opinions you can't take everybody's opinion on board, even if you wanted

to. Some people were independent learners, some people were better in a group. So, I think it just reconfirmed to us that we needed to make sure that there were a variety of different kinds of activities for them to do.

Commenting to her colleague, following a lesson she had observed, a newly qualified teacher said:

> It really surprised me how the students just got on and read their packs of information in their groups. I'm envious. What surprised me was the way you were able to give them instructions and rely on them to read through them. You have obviously been teaching them to be autonomous.

The next stage was to conduct a further cycle of lesson study research, building on the suggestions that had emerged from these various learner voice activities. By this time some Parkside staff had developed considerable experience of using lesson study for the purpose of teacher professional development. Consequently, it was decided to experiment with the idea of involving students themselves in the process. Specifically, the staff group decided to involve students in planning the research lesson and also for them to be additional observers of the taught lessons.

Early in the second year of the project, the approach was introduced at a professional development day for the whole staff, when time was given for groups to form and begin the planning of their lessons. The experiences from the first year were helpful in giving teachers ideas as to how to move forward.

Over the following months a range of activities took place, including:

- In the maths department, three groups of teachers worked on project activities. Each group was made up of three teachers and a teaching assistant. Their work was focused on the question, 'What engages students?' The groups each planned one lesson which required different approaches to learning (i.e. visual/audio/kinaesthetic). The planning was shared between the groups and student voice was a key factor in evaluating the impact. Specifically, students were asked to identify activities that went well and give ideas about what to change or improve. Teachers then made changes before the lesson was trialled again.
- In music, a group of teachers working with older students on a lesson about structure. The students themselves were required to take on the role of teaching the lesson to a variety of classes and contributed towards the development of the lesson plan. Class members were asked to give their views on which parts of the lesson they enjoyed (when it was taught to their class) and which parts they would have done differently.
- A trio of teachers in the science department worked in a slightly different way. Two teachers identified what they saw as a 'difficult' class and, together, they shared ideas on how to engage students in learning and, as a result, how to reduce off-task behaviour. The impact of these activities was evaluated through systematic observation.

It was significant that some of the groups experimented with involving students in their action research, an approach that might be viewed as radical and potentially risky. However, their conclusion was that all of this had been worthwhile, in the sense that the results were encouraging and that the teachers had witnessed the potential of greater student involvement in developing teaching practice. In particular, the teachers felt that it was significant that, in some instances, students had helped plan lessons that they imagined would not simply be about having more 'fun'. Rather, it had led to the development of lessons that they hoped would be more effective in facilitating the learning and progress of all of the students. Some of this focused on what proved to be important matters of detail. For example, when students recommended the use of group work, they did not merely assign students to work with their friends, but planned constructive groups that would motivate all students.

The staff involved also felt that it was important that student involvement in the planning and execution of lessons empowered them to have a practical influence over their own learning, as well as that of their classmates. A teacher of English, commenting on the impact on him and his partner teachers said:

> This has taken certainly two of us out of our normal ways of teaching and that was a good thing, 'cos it challenged us as professionals . . . it challenged us to do something different and that's a positive thing.

Other teachers noted similar impacts:

> To actually have some reflective time just as three professionals to share ideas and it is nice to be able to collaboratively plan with a colleague. That was a really positive experience as professionals.

> I know it's changed my practice. I do incorporate more practical work and kinaesthetic style activities, because they do enjoy them and do get a genuine delight out of doing them.

Students, too, seemed to recognise the benefits of their being involved in helping teachers plan their lessons. This led to what were seen as more engaging activities. For example:

> It's an easier way to learn, like, say if you just sit there and read through a book, you get bored and distracted and don't even read it, but say if you did something like a game or something else, then we'd listen.

> It was very good when we watched a film. It was much better than reading a book or explaining it to you. You actually watch it. So when we had the assessment it was so much easier to write it 'cos we remembered it.

At the same time, it seemed that many of their peers, knowing of their friends' involvement, seemed to be motivated to try their best in the lesson and for it to be a success. It was also apparent that students did not want the experiment to fail, since they looked for the initiative to be continued and for their turn to come to be involved in planning.

The evidence from these experiences at Parkside, alongside findings from the other schools involved in the study, suggest that the approach developed can be a powerful way of moving practice forward, using learner differences as a stimulus for innovation (Messiou & Ainscow, 2015). What was particularly distinctive was the added value that comes from engaging students themselves in planning the lesson study process.

Sadly, the enthusiasm and commitment of staff who were involved in these developments gradually faded. This occurred as Parkside went through a period of considerable turbulence related to changes in senior personnel, the story of which we tell in Chapter 6. During this period, increased anxiety amongst school leaders regarding the fragile nature of the school's examination results meant that risk-taking of any kind was viewed with suspicion. As a result, the tradition of top-down accountability and prescribed procedures for planning, teaching and assessment once again became the order of the day. Nevertheless, the period of experimentation had demonstrated the massive untapped potential that existed within the staff at Parkside and, importantly, amongst its students.

Conclusion

The story of the lesson study development closes our account of the extent to which Parkside Academy teaching staff had space to make decisions regarding aspects of their pedagogical practice. The evidence we have presented suggests that, despite the short-term success of the school's strategies for improving examination results, they may not be the way of ensuring longer-term improvements. It also leads us to challenge the assumption embedded in the academy policy rhetoric suggesting that increased autonomy would necessarily lead to greater freedom to innovate amongst teaching staff.

We concluded that teachers at Parkside were relatively autonomous in terms of the curriculum and other planning related decision making, as there was little school, sponsor or national level guidance in place that would have constrained their autonomy. However, although teachers were aware of this autonomy, they felt constrained in utilising it, due to pressures to improve examination results.

Our account has also thrown light on the way these pressures are created. In particular, we have shown how the standards-driven culture and highly regulated Academy-level assessment policy limited teachers' pedagogical decision making, not only framing their assessment practices, but impacting indirectly on their curricular decisions. This became most apparent through the ways in which planning and teaching were designed and conducted to most efficiently prepare students for examinations. Within this context, the overhanging fear of failure in examinations was seen to make staff reluctant to become involved in any form of risk-taking. This, in turn, led us to ask questions about the roles of management, leadership and governance at Parkside, and the extent to which these were determined locally, themes that we address in the next chapter.

Notes

1 In the English policy, a Key Stage refers to the grouping of students by age and setting the educational knowledge expected at that stage.
2 BTEC is a range of alternative qualifications for students taking their first steps into the world of work.

5

LIKE PLASTIC DOGS NODDING

The previous chapters have discussed the historical, political and geographical contexts in which Parkside Academy exists, as well as the extent to which its supposed autonomy has led to innovations in practice. This led us to consider how various pressures appear to limit the freedom practitioners have to explore new ways of addressing the diversity of learners within their classes. We have also described efforts to build on the collaboration that exist within the school in order to develop forms of professional development that support staff in moving their practices in a more inclusive direction.

In this chapter, we move on to consider the management context in which the school went about its business in an effort to understand further the nature and sources of the pressures that the Parkside staff and senior leaders experienced. This leads us to address the issue of governance, focusing specifically on the power dynamics between the school and its sponsor.

We begin by presenting an account of the sponsor's view of the role of local governance. This is followed by an analysis of the way in which this vision manifested itself in the contributions of Parkside's local governing body. From local governance, the focus shifts to the role of EfFT's central board, and, more specifically, to the mechanisms the organisation adopted, which are captured in its policies and other guiding documentation. As one of the key features of the English academies policy throughout its existence has been the autonomy academies have over teachers' pay and conditions, the final section of the chapter discusses the way these factors were handled at Parkside.

Local governance: an EfFT fantasy?

The overall governance arrangements in EfFT were such that each academy attached to the chain had a Local Governing Body (LGB) that is intended to oversee, as the term implies, local matters concerning each school. In the organisational hierarchy of EfFT, LGBs operate under central governance. The roles and responsibilities of the local bodies were described in some of the documentation produced by EfFT. However, these relationships were best summed up by the Parkside Principal, who in November 2011, when she was interviewed, had taken on the role of Deputy Chief Executive of the EfFT chain, alongside her work at Parkside, albeit on a part-time basis.

In the comment below, the Principal suggests that the existing structure was not the preferred model of EfFT. Rather, it would have preferred to rely solely on central governance but was forced by the requirements of government policy to establish some kind of local arrangements:

> So, the government said that with our academies, because there was always to be more than one, the arrangement that was fought for by the CEO then was to have all academies instead of being individual charities themselves, they should form one. That in itself meant that the governance was affected. So the department said every single academy must have a local governing body. . . . So each of the academies have their own local governing body, which I've described in some material I've just written as 'transformation champions'. They are the people on the ground, who are going to ensure that what the charity board intends with the academies, is actually happening. And if they are concerned that it's not, we have got the executive teams on the regional basis with a regional executive, who the LGB chairs, who can be used as a resource and also as holding the charity into account.

She went on to add:

> The LGB can hold the Principal to account in some ways in terms of questioning. What they [LGB] can't do is any formal process in HR, but if they are continuously unhappy, the regional executive knows about that and then the regional executive finds out why it's happening. Is it because you have a rogue bunch of LGB members; there's a particular dynamic for parts of local communities and they just want to take it over? Or is it the fact that the Principal is dissembling and is not doing the job right? So there's that triangulation all the time.

There are several points of interest in these comment, of which we focus first of all on the vision EfFT has regarding the role of the LGBs. In her description, the Principal, speaking now as Deputy Chief Executive of EfFT, makes it rather clear that the LGBs were intended to have little, if any, decision-making capacity. These 'transformation champions', she suggests, could be better described, to borrow business terminology, as having a consultancy or accountability, rather than executive, function, with a role in the overall accountability of the organisation. In this consultancy/accountability role, the LGB may question the Principal, but is not included in core decision making, such as appointment processes.

If we interpret the Principal's vision literally, in this consultancy role the LGBs are not entitled to an independent voice. Rather, she sees them as having an instrumental function in securing that the sponsor's policy and instruction are in place in each academy. As such, her view of the overall governance arrangements in the chain is a heavily centralised model, in which core decision-making functions are focused within EfFT. In this sense, local governance has a role in the overall accountability of the organisation, and is listened to, but only if in line with EfFT policy.

It became clear that members of the LGB were well aware of this thinking. For example, a local governor commented:

> I think EfFT have very distinctive and, to me, a not very well thought out view of governance in their whole structure. I think it's very hierarchical governance imposed from above, rather than a local governing body that has been given a responsibility to develop that school. That's how I see it.

This view of governance echoes with the original plan EfFT had over its organisational structures, since in its vision statements, governance is heavily centralised. Meanwhile, the accountability functions of the LGBs were further explained in an EfFT document, 'Principles for Principals', in the following manner:

> Within the Group [chain of EfFT academies], we are now proud of the quality and professionalism of our governing bodies. We have become increasingly focused on building the appropriate skills within LGBs, and have created structures, which are more closely aligned with academy processes. We believe we have recruited and trained governors who not only have strong local knowledge but also, who have a particular expertise from which the academy can benefit. We have created monitoring systems centrally, which ensure that chairs of governors and their fellow governors receive and are involved in the discussion, the analytical thinking and the successful delivery of their clear and unambiguous role of accountability. We know that strong governance plays a key role in leading the work of academy improvement and we have a very clear perspective on how robust governance is developed and maintained.

According to this documentation, the relationship between the local and central governance arrangements are clearly defined and consistent, and operations follow prescribed lines of accountability. Although the LGB is described as having little if any decision-making capacity, the excerpt suggests their contributions are valued in terms of Academy management, as well as with respect to EfFT central governance. Whether this is a true reflection of governance arrangements in other EfFT academies is beyond the scope of our research, but we will show how, in Parkside, the statement was fundamentally questioned by governors and staff alike.

Local governance: the Parkside reality

The Parkside LGB was formed by the newly appointed Principal at the time the new Academy was set up. Some of the governors from the predecessor school, Oak Drive High, joined the Parkside LGB but not all. Here one governor describes the way in which the LGB was formed and the governors selected:

> Right, I think you'll pick up on the course of the interview is that while I'm a strong supporter of the Academy, I'm not a particularly strong supporter of the governance arrangements. I'm quite critical of the governance arrangements, so, it's worth saying at the start, I think the Academy has done a wonderful job, to the local area and that's all very praiseworthy, I will also express some concerns and uncertainties about how clear the governance arrangements are within that structure. . . . So, people [governors] were pretty much handpicked by the first Principal, individual choices who she thought would be appropriate at that stage. I think there were two of us who transferred across from the old school, but the rest of us were all new. So they were personal choices of the new Principal really. That's how the governing body was formed.

It seems clear, then, that the LGB was set up by the Principal and it was through her invitation that new governors were invited to join. It is also clear that the group included members with an impressive range of expertise and contacts – locally and nationally. Indeed, it can be argued that this was another significant benefit of the school being designated as an academy in the sense that, in the past, schools serving highly disadvantaged communities have struggled to find governors with varied professional experience and connections.

As the group moved forward, it discussed many matters school governing bodies traditionally would, such as finances, teaching and learning, and local relationships. Since the matters concerning the school were numerous, in order to enhance an efficient way of working, the body was divided into subcommittees, each of which was overseeing a specific area of interest. Here, an assistant principal at the Academy, who at times attended the LGB meetings, explains their work:

> There's committees [in the LGB] for teaching and learning, community and welfare, and finance, and within that you basically attend as many as you can. So, I go to the teaching and learning one, because I'm particularly interested in it. I go to the community one because of the stuff in transition and respon-sibilities there, and I go to the finance one just for my own development. . . . There's usually few governors there. I suppose it reflects their interests in which subcommittees they attend.

The subcommittees were in place to enhance decision-making processes and to clarify procedures. However, it was reported by some governors that the ways in which they operated and, more specifically, the ways in which they reported to the main LGB were far from satisfactory. Here, for example, a governor elaborates some of the frustrations he and his colleagues had over the working of the subcommittees:

> A number of us think the subcommittee structure should be much more firmly in place. We never get subcommittee minutes to the LGB. So in a subcommittee meeting, you are accountable to have the minutes of the meeting and those minutes going to the LGB. That I think this has happened hardly at all. So I have no idea what the finance committee does, very little of what the discipline committee does. In fact, nobody knows what the discipline committee does, since no one sees the minutes.

Such inefficiencies in communication between subcommittees and the overall governing body were frequently reported and caused frustration amongst other governors. As a result, this lack of communication made the body rather disjointed, as the governors felt they were unaware of the working of the subunits they were not involved in.

However, it was not only the lack of communication between subcommittees which hindered efficient functioning of the body. Governors reported other issues, such as irregular meeting schedules, which, they argued, illustrated the poor organisation of the body. Generally, the governing body met about once every three months, however exceptions did occur as the break between meetings was at times much longer, as suggested here by another governor:

> Governing bodies are highly skilled. They would normally meet more regularly, so that's another issue with the LGB, the patterns of meetings. . . . So, I go to this meeting on the 24 March, having not been to the previous meeting. Now in the previous meeting, which would have been held on the 7 October.

The meetings mentioned had over five months between them. Such long gaps were considered to hinder governors' commitment, leaving them to feel that it was difficult to engage in the life of the Academy. Importantly, the period this governor refers to was during the recruitment process for a new principal, a process that is described in detail in the next chapter.

Considering the fierce pace of changes at Parkside during this period, the infrequency of meetings seems like a valid critique from the governors. Here a governor expresses his views on the pattern of meetings:

> I think we should meet more often. We hardly know each other. If you miss a meeting, you'll have a six-month gap. I think we should meet more often.

In his comments regarding the regularity of meetings, this governor also touches another issue hindering the work of the LGB: its membership. Governors reported that there was a lack of clear structures and processes in place regarding the introduction of new members to the body. The list on the Academy website indicated there was a stable presence of certain governors, but as the list was not updated regularly and due to the dynamic nature of the body's membership, it was not reflective of the reality. Here a governor describes some of the frustrations the governors had with the body's membership arrangements:

> The membership of the LGB has been, well, poor, to put it politely. Very little continuity, people coming, joining, no discussion who they are, then disappearing within a couple of meetings. So it's been very hard to form a stable body within the LGB I think. And the reason for that is that people are unclear about the role everyone has to play on the LGB. So we've had real problems in the membership. Working parties still to date struggle to operate properly. And I think something should be done about it really. And I think it's improved in the last 12 months. There's been improvements. . . . But I've been here for eight years and it's a long time to wait for improvements. I try to be very patient.

As described, the instability in LGB membership proved problematic to the functioning of the body, and was a source of frustration to its more committed members.

In addition to the lack of clarity about roles and the poor organisational arrangements, governors also expressed particular frustrations regarding the appointment of the chair of governors, a process that illustrated certain ambiguities in the EfFT accountability structures, which were outlined previously in this chapter. Here two governors describe the ways in which a new chair was introduced to his role by the sponsoring board, a process that sidelined the local governors completely:

> Going back to my story of the appointment of the chair, one of the governors raised the question: 'when will we have a say in who will be the chair' and of course he was told there will not be a discussion of who will be the chair and that the decision would be made by the EfFT board. And at the subsequent meeting, we were suddenly told who is the new chair. He's a senior member of a local law firm and had nothing to do with it [LGB] before. So how did he come to be there? How was he selected? Would be very interesting . . . but again, he's very keen, very enthusiastic, really seems to take trouble with things.

Another governor talked about this process:

> We've been through a very, very bad process of choosing a new chair. . . . I wrote to the EfFT about it and expressed my views on what happened was wrong. What happened was, a new chair was brought in and we had a perfectly competent deputy chair who could have stepped in, a local priest, a man of high regard, proven commitment to the school. And he was completely bypassed and unconsulted. I thought it was insulting. I said that . . . the process was not acceptable. It was a poor process.

INT: How was the LGB informed about this?

We were told that the EfFT would decide who the new chair would be and we would have to wait until we were told. I said at the time that the deputy chair should be considered as a new chair, as he had been supporting the school for six to eight years. And there was no response to my email.

INT: So was the new chair one of the existing governors?

No, unknown to anyone. Handpicked by somebody as a, presumably, very powerful businessman. . . . So, I agree with the choice, he's perfectly reasonable, and not a bad chair. But how that took place was disrespectful really, of the existing LGB. And our views were completely dissented.

As we see, the governors interviewed were rather content regarding the actual choice of the chair, but the process through which he was chosen was questioned. The selection of the chair of governors described here, to an extent, bears resemblance to the recruitment process for a new principal, described in the next chapter. In both appointments, decision making was centralised to the EfFT board, thus sidelining the LGB from the process and highlighting the lack of executive functions of the body, confirming what was explained earlier in this chapter by the Parkside Principal.

Nevertheless, it was stated in EfFT policy documentation, as well as by the Principal, that LGBs have an important accountability and consultancy function. However, as the appointment processes of both the chair of governors and the Principal followed a broadly similar pattern, they serve as illustrative examples of the power relations between the EfFT central board and local governance, and the ways in which the latter was completely sidelined from core decision-making processes. Rather illustratively of all of this, a governor summarised the role of the body in a passing remark:

So we [LGB] are a little bit like, you know, the plastic dogs at the back of the car nodding, like that.

The evidence presented so far has described the distant relationship the local governing body had with the EfFT central board, as their views and suggestions were consistently ignored and sidelined. To an extent symptomatic of this problematic relationship, the LGB sounded to be dysfunctional, with its unstable membership, infrequent meeting schedule and lack of communication within the body reported to hinder its work.

Rather unsurprisingly, considering the lack of communication within the LGB, as well as between the body and the central EfFT board, there was also very little communication between the LGB and the Academy staff, as noted here by two of the teachers:

You know I've had virtually no contact or communication concerning that [LGB]. Say for an election for a new member, or a re-shift of certain individuals, but no I don't know, probably through my fault of not finding out, but no I've had no contact.

INT: Are there are announcements in staff meetings or anything like that?
No.
INT: Could you name any members of the LGB?
It's interesting, because I remember from my own school career, a lot more a presence of the governing body, and here it actually feels quite separate, it's not a negative thing but just something I'm not aware of.

Another teacher offered a similar view about the local governing body:

No idea, we don't have any access, no reports are shared with us, or, I wouldn't know when they meet, I wouldn't know what their agenda was and I wouldn't know who's on the board.

All in all, the evidence presented in this section suggests that the local governing body was at the periphery of Academy-related decision making, with no executive role and very little, if any, consultancy or accountability functions. As we have explained, the executive functions were centralised to the EfFT central board, which are discussed in more detail in the following section.

The EfFT board

The description of the EfFT central governance discussed is this section is conducted from the perspective of those involved in the school. Through discussions with members of staff who had worked in other EfFT academies, we have been able to gain some sense of their different experiences of, and relationship with, the sponsor. Having said that, we stress that the analysis provided in this section only considers the functions of EfFT central governance that were distinctive in the organisation's liaison with Parkside. As such, it may not be representative of its governance arrangements with other academies in the chain.

The highest body in the organisational hierarchy of the EfFT chain was its board. From a Parkside perspective, it was a rather distant body, as it had no noticeable presence in the school. As a result, for the vast majority of the Academy staff, the board was as meaningless and distant as 'a list of names on the EfFT website', as noted by the teacher quoted above. During the later period of our involvement, the central governance of EfFT was being restructured and there was, we heard, a plan to distinguish a working group from the charity board to make the body function more efficiently. Here, the Principal, by this time the Deputy Chief Executive, explains the plans for restructuring:

Well, the governance arrangements in the charity is that there is a charity board, but then in order to make sure the business is done in an effective way they are creating a group board with functions dedicated from the charity board. So it's a smaller group of people who will meet more regularly. And they will be the ones who on the behalf of the charity board hold to account the executive team. And the governors [local] responsibilities discharge both through the executive team and the charity board and the group board.

As explained here, these proposals are rather difficult to follow. And, in fact, they continued to be debated as our involvement in the school drew to a close, with the exact functions and structures of different bodies still waiting to be clarified. Therefore, in what follows, when referring to the governance functions of the chain, the term 'central governance' is used. As such, this term refers to centralised chain-level strategic planning and decision making encompassing a variety of EfFT representatives.

In her explanation, the Principal also mentions the existence of an EfFT executive team, which, from the Parkside perspective, had a much stronger presence in the Academy than other branches of the organisation. The core members of the executive team were two regional executives, who line managed the academy principals in their regions. One of the regional executives had a background in education, having held an executive principal role in a local authority, overseeing several schools in a disadvantaged area; whereas the other regional executive joined EfFT from industry, having most recently held a management position in a department store chain.

Both regional executives were line managed directly by the Deputy Chief Executive, who, of course, was still the substantive Parkside Principal, and they, in turn, line managed the academy principals of their regions. This is how the regional executive looking after Parkside described his roles and responsibilities in the organisation:

> So, I line manage all the principals in the region, and therefore my responsibility is for 9,108 students, 1,284 staff and a budget of £53,500,000. So, as I'm not able to see all of them all the time, I'm very much a reporting line to [the Principal]. I would be the person to who people report, and then I'll report forward to [the Principal]. . . . the quality of leadership and the leadership team, because the academy is in a mess and it needs to recover, and we're trying to get things back to normal and trying to sort things out. In another academy, it was about attending to all issues from leadership to teaching and learning and behaviour of students. In another academy, we are dealing with specific issues to do with outcomes, and whether there is enough emphasis and rigour in pushing things forward. So, there's a range of issues, and none are the same, so my role tends to being put in into areas that struggle. . . . so we respond according to need.

In his comment, he describes the regional executive role as addressing a broad range of issues arising within different academies. The regional executives line managed all the principals in their region, and staff the regional executive liaised with in the academies he worked in were mainly senior leaders, but depending on each academy's individual needs, may have also included staff in other roles. At Parkside, for example, the regional executive liaised mostly with the senior team, but also communicated directly with other members of staff via email, as well as when leading staff meetings and assemblies. Within the EfFT central governance, the regional executives also liaised with a range of people in different roles, administrative staff in the central office, as well as the 'field force and consultants', as he described some EfFT staff working in and with different academies.

The consultants the regional executive refers to were employed directly by EfFT and held cross-chain roles, overseeing some key areas of the academies, with titles such as 'EfFT curriculum lead', 'EfFT assessment lead', 'EfFT data lead' and 'EfFT business and enterprise lead'. As described by here by the EfFT curriculum lead, they worked across the chain with different academies:

> So, how much I work with an academy to some extent is determined by them. Because my work isn't compulsory at the moment, so people don't have to work with me if they don't want to. I think over the last two years I've worked mostly with academies who have been in most need and academies that are managing changes in leadership.

It is important here to distinguish between the consultant and the EfFT executive roles, since the relationships academies had with these different actors were quite different in nature. Engaging with cross-group consultants was voluntary for academies, as the consultants' expertise was available for all those that, for one reason or another, had identified a need for additional support. As explained above, individual academies were drivers for these academy-consultant working relationships, as the need for the support was identified by the academies themselves.

The working relationships between academies and executives were, again, determined at the EfFT level and were more directive in nature, since the need for an executive intervention in individual academies was determined centrally. So, for example, in relation to Parkside, the arrival of the regional executive was not as a result of an invitation sent by the school, but rather in response to a need identified at the central governance level and imposed upon the Academy.

EfFT representatives, as well as staff in individual academies, were guided by a wealth of documentation produced centrally. This stream of documentation could be distinguished as two different elements: first, chain-wide policy documentation; and, second, guiding documentation for academy management, governance and staff. Focusing firstly on the latter, the first of a series of documents the EfFT central governance was developing for academy staff working in different roles was the document 'Principles for Principals', referred to earlier in this chapter. This was described by the regional executive as a 'diagnostic tool kit' for self-evaluation and management, designed for principals to identify areas of need in their academies. PfP was the first document published and was one of a series of other similar guiding documents developed subsequently. Indeed, it was used as the model for guidance documentation under production for local governors, as well as another aimed at middle leaders across the chain.

It is worth spending some time focusing on PfP here, as it provides further insights into the vision EfFT had regarding the relationship between central governance and individual academies, and, as such, also determined some of the interaction between the academies and the EfFT executives. This is how the curriculum lead described the document:

> So PfP is a guidance document for principals to follow. It's like a handbook for the principals of what EfFT expect them to be doing and what would be expected to be going on in these academies. And also there is a bit of a checklist so that they [principals] can see whether they are in line.

This 72-page detailed document was organised under 30 subheadings, encompassing different areas of the academy life. They were presented in this order: 'Educational Ethos, Christian Ethos, Academy-isation, Leadership, Governance, Academy Development Plans, Quality Assurance, Finance, Staffing Structures, Continuous Professional Development, Curriculum, Learning and Teaching' following up with themes such as 'Homework, Student Planners, Uniforms, Literacy and Numeracy, Inclusion, Displays, Business and Enterprise, Health and Safety, External Partnerships, Enrichment, E-Learning, Transition, Global Citizenship, Assessment of Learning, Assessment for Learning, Sixth Form Provision'. For each theme, there was a page-long description, encompassing the EfFT vision for each, followed by a 'Test Yourself' page, which principals could use to evaluate the current state of their school. In order to cast more light on the format of the document, we will focus on one of the themes it covered in more detail. The section titled 'Academy-isation' is chosen for this purpose, since the regional executive identified this part of the document as one of the most important ones, alongside with the one regarding ethos:

> There is something about the order and importance [of the themes]; there is a hierarchy, as I think there are important parts, like the ethos and academy-isation. If people are not academy-ised, so if people are not in terms of what we [EfFT] are all about, and behaving the way they should be, then it's much harder to move into the other sections. . . . It talks about academies as a part of a larger EfFT family: speech, behaviour, higher mutual respect. So there's a way of doing things. . . . This academy-isation section, for me is as much of page-turner, as the first lines of the American constitution. It's powerful stuff.

Notwithstanding the regional executive's apparent unquestioning emphasis on orthodoxy, it is true that the 'Academy-isation' section in PfP provided a clear statement of the vision EfFT had for its chain of academies. Specifically, it focused on the cultural change each school had to achieve in order to become an EfFT academy – abandoning old habits of predecessor schools and embracing what is seen as a new culture. Academy-isation was described as a long, ongoing process, which aims to articulate to the staff, students, parents and the whole wider community, alike, the significant changes that have taken place. This means that the school is following a new code of conduct in order to improve the education and life chances of its students.

This is how the document begins the description of what is meant by academy-isation:

> Academy-isation of students of staff and of parents is critical. When an academy opens, people see the same faces, often the same building, often the same timetable and certainly the same issues. Creating an understanding that things have changed and must continue to change in those circumstances is difficult. Assemblies, forums, consultations and PHSE lessons are obvious arenas for delivering messages of change, challenge and inspiration; but academy-isation needs to be a more powerful force if it is to enthuse, motivate, and develop a sense of pride and ownership in and through the community. It must establish and demonstrate a new form of educational life, new better ways of working and learning and a clear visible delivery system of high quality provision which has no toleration of mediocrity and complacency.

The description was followed with a list of expectations EfFT had of principals regarding the ways in which academy-isation should be achieved and led in each academy, articulated in the following manner:

> Expectations of the Principal:
>
> You take as your sole personal and professional responsibility the need for all students and staff to have a sense of pride in their academy and a feel of belonging. You do this by:
>
> • Promoting the academy as a family within a larger EfFT family. including the notion that once an EfFT student, always an EfFT student.
> • Being a standard bearer of corporate high expectations in all aspects of the academy provision.
> • Upholding particularly standards of speech, behaviour, dress and mutual respect across and from all in the academy.
> • Knowing the individual and group achievements and goals of students and how staff are meeting their needs.

Several other bullet points follow and the documentation goes on to provide a significant level of detail in the description regarding the manner in which the 're-culturing' of academies should be conducted.

The list of group expectations is followed by another page-long 'test yourself' section, according to which principals may assess how successfully the academy-isation process has been in their school. Below, we reproduce a few questions selected from the list to illustrate the EfFT vision regarding the ways in which principals may check the realisation of the change process:

- Do staff and governors understand and uphold our academy-isation pro-gramme?
- Would the public perception of our academy match my reality?
- Could the newest students tell me why they are pleased to be in the academy?
- Could the oldest students tell me why they are still pleased to be in the academy?

All the questions listed indicate that the perceptions stakeholders and the wider community have of the academy must be a serious concern for the principal, who should ensure these perceptions are managed and in line with the culture articulated by EfFT. The final two questions could be interpreted as being closed: indicating there is a correct answer that students should be able to provide when their opinion is asked.

Altogether, then, there is a strong notion of creating a public image and controlling the perception and opinion of stakeholders in the document. Certainly, it might be seen as being an effort to ensure a tight control over the schools that are part of the group. The fact that principals are encouraged to test whether their students are able to provide a suitable answer for a question regarding the culture of the academy also suggests that EfFT has an intention to hold power over the different stakeholders in its schools.

Such an authoritarian approach to governance echoes the broader develop-ments of the independent state-funded school movement in England and, indeed, in other parts of the world. For example, writing about academies in England from very different perspectives, Benn (2012), Adonis (2012) and Kulz (2015) all describe similar approaches, almost totalitarian in nature. These include reference to some highly performing academies, with their strict speech, uniform and behav-iour policies, as well as in their thoroughly constructed public image. Certainly, there is no doubt that, as far as Parkside was concerned, the term 'academy-isation' related directly to various processes in place, some of which have already been described in the previous chapter: the construction of public image through 'an official story'; external branding; and the rigid behaviour code for staff and students alike.

The academy-isation section in Principles for Principals described here is only one of the 30 themes listed in the document, all of which are dealt with similarly detailed guidance for principals to run the school in line with the EfFT vision. As such, it goes into a significant level of detail regarding what might be seen as the micromanagement of its principals, as the document portrays an image of heavy-handed governance and management culture within the organisation.

However, PfP and other related guiding documents were only one stream of documentation produced by EfFT to guide and frame practices in the academies. As PfP was described as a diagnostic tool, the use of which was voluntary in nature but strongly encouraged by EfFT executives, as explained earlier by the regional executive, there was also a strand of what the assistant principal, referred to earlier, called 'non-negotiable' policy documents. These were developed at the central governance level and all academies in the chain had a responsibility for 'localising' them according to their needs. This is how a member of staff expressed his view on these documents:

> . . . . there is a policy for everything in this school, absolutely everything. They are all online, but honestly, I'm not quite sure what's in them. There's too many.

Like this teacher, other members of the Academy staff, as well as some of the governors, repeatedly referred to EfFT as a policy heavy organisation, as there were hundreds of pages of documentation available. Many of the chain-level policies, or possibly all of them, were available on the staff shared area, encompassing a variety of issues, from bullying to insurance on vehicles and, again, to educational ethos. These 159 separate policy documents were distinguished as follows:

Policy	No. of documents available
Company Secretary	6
Education	24
Governance	2
HR	79
ICT	4
Insurance	44

(Withdrawn from Parkside Academy staff shared area 10 May 2012)

The sheer volume of policy documentation EfFT produced could be interpreted as symptomatic to their approach to governance and their strong intent to direct the operations in individual academies from the centre. However, as the teacher's comment suggests, most of the staff were oblivious to the content of these policies, especially if they were not involved in senior management. In the next section we look more closely at one of the most significant of these policies, as perceived by the Parkside staff.

Pay and conditions

One of the key features of the academies programme throughout its history has been the autonomous nature of these schools regarding teachers' pay and conditions (Blunkett, 2000; DfE, 2010). As the human resources functions in the chain were centralised, EfFT determined the contracts for the staff working in all of its schools. This meant that all new staff appointed signed their contracts with EfFT, but as this teacher, who is also a union representative, explains, the members of staff who transferred across from the predecessor school also had the option to remain under their original contracts:

> So I kept my contract when I transferred [from Oak Drive High to Parkside], TUPEd[1] across. A lot of us who transferred did that: stayed under the same teaching pay and conditions as we had under LA control, and that was something they [EfFT] couldn't change. They wanted us all to sign new contracts, but many of us didn't.

The shift from the maintained sector to the independent state-funded sector puzzled staff across the Academy, with veterans as well as newly joined staff expressing their concerns regarding their contracts under EfFT. As staff discussed their pay, the comparisons they frequently drew were between Parkside pay and conditions and the conditions they would have in similar roles in the maintained sector. In these comparisons, the staff identified some differences regarding teaching time, holidays and pay.

Focusing firstly on salaries, the junior members of staff seemed generally content about having EfFT as their employer, since their annual pay in the Academy was reported to be somewhat higher than it would be in a similar role in the maintained sector, as explained here by one of the teachers:

> In comparison to a more traditional school, we [teachers] get paid more here. Like I would get paid £25,000 per year in a traditional school, but here I get paid £25,500.

Such approaches to teachers' salaries have been reported elsewhere, as in the case of a chain that was suggested to 'lure in best teachers' with higher entry salaries (Garner, 2013). However, teachers were also keen to remind us that, although on a higher salary, they were expected to work for longer hours than their colleagues in a maintained sector:

> Up to main scale 6, which is the normal standard teacher not with any responsibilities or anything, I think the salaries are slightly better, but the hours expected are much longer; you know, the day length. So it works out that the hours over the year are more. Because here, the days are from 8am to 4pm, but most other schools it's from 8am or 8.30am to 3pm. And when it first became an academy it was from 9am to 3pm. And then we were told we must be in line with all other schools around us and start at 8.30 and finish at 3. And then finally they made teachers stay until 4pm. It was put into contracts. So the teacher's pay, before any responsibilities, is a bit better but with longer directed hours.

As suggested, the slightly higher pay offered for the most junior members of teaching staff was to compensate for the daily 'extra hour' that staff were expected to stay after they had finished teaching. This was dedicated to lesson planning and meetings, and it was an expectation that all staff would be present. The extended school day rather unsurprisingly led to mixed feelings amongst staff. According to opponents, planning took up teachers' time in the evenings and weekends regardless the dedicated hour for it, and that it was an unnecessary constraint to be told to stay behind rather than conduct the planning in another location. However, according to members of staff who had worked in other EfFT academies, the extended school day was a Parkside specific policy, as other academies they had experiences of had a shorter school day.

Another, possibly more significant, issue that Parkside staff reported regarding was in relation to pay structure and progression. Generally, the staff seemed to be oblivious to the pay structure and there seemed to be widespread confusion regarding progression. Some members of staff reported their attempts to contact the EfFT central office for clarity in the issue, but all the attempts reported to us had failed, as the EfFT human resources section had not been able to provide Parkside staff with sufficient information regarding progression. Here, a union representative describes some of the issues regarding the lack of clarity regarding pay structure:

> People have come to me because they are really confused about the pay structure: the progression of pay scale, threshold, performance management and all that. . . . The problem is there is no set grade like there is on the LA pay scale. In the EfFT one, it just goes from here to here, [hand movements] and whatever they think your role is they'll put you on a pay according to that, and then people don't know where they are in the scale and they don't know how to get higher. . . . So I've asked the senior management or people from HR to come and explain the pay scale and explain the threshold, and I know it's going to happen, but just hasn't happened yet. But I did ask for this a couple of years ago, asked for the pay scales to be explained and they still haven't been.

The issues described here applied to teaching and support staff alike, as members of staff who had worked in the Academy for more than five years had experienced difficulties in their attempts to negotiate progression. Here, for example, an experienced teacher, who had worked in the school since the Oak Drive High days, explains the difficulties she faced when negotiating progression:

> I haven't had a pay rise for a long time. I was on threshold in 2005, so six years ago, then you should have one every three years if this was an LA school, and I haven't had one. So I've done my sums and I've lost about £10,000–£15,000 in that time. Here they don't tell you that you are eligible for them. You need to find out all yourself. And when you try, it's not clear how it works. Finally, I got one [paystructure] from the HR, but when it was already out of date when I got it. They just haven't made it clear.

As noted previously, the teaching staff in the early stages of their career received somewhat more generous pay than their colleagues in the maintained sector, but the more teaching years they gained in Parkside Academy, the less attractive the pay became in comparison. Lower pay was not only troubling to members of staff with several years of teaching experience, but also to those who had taken leadership roles in the Academy. For example, assistant principals were paid less than their colleagues in the maintained sector, as explained here by an assistant principal:

> We're [senior leaders] paid less, much less. If I went to be an AP for an LA school, I would be paid at least £5,000 more. Also maternity pay is less. We don't get the same LA allowances if we were an LA school.

In addition to lower pay, senior members of staff also reported differing conditions EfFT offered for assistant principal holidays. In comparison to the maintained sector, the academic year in Parkside was the same length as in any other school, and teachers were entitled to the same holidays as their colleagues working in local authority maintained schools. However, the same conditions did not apply to senior members of staff whose holidays were significantly shorter. Here an assistant principal explains the senior leaders' holidays:

> We [senior leaders] are not allowed to take full holidays. I get to take 40 days, so that's eight weeks, whereas I should have 12 or 13 weeks if I worked in any other school. So, you have to bank up your holidays as well. You can imagine when the Ofsted went on in January, and we had a February half term straight after, when some of us [senior leaders] had to come around to work for a few days. This is because there must always be a senior member of staff in the building during the holidays. So you can imagine what that does to my morale.

As suggested, senior members of staff were not overly excited about their reduced holidays, but there was a general acceptance of them since they were all in a similar situation. Due to the lack of detail in the EfFT teacher pay scale document regarding senior leader pay, it is not possible to discuss the pay and conditions of the Academy Principal or executive figures, such as the regional executives, who were directly responsible to the EfFT.

Similarly, we are not sure whether the Academy was financially an attractive option for a principal to join, although indications across the field lead us to guess that it was. Certainly the person who was to replace the principal left his position as a principal of an inner city school, moving hundreds of miles away from his young family to join Parkside. Inevitably this created some whispers amongst staff, suggesting that the principal's salary was significantly higher than in the maintained sector. This would not be completely unheard of in the independent state-funded independent sector, as national media has reported exceptionally high pay of senior staff in some sponsored academies (Paton, 2012; Northen, 2011; Clark, 2012). These developments have taken place mostly within groups of academies, where even higher salaries are often paid to executives, something that has also led to considerable media attention and controversy (Mansell, 2016). However, as there is no data to back up the whispers of the staff, the salary of the new Parkside Principal, as well as the EfFT representatives with executive roles, remain a matter of speculation.

Altogether, the experiences of Parkside Academy staff over teaching pay and conditions echo broader developments at the national and international levels. For example, literature regarding independent state-funded education elsewhere, such as in Swedish free schools, have suggested similar patterns (Skolverket, 2010). And in England where similar developments regarding staff pay and conditions have been reported from other sectors of public services subject to privatisation (Mills, 2013).

As we have seen, EfFT identified senior staff within their schools to take on wider roles across the chain, as well moving staff from one academy to another to lead on particular themes, fill gaps and address problems. The groups EfFT policy document regarding management staff recruitment states the following:

> The appointment of Leaders and Managers may be from a pool of either external and/or internal candidates. EfFT will encourage principals to use the promotion route as a means to recognise excellence within the existing teaching staff, to offer promotion, to provide development opportunities for teachers who demonstrate exceptional abilities and to plan for succession. Where it is proposed that an internal appointment is made, that position will not normally be advertised externally.

It goes on to say:

> Principals will also be encouraged to make available opportunities for teachers to apply for appropriate Leader and Manager vacancies within other schools or Academies within the group. Such positions might be made available as a secondment or as a temporary contract. Where such a position arises, that position should be advertised within the group.
>
> *(EfFT Leadership and Management Policy)*

During the period of our involvement there were many examples of teachers, as well as senior leaders, being promoted from one academy to another, at all levels of the management hierarchy – something staff mostly considered as a positive feature of being employed by the chain. All of this resonates with the statements the proponents of academies, especially chains of sponsored academies, have made with regards to positive effects regarding pooling resources and benefitting from economies of scale (Hill, 2010; Hill et al., 2012; Adonis, 2012; Husbands et al., 2013). However, not all such movement of staff between different EfFT academies followed the will of the staff, although there were examples of exchanges of staff involved in various projects and support roles, as well as for career development, which were regarded positively by those involved.

Conclusion

In this book autonomy is understood as a multidimensional concept, which, in a complex social system such as a school, means that the actions of some may limit the freedoms of others (Gewirtz & Cribb, 2009). The accounts presented in this chapter indicate that EfFT embraced the autonomy they were entitled to regarding management by setting up highly centralised governance systems, experimenting with leadership approaches and establishing new teachers' pay and conditions.

This evidence portrays an image of an organisation with a heavily centralised approach to governance. In particular, we have shown how decision making regarding leadership recruitment and the membership of local governing bodies, plus the existence of a powerful executive board, are symptomatic of an organisation holding significant levels of central power. And, inevitably, this means that less space is left available for those stakeholders away from the centre.

The existing research base regarding governance arrangements in chains of academies suggests that substantial differences in governance strategies and mechanisms between academy chain sponsors exist (Hill et al., 2012; Salokangas & Chapman, 2014). When compared to other English academy chains, EfFT would be located towards the centralising end of the sponsor spectrum.

Another area of centralised decision making is with regard to the finances of EfFT, a theme that would have naturally complemented the issues discussed in this chapter. The reason why this is not discussed here is that the material available regarding Parkside's and EfFT's finances was not available for our research. So, for example, the staff online-area to which we had access contained no information regarding finances. Meanwhile, those who could have cast some light regarding the issue, denied access to such information by either directly refusing to take part in an interview (the business manager), not responding to an interview request (the LGB chair of finances) or by expressing their lack of interest in discussing financial arrangements (the Principal and the regional executive).

It is not within the scope of this book to discuss the finances of the organisation in more detail. We should stress, however, that there is no reason to believe that there are any particular reasons for those involved to withhold this information. Given the frequent scandals in the national press regarding the use of funds in other academy chains, however, this is an area that always warrants investigation.

The accounts we have reported indicate that EfFT did embrace the autonomy to which academies are entitled in dealing with various factors to do with the running of Parkside. In particular, we heard how staff reported lower pay and longer hours than their colleagues enjoy in the maintained sector. How far these differences are notable and, as such, how significant are the savings EfFT gains from these contracts and in what ways these possible gains are spent, are, once again, questions beyond the scope of our research. However, it can be argued on the basis of the information presented in this chapter that EfFT embraced the autonomy they were entitled to in relation to teaching pay and conditions, and, in this way, actively enacted this aspect of the academies policy (Braun et al., 2010). This feature becomes even more apparent in the next chapter, where we describe a year in the life of the school that led to considerable organisational change and turbulence.

Note

1 As Parkside Academy opened, the staff from Oak Drive High transferred to the new academy. In this process the Transfer of Undertakings (Protection of Employment) Regulations (TUPE) applied (www.legislation.gov.uk/uksi/2006/246/contents/made). This ensured that when schools converted to academy status all teachers and support staff employed by the maintained school would become employees of the academy and they would retain their current contractual status.

6

A TURBULENT YEAR

So far we have told the story of Parkside Academy over a period of ten years or so. In so doing, we have looked specifically at the extent to which the autonomy that is said to be the feature of such schools had led to innovations in terms of the work of teachers and those involved in leadership roles. Our conclusion is that pressures created by national accountability measures, as they have been interpreted by the school's sponsoring organisation, left little space for experimentation to take place. In its place the sponsor adopted a centralising stance, which imposed policies and practices on the school in an attempt to improve its performance on national examinations and during inspections.

Clearly this approach paid off, with Parkside's results improving significantly in a relatively short time, leading the school to be recognised as being outstanding by Ofsted, the national improvement agency. A concern we have raised, however, is that these strategies may not be sustainable over a longer period, not least because they place intensive pressures on practitioners, who, sooner or later, may decide that there are job opportunities in other schools where life is much easier. We also worry about the failure to make better use of the latent creativity within the staff, and amongst the students, the governors and, more widely, in the local community.

Where the autonomy associated with academies has led to a degree of innovation it is with respect to the ways in which the sponsoring organisation operates. In particular, we have shown how, at Parkside, the sponsor took the opportunity to experiment with management approaches, as well as setting up highly centralised governance systems. At the same time, it introduced new arrangements for dealing with the pay and conditions for teachers.

In a way that we had not anticipated, the school year 2010–2011 brought a period of significant change and, indeed, turbulence at Parkside. This threw further light on the role of management and leadership in the school. It also led us to look more closely at the complexities that are involved when major policy decisions are necessary.

The sense of turbulence was created when it gradually became evident that this was to be the final year in post of the first Parkside Principal. This was a culmination of a period of some months during which her role in the EfFT central governance grew and, as a result, her absence from Parkside created a vacuum in the Academy's senior leadership arrangements. The process of succession that followed provided remarkable insights into the ways in which Parkside EfFT actors interpreted and enacted increased autonomy in relation to management, leadership and governance. We tell the story of this event in relation to a series of changes made in management and leadership arrangements within the school.

Management and leadership

The story of what occurred regarding management and leadership over the ten years of our involvement at Parkside is complex and, at times, confusing. It involved considerable changes in the structure of the school, culminating in the messy process of appointing a new principal in 2010, the full details of which remain something of a mystery even to this day.

In order to help readers to track this complexity, throughout this chapter we map the evolving structure of these arrangements in the form of a series of charts. We designed these displays from multiple sources of data. To secure their accuracy, they were presented, discussed and developed further with the staff involved at various times. As these discussions developed, we kept in mind the ideas of various proponents of the independent state school model, particularly their thoughts about management and leadership, such as:

> Independent management is vital to their [academies] success, generating ambitious school leadership and sponsorship – from within and beyond the existing state system – and with a vision and ethos focused on rapid success.
>
> *(Adonis, 2007)*

For the first seven years of its existence, Parkside Academy operated under the leadership of its first principal. As we explained in Chapter 3, she was described as a strong leader, known for her directive leadership style and persistent focus on routines. The two Ofsted inspections carried out in her time rated the leadership of the Academy 'outstanding', describing her as being seen as inspirational by many staff. The second of these reports concluded that she had secured the loyalty of students and staff and united them in a drive to raise standards, setting high expectations. Mention was also made of her as an excellent role model, providing clear direction and a well-considered approach to improvement, that she had communicated effectively to all the stakeholders. Given the comments from some of the teachers we have reported, it was noticeable that the inspectors also felt that the Principal had 'rightly concentrated' on establishing the academy's ethos through demanding that policies are implemented consistently, with a relentless focus on routines.

The chain of command under the Principal's leadership was organised so that she directly line managed ten assistant principals, who were all overseeing different areas, such as: curriculum, assessment, teaching and learning, data and the sixth form. Throughout the Academy's history, the structure of the SLT had remained similar, although it had undergone some changes in membership as well as cabinet reshuffles, in which the remits of the assistant principals had been redefined or reallocated. Below this structure of the senior leadership team were the middle managers, including heads of department who line managed teachers and support staff. Many teachers would have held other management responsibilities, such as second in department or head of year, but as the main focus of this chapter is on the senior leadership team, more attention is paid to the top end of the management structure.

The Principal was sometimes described as an outward- and forward-looking leader, who engaged actively with the central governance of EfFT, and was very keen to develop local, national and international relationships with a variety of relevant individuals and groups. During her years in post, she represented the Academy frequently in local and national media, and was a sought-after speaker for educational events. The work she did on external relations, combined with the success story of the Academy, attracted visitors on a weekly basis to Parkside, which under her leadership was recognised as the 'flagship academy of EfFT'.

As we have explained, during her last few years as principal, she became more and more involved in the central governance of EfFT, which required that she spent increasing periods of time offsite. The comment below from a senior member of staff summarises how the process was viewed by many members of staff.

> The person in charge [the Principal], took more responsibilities [in EfFT] and sadly couldn't give up the day-to-day running of the Academy, which I think was a big mistake. You know, when people become so fondly attached to a place they can't let go. I think that's what happened here.

The following section describes some of the implications her extended absences had for staff and students of Parkside Academy.

A dual role

In September 2010 the Parkside Principal was promoted to a senior position in EfFT and for the duration of the academic year that followed, she had a dual role, as principal of the Academy and deputy chief executive of EfFT. Figure 6.1 illustrates the SLT structure at the start of that school year, showing that the Principal had support from ten assistant principals.

Other stakeholders involved in Academy-related decision making not included in this display are the central governance of EfFT, in the form of its board, and the local governing body (LGB). In her role, the Principal was directly accountable to

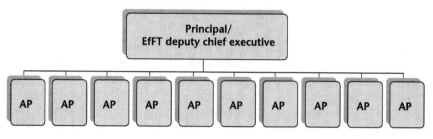

FIGURE 6.1 SLT structure September 2010

the EfFT board, which, if included in this display, would therefore be located directly above her in the hierarchy. As we reported in Chapter 5, the role of the local governing body is not quite so straightforward to define, and therefore more difficult to locate in the display.

The first significant restructuring of the SLT took place in October 2010, just after the Principal took on her dual role. At that time, a new layer was created, as two of the former assistant principals were promoted to acting vice principal roles, to oversee some of the responsibilities of the Principal while her duties occupied her elsewhere. Simultaneously, two of the former assistant principals were promoted to EfFT roles: one overseeing the curriculum, and the other taking responsibility for assessment across the chain. In their new roles, the EfFT curriculum and assessment leads were still based in Parkside Academy, sharing an office in the school building, but as these roles entailed supporting all EfFT academies, they were no longer present in the Academy on a day-to-day basis. Figure 6.2 illustrates these changes.

The restructuring of the SLT was discussed in the local governing body meeting in the October and the governors were made aware of the changes in leadership roles. However, they were not involved in the decision-making process regarding the restructuring, as one of the governors here clarifies:

> There was a notion of restructuring the SLT, various things about different roles, and mentions about [the Principal's] growing role in the EfFT in the October LGB meeting.

During the following months, the Principal's role in the EfFT seemed to require progressively more of her time and, as a result, her presence in the Academy became much less frequent. As her growing absence was a gradual development, rather than a sudden move, students and staff became used to her infrequent presence. Her main method for keeping in touch regularly with students and staff during this period was a weekly video recording known as the Principal's Broadcast. These five- to ten-minute clips served to a great extent the purposes of more traditional assemblies, as they addressed timely topics, such as mobile phone and headphone policies, and were shown to all students in classrooms on Friday mornings.

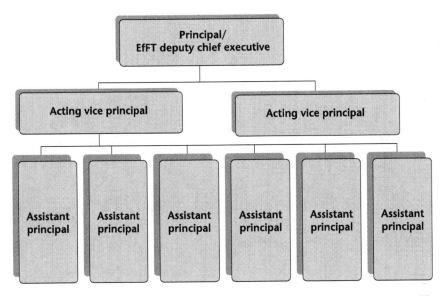

FIGURE 6.2 SLT structure October 2010

Note: One senior leader became EfFT assessment lead/Parkside assistant principal, and another became an EfFT curriculum lead/Parkside assistant principal. Neither appear on this display.

Despite these structural changes, the first term of the year appeared to be rather stable as far as senior leadership was concerned. The acting vice principals, assistant principals and the EfFT curriculum and assessment lead roles were all carried out by staff with experience of Parkside, and who knew the Academy and its students and staff. The actual involvement of the Principal during this period could be described as the final line of reporting for other senior leaders, with her holding the ultimate decision-making capacity over policy-related decisions. As such, she retained the responsibility for making the final decisions on all Parkside Academy issues, liaising mainly with the acting vice principals and the EfFT leads, and sometimes directly with the assistant principals. This hierarchical structure was a more or less stable condition until the end of the autumn term 2010. However, this was to change in significant ways following the Christmas break.

Who is the Principal?

In February 2011, the Principal contacted the Academy staff through a group email, which firstly explained her departure and then outlined her plan for the succession process of the headship. It is worth spending some time on the letter, since it outlines the plan put in place to replace her. In it, she explained that, in her absence, the only time many would have seen her over previous months was through 'the magic of technology', i.e. a Friday broadcast that was viewed across the school.

A document attached to the email provided an explanation for the Principal's absence from the Academy. She explained that, as a result of changes going on regarding the overall management of the chain, more of her time would be required at that level. In the note she provided the context for her increased role within the EfFT central organisation, leading her to suggest that it was time to consider how best to secure the medium to long term, so that Parkside Academy was not disadvantaged by her having to give all her time and energy to the post of deputy chief executive. She explained that the Chief Executive was due to leave his post in the summer and that, as yet, there was no replacement appointed because of the decision by the EfFT Board to review its central governance role and that this had delayed the appointment process.

This email confirmed rumours that had been circulating amongst staff regarding the Chief Executive's retirement. This underlying recruitment process of the new chief executive and the restructuring of the EfFT central governance undoubtedly required the Principal's attention in her deputy chief executive role. However, it also fuelled more rumours amongst staff about her possible interest in the chief executive position herself.

Whatever her actual personal career plans were, they were not addressed officially. However, in the same letter she expressed concerns regarding her absence from the Academy, as well as her plan for how best to secure Parkside's future leadership arrangements. She would, it was suggested, be looking to recruit a 'head of school'. In the first instance, this would be from those within the senior leadership team who could demonstrate at interview that they had sufficient relevant experience to fulfil the role. She added that a permanent and substantive replacement might be recruited subsequently but a decision on this would be made at a later date. The actual process which will be followed was set out at the end of this note.

The plan for succession outlined in the email may be interpreted as involving two phases. First, a 'Head of School' was to be filled from within the staff. Meanwhile, she would remain as the Academy principal but, due to her dual role, would not be able to carry out some of the duties involved. Second, the decision regarding her permanent replacement once she moves on would be made at a later date.

It was also explained that the interviewing panel would consist of a member representing the EfFT executive team, the chair of the Local Governing Body, or another governor representing the LGB, and a representative of the EfFT Board.

This rather unusual selection process for the head of school role was to take place in the following months, and the future leader was to be selected amongst the existing Parkside Academy senior leaders. The different phases of the selection process were to include psychometric testing, shadowing applicants, interviews and presentations, and, rather interestingly, a '1 on 1 lunch or dinner with the chair of LGB'. Clearly, the purpose of the email message was to communicate to members of staff the forthcoming succession process and, as such, it was one of the few attempts made to inform stakeholders about the process.

In addition to this announcement regarding the succession plan, various informal conversations took place regarding both the short-term arrangements and the eventual replacement of the Principal. One of these conversations regarding the succession plan involved the Principal and the EfFT assessment lead regarding her interest in taking on the proposed interim headship role:

> In the run up to the February half term, I had some conversations with [the Principal] about taking on a bigger leadership role in Parkside Academy, a sort of head of school kind of role, and those were obviously confidential discussions . . . and we got as far as the job being advertised and a couple of people applying.

As the assessment lead points out, the conversations regarding the succession plan took place in late February, following the advertisement of the post. This conversation was, of course, private in nature. Indeed, according to the governors we interviewed, the LGB was not included in any of these early conversations.

The next LGB meeting following the Principal's letter took place in late March. To the surprise of the governors, some of whom had by that time become aware of the content of the letter, little attention was paid to the succession plan at that meeting. One governor described the ways in which the topic was covered:

> So I went to this meeting [local governing body] on the 24 March thinking that this [succession plan] will be mentioned. And it wasn't mentioned at all until the final minutes of the meeting, under any other business. And the implication we got was that very little had happened, and nothing significant is happening. I knew for a fact she [the Principal] had resigned from her post and that there had been a discussion about who would be replacing her and that they will advertise, but none of that was discussed with the governors.

As this governor suggests, it had become obvious by this meeting that the governors were not to be included in the decision-making process regarding the Principal's succession plan. Indeed, this lack of involvement suggests that their role in the process was seen to be of no relevance and that the decisions regarding the future of Parkside Academy leadership were to be made by the EfFT central board.

However, the story then became even more complex, since the process did not materialise quite as outlined in the Principal's letter. The details of the actual process were poorly communicated, not only to the LGB, but also to members of staff. Thus, the succession process that actually took place, as opposed to the plan articulated in the letter, is described next as explicitly as the extent of our information allows.

One possible reason explaining the exclusion of the governors from the succession plan at this particular stage, as well as the poor communication with staff, was that an unexpected incident had taken place in the Academy just prior to the LGB meeting. This event altered the course of the succession plan outlined in the Principal's letter, delaying the process and eventually changing what actually occurred. Here the assessment lead provides some insights to this unexpected turn of events and the ways in which it affected what happened:

> There was an inappropriate email sent from a junior member of staff . . . to half of the SLT about another member of SLT, which is one of those things you can't really do anything about after the fact, that once it's sent, it sort of damages everybody in the email. So we [SLT] were all affected and the response to that was to suspend the recruitment process, on the grounds that, this email had made [the Principal] think about us all differently. It's one of those things, which is difficult. You know, by the letter of the policy, I did exactly what was required. . . . So on the one hand it was frustrating really. . . . I didn't do anything wrong, other than just to have the misfortune of being copied in. However, I can see it from [the Principal's] point of view as well, which is that she felt that it was symptomatic of a problem in the Academy that the staff were too close to each other. . . . And she wanted a much more kind of directive, or a distanced autocratic leadership.

Even though the incident in itself was not reported to be significant to members of the Academy leadership team, it seemed to have an impact on the ongoing recruitment process.[1] According to the assessment lead, it led the Principal to conclude that members of the Academy staff, particularly those in senior positions, were too friendly with one other. Therefore, she decided that the original plan of promoting one of the existing senior leaders to the head of school role should be reconsidered.

The developments that were to follow support this view. The recruitment process was indeed suspended, and instead of promoting one of the existing senior leaders to be the head of school, the EfFT response was to introduce external support for the Academy leadership. Why these external actors were brought in, and what their purpose was to be, was communicated in what can only be described as a confusing way to the staff and students.

During the final week of March, two new people were introduced into the senior leadership team, such that another layer in the SLT structure was created. The first of these new senior leaders had previously had some involvement in Parkside in his role as a member of the EfFT central team. The second new member of staff was a private education consultant. They were each designated as associate/ acting principals, titles that seemed to signal a sense of uncertainty and, indeed, ambiguity about what their status was to be. This is apparent in the amended display of the SLT hierarchy, where they are positioned 'above' the existing associate/ acting principal roles, as shown in Figure 6.3.

The reason why the four leaders are all titled acting/associate principal in the display is that, as far as we could determine, they used these titles when referring to themselves and each other, causing inevitable confusion amongst the staff. In this respect, the display did not resolve the apparent uncertainties regarding seniority, leaving members of staff to have differing views of the line of command.

All of this is interesting in relation to two themes – the centralised decision making of EfFT and consequent down-playing of governor and staff involvement, and the changing role of school leaders in England. In particular, the Principal could

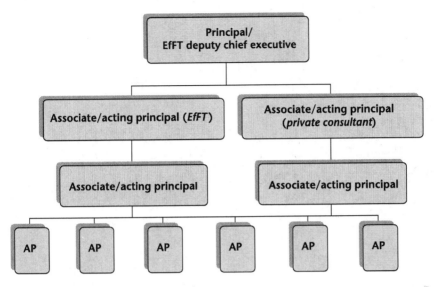

FIGURE 6.3 SLT Structure late March 2011

Note: The roles of the EfFT curriculum lead and the assessment lead remained unchanged, and are not mentioned in this table.

only absent herself from the school because headteachers are no longer regarded as having to use their professional skills and judgement on a daily basis to make a school work. Instead, leadership is increasingly systematised, so that the primary task of leaders is to set up efficient systems which can then be left to run without their continuous presence. In this way, leaders can take on two or more schools and/or 'turn schools round' in short order, then move on to other schools. In the meantime, other senior staff – 'heads of school', 'acting heads', 'assistant principals' – can be left to run schools because all they need to do is follow systems.

What is more descriptive of the reality is that it was made clear that the two new arrivals were introduced to oversee the Principal's duties whilst she was elsewhere. Here, for example, a senior leader explains her understanding of the involvement of one of the associate/acting principals:

> She came in as a sort of associate principal, in the interim period while the Principal moved on to do her role [in EfFT] and no recruitment took place for the head of school.

This comment implies that the new colleague was seen as being there to take responsibility for the day-to-day running of the Academy whilst the Principal was absent. This role was to be shared with the other associate/acting principal, who clarified his role and responsibilities in a letter addressed to all members of staff on 29 March. The letter, provided some insight into the dynamics of his move to the Academy, suggesting that EfFT had introduced him into Parkside for a specific purpose, rather than him, say, having applied for the post. However, there was no indication in the email of how the decision to introduce him into the Academy came about, or who had assigned him to the role. Further on in the email he outlines initiatives he would be working on, as well as some objectives and milestones set for the improvement of teaching and learning in the school. Despite this note, there remained some confusion amongst staff regarding the new arrangements, as the line of operations, the purposes of the introduction of new members of the SLT, and the roles of senior leaders, were still far from clear.

At the beginning of April, in the week following this letter, Parkside received another visit, this time from the regional executive of EfFT. It will be recalled that his responsibilities in the organisation entailed overseeing ten of its academies. On the morning of his visit, the assistant principal leading the day's morning briefing session sent an email to all staff in which the regional executive's visit was mentioned. It noted that he and other visitors would be in school, adding that everybody should ensure that the school was seen at its best: by meeting and greeting, checking uniform and ensuring students do not have drinks, mobile phones and headphones visible. Staff were also asked that no students were sent out on corridors, or allowed to go to the toilet during lessons. It was noted that there had been a marked improvement in all of this over the previous couple of days, because everybody had been proactive.

The full email consisted of ten announcements in total, of which the regional executive's visit was one. The actual purpose of his visit was not made clear. However, the staff were used to visitors on a weekly basis, and these were usually announced in a similar manner. There was, therefore, no reason for staff to pay more attention to this particular visit than to any other.

During the week following this visit – more precisely on Wednesday the 13 April, during the week before the Easter break – all members of staff received an email from the regional executive regarding Parkside's detention practices. The was a response to an email by one of the assistant principals which commented that the consistent use of the approach to data entry would assist greatly in monitoring and tracking affected students – thereby leaving all types of detainees (one-off and repeats) with 'nowhere to hide'. The regional executive went on to commend their use and to encourage all staff to trial the system, when needed.

In this email, it is noticeable that the regional executive addresses specific Parkside policies and, in so doing, appears to guide the staff directly on how to operate in a particular situation. What was significant about this was that the staff were not used to the direct involvement of representatives of EfFT in such day-to-day procedures. Rather, they were usually discussed at the Academy level, with one of the SLT then communicating them to the staff. Therefore, the tone and content of the message suggested that, yet again, some changes had taken place in the dynamics of the school's management system, even though these had not been communicated to the staff.

This first email sent by the regional executive was followed soon after by a series of similarly notes to staff regarding a variety of specific topics, such as student behaviour, staff holiday procedures and even the staff dress code. The tone of these emails was directive, all implying an expectation that the staff would follow the given guidance. All of this indicated that he had now taken on a more direct role in the Academy, not as a regional executive, as his title indicated, but as one of its managers. Simultaneously, there was very little, if any, email correspondence to staff from the two recently introduced associate/acting principals.

Two days after the first email to all staff from the regional executive had arrived, it was announced in a staff meeting prior to the two-week Easter break that he had taken a role in the Academy as an associate principal and, as such, had replaced one of those who had been in the role since late March. These changes were described by one of the teachers in the following way:

> And in that time, [the last week before Easter break], [one of the associate/ acting principals] was off on a pre-booked holiday and [the regional executive] came into school and was announced, on the last day of term as a different associate principal, or an additional associate principal, and in the meantime [the other associate/acting principal] was also there. So it was a kind of mess and nobody really knew. But I think the idea was that they were both overseeing different parts of leadership team. I'm confused.

As implied by this teacher, the final week of term was, to say the least, a time of confusion for the staff and, indeed, for the students. During that week, the regional executive was frequently seen patrolling corridors, and instructing members of staff via email, even though he had not been formally introduced to the school. Meanwhile, senior leaders also had difficulty in keeping track of developments within their team. This is how one of the assistant principals explained the situation as he saw it:

> We went through a stage in which we saw [an associate/acting principal] being brought to the Academy, then [the regional executive] being brought to the Academy, [the other associate/acting principal] coming in and out. . . . You know there was a series of assemblies in April 2011 in which I first introduced [an associate/acting principal] as a principal and then the following week, in another assembly, [the regional executive]. And I had kids coming to me saying: 'Sir, first you say it's her and now you say it's him'.

Confusion regarding the membership and structure of the SLT escalated progressively during the first two weeks of April, as members of staff, students and even senior leaders were not sure who was actually leading the school. Meanwhile, throughout the period of these changes and introductions of new senior leaders, the Principal's name remained on the door of her office, even though her visits to the building were, by this time, rare.

On the basis of information provided by senior leaders to the staff, the SLT structure on the last day of the spring 2011 term is outlined in Figure 6.4.

With these changes in the structure and membership in the SLT determined, the staff and students left for their two-week Easter break. It had been a hectic and, at

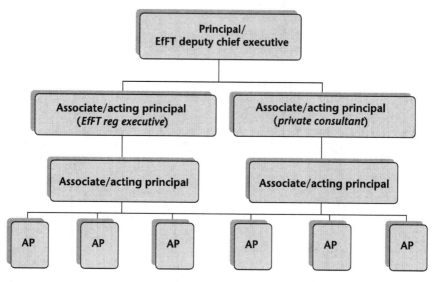

FIGURE 6.4   SLT structure on 15 April 2011

Note: The roles of the EfFT curriculum lead and the assessment lead remained unchanged and, once again, are not mentioned in this display.

times, bizarre term, which had left staff and students confused. Unsurprisingly, student behaviour had been in decline during the last couple of weeks of the term and the SLT addressed this by introducing new behaviour policies.

The Easter holiday provided a break for staff and students alike, and it offered the school community an opportunity to reflect on the developments. Meanwhile, as teaching staff and students went on their well-deserved break, the SLT and the central governance of the EfFT carried on working, presumably attempting to find a solution to the situation Parkside Academy was in. More complexities were to follow as efforts were made to solve the problem of the school's management arrangements, including the question of how a new principal was to be recruited.

More and more change

Whilst the students and staff were on their two-week Easter break, further decisions were made by the EfFT central board regarding the structure and membership of the SLT. As a result, by the time that staff and students returned to the Academy, there was, yet again, a new SLT in place. This time the changes were even more significant, as some members of senior staff had been demoted and others had swapped places with senior colleagues in other EfFT academies. This resulted in further changes in the structure, as illustrated in Figure 6.5.

To clarify the changes in the leadership team, we begin with the two new introductions to the Academy. They were brought into Parkside from other EfFT academies to take on vice principal roles. Both had held senior leader roles in their

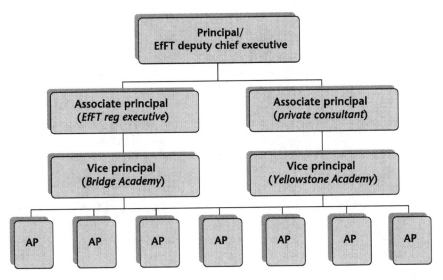

FIGURE 6.5 SLT structure on 2 May 2011

Note: An associate/vice principal had left to join Yellowstone Academy; the EfFT assessment lead/NA assistant principal had moved to Bridge Academy; the EfFT curriculum lead/NA assistant principal, remained in her role

previous schools. In the management hierarchy, they were positioned directly below an acting principal and an associate principal: one with a dual title of acting principal and EfFT regional executive, and the other with the title of associate principal.

The two new vice principals replaced the associate/acting principal roles held by two other senior staff members prior to the Easter break. This meant that they were, in effect, demoted back to their original assistant principal roles. However, instead of moving back to his original post, one stepped aside and moved to Yellowstone Academy, from where another had arrived. Here an assistant principal gives his view of the motives and practicalities behind this move:

> As I saw [the assessment lead] going to Bridge Academy, I decided I had had enough and went to Yellowstone. You know, [the vice principal of Yellowstone Academy and former assistant principal of Parkside Academy], a former colleague, was here in Parkside Academy one day. When she saw me she asked: 'What is going on in here?' and then she realised what the situation was and contacted them [the Principal and regional executive] and said she's got a job for me in Yellowstone, and would they let me go. It was her sort of pulling me out for a while, that's how bad the situation was.

As indicated, this senior member of staff saw his move to Yellowstone Academy as an offer of help from a former colleague, to distance him from the turbulent times of Parkside. The move was seen as being temporary in nature, and certainly his aim was to return once the leadership of Parkside had been settled. How the move of a member of staff from Yellowstone to Parkside Academy came about remained somewhat unclear, as she did not accept our interview invitation, and the members of staff interviewed were unable to clarify this for us.

Other swaps referred to concern the move of a staff member from Bridge Academy to Parkside, and the assessment lead's move from Parkside to Bridge Academy. Even though she had not been fully involved in the Parkside SLT structure since her promotion to EfFT assessment lead role in October 2010, her office had remained in the Academy and she had been closely involved in its senior leadership arrangements. This is how she explained her new role in Bridge Academy:

> I was sort of embedded as a kind of '[EfFT] system principalish' level, within the senior leadership team, still doing my EfFT assessments over the top but with a remit in Bridge as well, developing middle leaders . . . those sort of things, so back in a sort of a dual role, but the academy role being Bridge rather than Parkside Academy.

At this stage in the story it is important to remember that this individual had been approached by the Principal during the previous term regarding her interest in applying for the role of head of Parkside. Her sudden move was, to say the least, a surprising turn of events. She explained her perspective on all of this as follows:

> So [the Principal at Bridge Academy] agreed about the swap, and so did I really. Not out of any massive motivation to move necessarily, you know, I felt a lot of not being in this school, quite a lot really. But I could see that in this situation, for me this was probably the best thing. And it didn't really matter which academy I worked from in order to fulfil what EfFT expects from my contract. So I agreed the swap and that's fine. The original swap was for a term. [The Bridge Principal] and I both agreed for one term. . . . If you think about it, from a personal point of view, in the course of a week, I went from having fairly regular conversations with [the Parkside Principal] about: the ways she wants things to run here [Parkside], about other academies, about EfFT all sorts, and at that point she valued my view. In a week, that all changed completely. I think she associated me too closely with people she no longer rated, and for me I'm not quite sure if that was a fair reflection.

The purposes of the assessment lead's move, as well as other changes in the SLT, were once again poorly communicated to the staff and students. However, it is worth noting that during these turbulent spring months, the staff and students were rehearsing for the Green End Musical, which we described in Chapter 3. As the assessment lead had a central role in the production, regardless of her move to Bridge Academy, she spent every Friday of the third term in Parkside Academy rehearsing for the musical. Nevertheless, the official structure of the SLT remained as described above, with four senior leaders managing the team of assistant principals.

During early July, another change became apparent. At that time, the assessment lead was seen to have a more visible presence once again in Parkside, patrolling the corridors during break time and working from one of the assistant principal offices during lesson time on other days than Fridays. Then, on 11 July, she sent her first email to all staff from her Parkside account in which she indicated she was back full time at the school in a senior leadership role. From then on, she was involved in the day-to-day running of the Academy, dealing with issues such as student behaviour and staff meetings. Meanwhile, the four designated 'principals' referred to in Figure 6.5 were also involved in leadership tasks, as well as all the assistant principals.

To clarify the structure and membership of the senior leadership team for the upcoming academic year, 2011–2012, the assessment lead sent Parkside staff an email towards the end of the term, with the SLT arrangements for September (see Figure 6.6).

The new structure, with its expansion of leadership roles, confirms the assistant principals' roles and that the same people will fill these posts. Above the AP roles in the management hierarchy there is the principal and vice principal but, at this stage, no indication given regarding who would fill these roles. The roles of EfFT curriculum lead and EfFT assessment lead are not mentioned in the display, but the same two individuals were to carry on in these roles for the upcoming year.

With this structure in mind, the staff and students embarked on their summer holidays. The turbulent year had undoubtedly had an impact on staff and students alike, as both student behaviour as well as staff morale had noticeably declined. There was a 'cloud of frustration hanging over the staff room', as one teacher phrased it, with the sense of insecurity and confusion regarding the leadership arrangements lingering over several months.

The constant changes in management arrangement had also led to frequent changes in school policy, as new leaders brought new ideas and initiatives with them. Consequently, by the end of the school term, staff appeared to be exhausted by the instability, and symptomatic of this, morale had sunk rather low. Some of

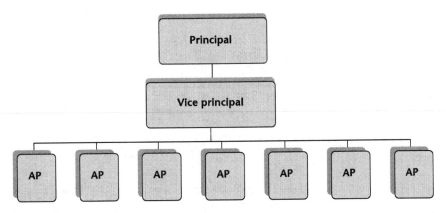

FIGURE 6.6   SLT structure as planned for September 2011

the frustration of staff could be explained by the deterioration in student behaviour, and the general consensus the staff had that the senior team was not supporting them. Here a member of staff gives a sense of these frustrations:

> Management structure is the key, and you know what happened here: they came in, all these people came in. It was almost like they came in to save us because they thought we were almost in special measures, but we weren't! We were not! We were fine before these people started coming in. But that was the attitude they had. What they put in place was that we faced a lock down, we had to get students to line up in the yard, and all that we didn't need to do anymore, but we went back to that. . . . Even the phrases they used, 'get the kids out, get them out', that kind of language, we were not used to it, there was no need for that. There was a time, years ago, when there was a need for stricter discipline, but we had moved beyond that a while ago. Until all these new people came in, and then there probably was a need again, the students aren't stupid, they pick up on the vibe. . . . And, you know, at least one of those senior managers came here from a school that was in special measures itself, so I don't know what they can bring to the school, apart from, shout a lot.

The sense of uncertainty was to continue into the following school year, as the process of finding a new principal for Parkside became even more urgent.

Waiting for the mystery man

After the summer holidays, there were two inset days for staff. As an annual tradition, on the first of these days there is a staff meeting, at which the Principal begins with a welcome speech and introductions of the new members of staff. In September 2011, the Regional Executive gave the welcome speech, in which he addressed various general topics, such as the exam results, reports on some events in which former and current students of the Academy had been involved during the summer months, as well as general issues relating to practice.

At the end of his 45-minute speech, the Regional Executive spared two minutes to explain that a new principal had been appointed. He also mentioned some of the practicalities regarding the ways in which the transition would be organised. One of us made notes describing what happened at the time:

> Parkside Academy Principal Welcome Speech: last two minutes of his speech [the regional executive] spends explaining to the staff about the appointment of the new principal. He refers to the new principal as the 'mystery man', 'Peter', and explains: 'everything is more or less agreed with him at this stage'. He will begin in his new role as the principal of Parkside Academy on 1 November after half term and until then [the regional executive] will serve the Academy as an acting principal five days a week.

Once the new principal begins in his role, [the regional executive] will be present in Parkside Academy in the principal's office two days a week. However, the Academy staff will have a chance to meet Peter when he visits the Academy on 29 September.

There are three significant points regarding the way in which this topic was dealt with that are worth noting. First, the presentation was addressed to all staff, but certain senior leaders were absent: the EfFT curriculum lead/AP, as well as the EfFT assessment lead/AP, (who had returned from the Bridge Academy in July) and the Principal/deputy chief executive. Her name was listed on the pre-circulated programme for the day, but no explanation was given to the staff about why she was absent. Second, the way in which the regional executive introduced the topic of the new principal in the last two minutes of his 45-minute speech: prior to this he had talked about several far less significant issues, as well as sharing some personal stories in his speech. The fact that the new leadership of the Academy was mentioned so briefly, at the end of the talk, made it seem like an afterthought regarding what might be regarded as an insignificant issue. Third, the Regional Executive explained nothing about how the new appointment had been made, nor anything about his background or experience. All that staff were told was his first name and, as we have mentioned, the references to him as a 'mystery man'.

In the period prior to the arrival of the new principal, the impression given was that the existing Principal would continue in her role. This being the case, the overall arrangements seemed to be as laid out in Figure 6.7, remembering, of course, that the Principal was rarely to be seen in the school, leaving the regional executive to continue as acting principal.

The roles of the EfFT leads still exist, with the same two people carrying on dealing with curriculum and assessment. At the same time, the assessment lead was to return to the Academy for the time being, until the arrival of the new principal. In the management hierarchy, she was placed above the assistant principals, alongside the regional executive, taking care of the day-to-day management of the

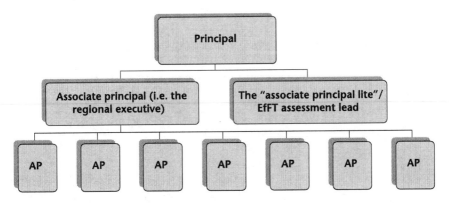

FIGURE 6.7 SLT structure September 2011

Academy in collaboration with him. Talking of her rather ambiguous status, she commented:

> In this meeting with [the Principal] about my role in Parkside Academy for the next while, I asked her what should I call myself, and she says: 'how about Associate Principal Lite'. Seriously, you know, lite as in cheese, like Philadelphia Lite.

It seemed to us that, by this stage, EfFT was running out of titles for its senior school leaders.

The formal announcement to members of staff from the EfFT chairman regarding the changes in Parkside's leadership arrangements took the form of an email headed 'APPOINTMENT OF PRINCIPAL AT PARKSIDE ACADEMY'. This appeared six weeks after the beginning of the term and ten days prior to the date that the new principal was to arrive. It explained that, over the summer, efforts had been made to identify a suitable candidate to lead Parkside Academy on 'the next stage of its journey as an outstanding school'. This had not been an easy task, it was noted, since what was wanted was an individual with the strong leadership skills, the charisma and the energy to lead a 'flagship academy'. The email also commented on the fact that, over the previous 12–18 months, all at Parkside Academy had tolerated a great deal of turbulence, as senior staff had moved around the group, spreading the best practice that had been developed at Parkside.

As the staff returned from the half term break, at the end of October, the new principal took up his post. He had briefly visited the Academy in late September, so the staff had had a chance to meet him in person before he started.

The role of the members of the local governing body in this process of appointing the new principal was difficult to follow. As we have already explained, they did not seem to be involved in the actual decision-making process, nor were they informed about its developments until after the decision was made. One governor commented as follows:

> During the last year [2010–2011] the LGB virtually didn't know who was running the school. . . . We weren't informed when the principal finally left. And until very recently we had no idea who was the principal or the deputy principal.

However, it later emerged that certain members of the LGB had been included in the decision-making processes, at least to some extent, as this conversation with one governor revealed:

> Three of them did. One of them was the chair of LGB, one was the deputy chair, and then the chair of finance. How they were selected? I don't know but probably by [the Principal] and [the regional executive]. And [the Chief Executive] probably involved as well. So they all had lunch together.

So there you go. But we [the rest of the LGB] didn't know at the time what was going on.

This story adds further complexity to the account of the local governance arrangements and the role of the local governing body that we explained in the previous chapter. It reminds us that, even today, we do not have the full details of what happened.

Conclusion

In this chapter we have described changes in the roles of senior leaders during what proved to be a year of remarkable turbulence at Parkside Academy. These change processes regarding the formal leadership structures were described here in some detail in order to cast light, first, on the ways in which the succession process was handled, and, second, where the decision making for the process was located. As we have illustrated, the significant staffing decisions that were made impacted on the whole school community. They were also made at a rapid pace (in March and April the Academy welcomed five new senior leaders) and sometimes in ways that seemed to disregard the professional interests of the staff involved (such as the assessment lead's move to Bridge Academy in May). These events are, we suggest, indicative of a heavily centralised operation, in which much of the Academy related managerial decisions were made well away from the school by those involved in the central governance of the sponsor.

These changes reflect the increased autonomy of academies, particularly when it comes to decisions about major areas of policy. Significantly, they took place in the absence of the involvement of a local authority that might have been in a position to offer constructive advice from a more detached perspective. We assume, for example, that the decisions regarding the senior leader moves from one academy to another at short notice would be, if not impossible, at least more difficult to negotiate in the maintained sector. Similarly, promotions and demotions of senior leaders from one role to another, jumping up and down in the organisational hierarchy over short periods of time, and lacking transparent application processes would previously have been hard to negotiate.

Meanwhile, the methods applied in the principal recruitment process are also symptomatic of significant managerial autonomy at the sponsor level. The fact that local stakeholders with a greater knowledge of circumstances within the school community – particularly the local governing body – were largely excluded from the process and, indeed, not even informed it was taking place, indicates that decision making was taking place at the EfFT level. In a maintained sector structure, the approach EfFT took would be unheard of, as these processes would be steered by guidelines outlining the stages of the procedure, requiring an involvement of stakeholders. These processes would also require transparency in terms of a recruitment and interview procedures, and would be documented and open to the scrutiny of a much wider audience, rather than just a few powerful system-level leaders.

By explaining all these processes, this chapter has thrown further light on whose voices are heard within an independent state school. In the case of this particular school, it has shown that there was a degree of autonomy in relation to overall management decision making. We contrast this with the limited space available to practitioners and school leaders that we reported in the earlier chapters.

Our account also throws light on processes which can lead a school that has been 'turned round' to go into decline. The idea that schools regress to the mean is far from new but, to our knowledge, there are few if any ethnographic accounts of how the process of regression actually happens. It seems here that the erosion of 'professional' autonomy may well have been a factor in the school's regression. Once professional autonomy has gone, we suggest, the school has less resilience to deal with the difficulties it faces.

In such contexts, schools need to be autonomous only insofar as this means being free (and competent) to follow instructions from above. There may be some real autonomy at different levels, but the autonomy is always prescribed. If the instructions from on high are flawed, or if they fail to deal effectively with local circumstances, there is nothing else for the system to fall back on.

In the next chapter we relate our account of Parkside to evidence from elsewhere in order to consider possible implications for future policy and practice in the field.

Note

1 Details of the incident remain a mystery to us, as our participants were not willing to share the details of it with us.

7

THE REALITY OF LOCAL AUTONOMY

In the previous chapters we have revealed a sense of what day-to-day life was like for those involved in Parkside Academy over a period of ten years. We have also described the way that the school improved student attainment, such that it came to be recognised as something of a success story of the early English academies policy.

We went on to describe in some detail the way that decisions were made within the Academy and by its sponsoring organisation, as those involved responded to external pressures to raise standards. The complexities involved in all of this became particularly evident when it came to the appointment of certain key posts.

In this chapter we reflect further on our account, using various thinking tools derived from international research in order to analyse these developments. We look, in particular, at the extent to which the various stakeholders were free to influence decisions regarding policy and practice. In so doing, we continue with our focus on the idea that school autonomy will provide freedom to innovate. First of all, however, we start by reminding readers of the thinking that led to the introduction of the first group of sponsored academies in England.

Early academies

In Chapter 1, we suggested that the first academies initiated in the early 2000s were seen as a remedy to cure some of the ills in the English education system. The logic was that, if certain steps were taken in relation to administrative and governance arrangements, schools would be in a better position to educate their students, particularly those from economically disadvantaged and minority backgrounds.

In summary, the steps taken to achieve this overall goal were:

- **Making schools more autonomous.** The logic was that giving schools more freedom would put them in a better position to address the needs of their particular students. In this way, it was assumed, most decisions would be made by the people involved in schools, rather than by administrators at the local authority level. The early academies were therefore made more autonomous over educational matters, particularly the curriculum, and administrative arrangements, such as finance and regulations concerning staff recruitment and contracts.

- **Bringing new actors into the management, administration and governance of schools**. The early academies were removed from the control of local authorities and paired with a sponsor. Sponsors included organisations and individuals who had not traditionally been involved in the management of publicly funded education, such as: charitable trusts, religious organisations and wealthy philanthropists. These new actors, it was argued, could bring fresh ideas that would inject new energy and more efficient ways of working into public education.
- **Maintaining heavily regulated quality assurance and accountability systems**. Here, the aim was to make the schools' performance transparent for wider audiences. In England, this was relatively straightforward since academy students sit the same national tests as those in other state schools, and are subject to similar school inspections as others. As we have explained, the results of both the testing and the inspections are made publicly available in order to inform decision making, not least amongst parents.

Keeping these steps in mind, this chapter analyses how the introduction of the remedy operated at Parkside.

Thinking tools

In order to probe the impact on the various stakeholders, we utilise some conceptual tools from school and teacher autonomy research to guide our analysis. This helps us to steer away from normative connotations often associated with the concept of autonomy – as something that is always positive, something to strive for – and to focus on what autonomy means for those involved. This leads us to demonstrate what the freedoms associated with academies meant for stakeholders, as well as casting further light on the nature of the involvement of the 'new actor' – its sponsoring organisation, the EfFT. It also reveals the complex ways in which the various national accountability systems affected the work of the Academy.

We take schools to be complex social systems in which the various actors, such as students, teachers, school leaders and support personnel, operate with a range of agendas. Therefore, when examining school autonomy, it is, we believe, essential to acknowledge this complexity. International research literature is helpful in this respect. In what follows we outline how we have tried to capture this complexity in our analysis of Parkside.

A helpful starting point for our analysis is provided by the work of Gewirtz and Cribb (Gewirtz & Cribb, 2009; Cribb & Gewirtz, 2007) on dimensions of school autonomy. Drawing on their ideas, we suggest that it is important to consider different dimensions of school autonomy through asking the following questions:

Who is autonomous? Over what matters are they autonomous? How is their autonomy exercised?

This implies that who is autonomous will depend on local context and suggests that there is likely to be a number of actors involved. It is therefore important to remain sensitive to the context under focus. Applying this to Parkside, the ways in which increased decision-making capacity associated with the academies policy affects different people at a local level is therefore a starting point for our analysis.

Our involvement in Parkside over the years indicated that there were four distinct groups of adults on whom we should focus: teachers, school leaders, sponsor representatives and members of the local governing body. Had the Academy operated differently and included other groups in decision making – such as students, support staff and parents – the inclusion of these other stakeholders would have been justified. And, on reflection, we recognise that it is a major limitation of our work that their voices are not heard in this book.

Moving on to analyse the matters about which actors are autonomous, we have to pay attention to different areas of decision making. International literature on school and teacher autonomy offers helpful starting points for distinguishing these different areas. As we noted in Chapter 1, the early work on charter schools of Lubienski (2003) distinguishes autonomy in relation to two domains: *educational* and *administrative*. The former refers to matters directly related to teaching and learning, including but not limited to planning, classroom practices and the forms of assessment/evaluation used to monitor progress. The administrative domain refers to aspects of the work of schools that are intended to facilitate teaching and learning but are not directly related to classroom practice, including, for example, timetabling, and financial and contractual matters. As we have explained, the early academies policy focused on increasing educational and administrative autonomy of these schools, which justifies focusing on these two areas. Consequently, this division is used to structure the overall discussion in this chapter.

In order to capture the nature of autonomy in schools, we must also examine how different actors exercise their increased freedom. Again, there may be local variations in how this is exercised, which is why when examining the nature of autonomy in particular contexts, the analysis should remain sensitive to local practices. In the case of Parkside, we found Bailyn's (1985) ideas about professional autonomy helpful. She distinguishes decision-making capacity to be either: *strategic*, referring to a capacity to influence agenda and policy; or, *operational*, referring to the capacity to make decisions within set agenda. Applying this formulation to our analysis of developments at Parkside, we focus on the extent to which those involved are able to contribute to the future direction of the school more widely, as well as more specifically within their own remit. Using teachers' educational autonomy as an example, we understand this to involve *developmental autonomy*, referring to the extent to which stakeholders are able to contribute to school-level policy that is intended to frame educational practice. This means that *operational autonomy* refers to the extent to which they may be in charge of educational matters within their classrooms.

	Teachers		School leaders		Governors		Sponsor representatives	
	DA	OA	DA	OA	DA	OA	DA	OA
Educational								
Administrative								

FIGURE 7.1 A framework for analysing autonomy

Drawing together these various thinking tools, Figure 7.1 illustrates how they were used to guide our analysis. The horizontal lines indicate the different areas of autonomy. In our study, these areas are educational and administrative. The vertical columns point to the different actors whose autonomy is in question. In Parkside we focused specifically on: teachers, school leaders, local governors and sponsor representatives. The vertical columns also indicate the ways in which autonomy may be exercised, as in the extent to which their agency has the capacity to contribute to decision making regarding the development of school-level policy (DA) and in regard to operational practices (OA). Later in the chapter, we explain how the thinking tools mentioned in the table helped us to analyse our observations at Parkside.

Keeping this overall framework in mind, in what follows we begin our analysis by analysing the nature of teachers' autonomy over educational matters, before moving on to discuss the administrative autonomy of the academy-level leadership, and its sponsoring organisation. This leads us to cast further light on the ways in which decision making was distributed amongst the various stakeholders.

Autonomy over educational matters

To examine the boundaries of Parkside teachers' autonomy, we have collated the findings presented in Chapters 2 to 6 in Figure 7.2. This illustrates by whom and over what matters teachers' autonomy was regulated. All the constraints presented in the table are directed at the teaching staff, either as individuals or as a professional group, and relate to school, sponsor and/or national policies. The table does not present an all-encompassing list of constraints framing teachers' day-to-day practice. However, those included in the table are all mentioned in the previous chapters and, as such, illustrate some of the boundaries within which teachers operate.

Constraints

In order to better understand the ways in which the constraints mentioned in the table bound teachers' pedagogical autonomy, we start by approaching them from the bottom-right corner – that is, from the angle of the individual teacher. In all pedagogical activities, including planning, teaching and assessment, the teacher was expected to take into consideration the instructions and guidance set within the Academy and by EfFT, as well as in national regulatory frameworks.

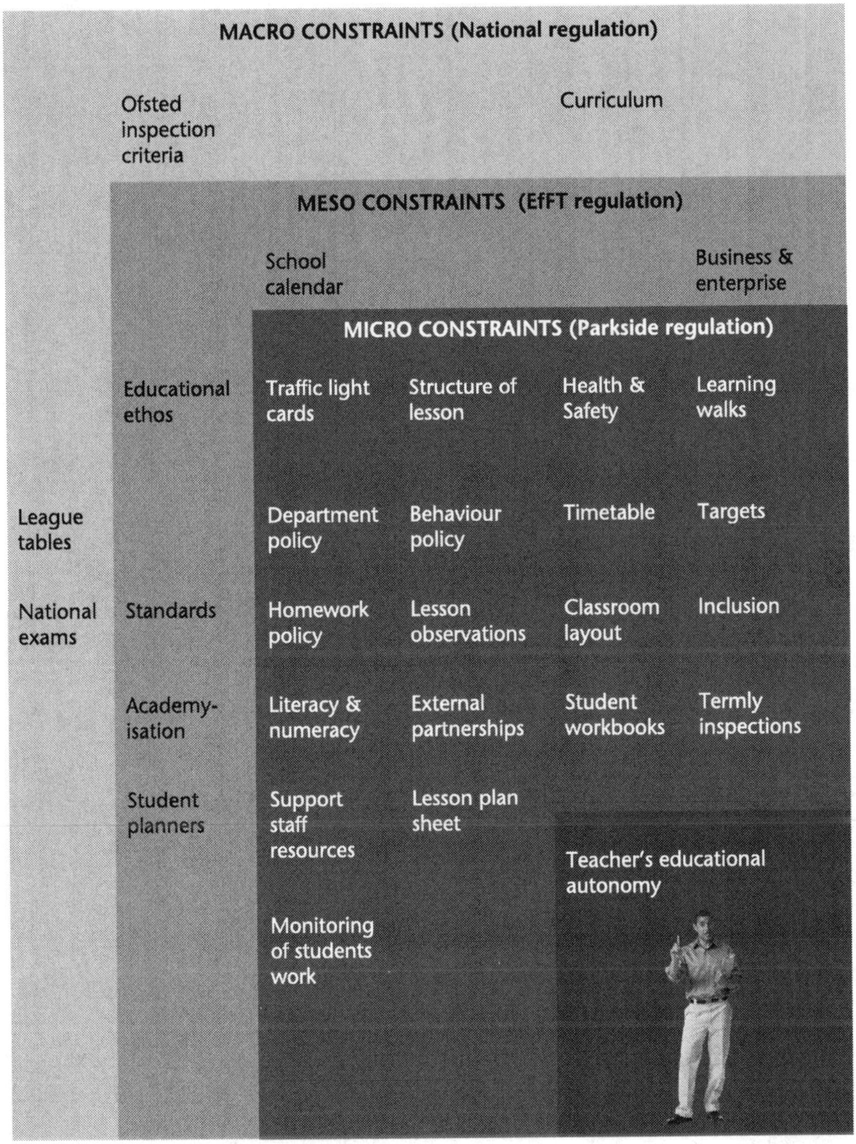

FIGURE 7.2 Constraints on teacher autonomy

In light of the accounts presented in the previous chapters, in what follows we offer a brief description of teachers' lesson planning and the ways in which this appeared to be constrained, in the form of a synopsis:

> When a Parkside Academy teacher planned a lesson, she or he must ensure that its content was in line with what was articulated in curriculum guidelines, which was mostly in line with the national curriculum. For every lesson taught, teachers were expected to fill a common lesson plan sheet. This required them to make explicit the content, objectives and methods used in the lesson, and the progress the students were intended to make. Teachers were expected to incorporate certain initiatives articulated in the school's policies in their plan, such as the use of the traffic light cards and the suggested structure of lessons. Teachers also needed to take into consideration the fact that students' desks and chairs were organised in a particular manner, according to Parkside policy.
>
> Students were required to produce work in their workbooks, using only black and blue ink, and not to illustrate them with images. The student workbooks were checked by the head of department fortnightly and by senior staff during termly observations, something the teacher might wish to keep in mind when planning a lesson.
>
> In addition, teachers were expected to: incorporate the Academy ethos into their teaching; follow the behaviour policy; and, perhaps most importantly, show the progress that students would make. When planning a lesson, teachers must also take into consideration that students' home-work is assigned by a member of staff with specific responsibility for the whole department, which may be somebody other than the teachers in question.
>
> When planning a lesson, teachers may wish to take into consideration that at any moment they may be subject to a learning walk visit by a senior colleague, and that on a termly basis they were subject to a 'mock Ofsted inspection' carried out by an Academy observation team. Last but not least, when planning a lesson, a teacher was expected to keep in mind that students' learning will be assessed in a national examination that has been written and marked by somebody other than the teacher.

Although this brief synopsis only illustrates some of the main guidance binding Parkside Academy teachers' lessons planning, it captures the ways that teachers operated within a heavily constrained environment.

Some of the constraints are not directly related to the school's academy status, but consist of more general requirements placed on teachers in other types of English state schools, such as inspections and pressures to improve examination results. Nevertheless, there is a considerable number of factors that were particular to Parkside. Furthermore, it is possible to argue that these relate to the school's status as an academy and, indeed, to its membership of this particular chain.

We observed that the constraints we have summarised were imposed upon teachers through two different means: *formal policy* and *direct interventions*. These were mainly developed by senior leaders, as well as within the subject departments, encompassing regulation and guidance regarding issues such as homework, student workbooks and student progress. As we saw in Chapter 4, the specific policy was extensive and detailed, including hundreds of pages of guiding documentation. In addition, teachers' decision making was informed by guidance and regulation articulated by EfFT, encompassing instructions regarding educational ethos, and business and enterprise education in the chain. Last but by no means least, national policies were always there in the background, steering teachers' pedagogical decision making related to the need to take account of national examinations, and ideals of pedagogical practice as articulated in the Ofsted criteria use during inspections.

Some constraints were not solely articulated in policy but also materialised through direct interventions, as teaching staff were subject to regular scrutiny by a variety of Academy and sponsor representatives, as well as through occasional inspections. As we have explained, lesson observations took place on a termly basis, which, depending on the outcome, might lead to further intervention in the form of compulsory weekly training. In addition, there were weekly learning walks carried out by senior staff.

Such pedagogical interventions were generally considered as accountability mechanisms, utilised to make classroom practice transparent. These interventions were conducted by the senior leaders and/or middle leaders, rather than by sponsor representatives. As such, direct EfFT-level intervention in these processes was rare, although not unheard of, as with the involvement of the Principal in the Green End Musical, highlighted in Chapter 3.

Teacher responses

So far, we have treated teachers as a group and examined the extent to which they were able to use their judgment. The analysis has focused on the formal boundaries of teacher autonomy. However, it is important to recognise that actors may respond differently to reforms at the local level and negotiate the guidance imposed upon them (Braun et al., 2010; Braun et al., 2011). Certainly, at Parkside, teaching staff responded to constraints differently, such that they were seen to negotiate and redefine their boundaries of autonomy.

In this context, it became obvious that some teachers were more resentful towards the constraints that were imposed upon them, whereas others accepted, or even embraced, the external guidance and interventions to which they were subjected. However, as we saw in Chapter 4, the constraints teachers negotiated, questioned or ignored tended to be Parkside initiatives regarding particular teaching methods or the layout of classrooms. According to the evidence, teaching staff were much less reluctant to ignore or challenge macro-level constraints, such as the requirements of examinations or inspections, and actually such macro constraints were often referred to as the main drivers of practice, towards which teachers usually worked really hard.

To an extent, there was a pattern in which the staff exercised agency over the constraints imposed upon them. What we mean by this is that experienced teaching staff tended to be more likely than their junior colleagues to question, ignore or challenge Parkside and EfFT guidance and interventions. The teaching staff who talked of ignoring, questioning or challenging these policies were more senior in the profession and had worked in the Academy for at minimum three, some of them over ten years. Nevertheless, although teachers negotiated and adjusted their boundaries of autonomy, it can still be argued that the constraints they were negotiating set tight boundaries on their professional decision making. As we have explained, some of the constraints limiting teachers' autonomy over educational practice were rather general and would be recognisable to teachers working in different types of state-funded schools across the country.

In principle, the teaching staff of Parkside held some of what we identify as developmental autonomy, as they were able to contribute to the school's curricular policy, which was mainly developed within the subject departments (see Chapter 4). In addition, they had a degree of operational autonomy, since in their day-to-day practice they had the capacity to make curricular decisions.

The influence that the teaching staff had over curriculum was a result of the autonomy academies have from the national curriculum, as well as the EfFT and Parkside policy frameworks regarding curriculum being rather loose and general. Teachers acknowledged the capacity they had to experiment with curriculum, and reported some alternative approaches they had adopted with classes of younger students. However, it was noticeable that with the approaching examinations, the national curriculum was more rigorously followed with older classes across the different subject areas. As such, teaching staff were conscious of their 'theoretical liberty' to experiment with curriculum, but had an overhanging fear regarding examination results. This tended to prevent experimentation, which was considered to be too risky. It seems likely that such a stance would be more apparent in schools that are seen as performing poorly.

Levels of involvement

Although our analysis so far has focused on teachers, our account of developments at Parkside has shown that curriculum, teaching and assessment-related decision-making processes in the Academy were also the concern of senior leaders and EfFT representatives alike. Within English traditions it would also be expected that governors would have some involvement, although, as we have explained, this was far from the case at Parkside.

Figure 7.3 illustrates the involvement of different actors in teaching and learning related decision making, and the extent to which these different groups were actually involved in making such decisions. The horizontal lines in the table refer to areas of educational practice: curriculum, teaching and assessment. The vertical

	Local governing body		Teachers		School leaders		The sponsor	
	DA	OA	DA	OA	DA	OA	DA	OA
Curriculum	none	none	some	some	some	some	high	high
Teaching practices	none	none	some	some	some	some	some	some
Assessment	none	none	some	some	some	some	some	none

FIGURE 7.3   The involvement of different actors

columns display the different actors involved in the school: local governors, teachers, school leaders and the EfFT central governance.

The vertical columns also present the ways in which different groups may contribute to decision making regarding these issues in the school. In making this analysis, we draw on Bailyn's (1985) distinction, referred to earlier. That is to say, we use *developmental autonomy* (DA) to refer to the capacity to influence agenda, and *operational autonomy* (OA) to refer to the capacity to make decisions within a particular agenda.

The scale used in the table describes levels of autonomy: *high*, indicating the capacity to overrule the decisions of other stakeholders, if it is considered to be necessary; *some*, indicating decision-making capacity that may be intervened and overruled by other groups; and *none*, indicating lack of involvement in the decision-making processes.

Making decisions

Typically, key decisions regarding the *curriculum* were made by the heads of subject departments (sometimes in consultation with teachers), verified at the senior leadership level, and, if thought necessary, checked by the EfFT curriculum lead. However, as we reported in Chapter 4, standards in Parkside were on the rise, which was considered an indicator of successful curricular policy and practice. A question can therefore be asked regarding the extent to which the Academy staff had earned their autonomy over curriculum through rising standards (see, for example, Whitty, 2007; Beck, 2009; Storey, 2009).

As we explained, at various stages the EfFT curriculum lead and members of the sponsor executive team worked closely with less successful academies in order to provide additional support. However, had results dropped in Parkside, would EfFT have taken more control over curriculum and limited the curricular autonomy of teachers and senior leaders? Answers to such questions were beyond the scope of our research and therefore remain unanswered here, although they would contribute to our understanding of the dynamic nature of independent state school autonomy reported elsewhere (Finnigan, 2007).

Various actors were also involved in developing *teaching practices*. As with the curriculum, key decision making regarding teaching and learning was usually made within the subject departments by teachers and heads of departments, and then verified at the senior leadership level. Although the teaching staff were actively developing teaching materials and methods, and were able to contribute to policies and practices both within their classrooms, as well as within their subject departments, there was always a chance that these decisions would be overruled by senior leaders, or by sponsor policy or intervention. Moreover, as we saw in Chapter 4, it was notable that the 'invisible hand' of the inspectorate was constantly steering this line of work across the Academy. Indeed, we argue that the most powerful actor in terms of teaching and learning was the inspectorate, as the Parkside and EfFT practices and policies were heavily steered by Ofsted intervention and guidance. In this sense, it seems reasonable to argue that the final say on what happened in classrooms was in the hands of the inspectorate.

Assessment practices were also dominated by the requirements of national examinations. Within this sphere of influence, Academy staff were able to develop continuous assessment, however, this was all done in line with the expectations of the examinations. This also applied to EfFT-level policy and interventions to assessment practice, as these were basically conducted to reinforce the existing framework.

In summary, then, it can be argued that although academies are legally autonomous from the national curriculum, which arguably gives these types of schools a greater scope of action to experiment with educational approaches and practices, this autonomy is largely theoretical. Based on our evidence from Parkside, we argue that because an academy's performance is measured against the same national performance indicators as other schools, in reality, examinations and inspections set a tight frame for educational practice in these schools – a case of 'what gets measured gets done'. Commenting on all of this, Exley and Ball (2011) and Goodman and Burton (2012) have challenged the paradoxical dual existence of purported increase in school autonomy and tight governmental grip through performance testing and targets (cited in Kauko & Salokangas, 2015, p. 1110).

It is worth noting at this stage in our argument that these observations regarding the situation at Parkside resonate strongly with international literature focusing on teacher autonomy in other education systems with high-stakes accountability and quality assurance procedures. So, for example, Wills and Sandholtz (2009) have suggested that teachers' professional autonomy in such contexts is compromised by accountability mechanisms, standards-based testing and an increase of administrative workload. We return to these international trends in the next chapter.

Autonomy over administrative matters

Moving on, this section focuses on the scope of action Parkside stakeholders had with regard to administrative work. Stakeholder groups assigned with administrative duties, rather than educational roles, included: school leaders, local governors and the EfFT central administration.

The analysis focuses first on the senior leadership team, which consisted of the principal and a team of assistant principals. They were contractually based in Parkside and not usually assigned there by EfFT on a short-term basis, although, as we have explained, sometimes the sponsor stepped in to enforce changes. We begin this section by focusing on constraints framing senior leaders' practice. As established earlier in this chapter, formal EfFT and Academy level policy and direct interventions set a framework for practice at Parkside.

Policy formulation and implementation

It is worthwhile first of all to spend some time on policy formulation and implement-ation processes. As mentioned in Chapter 5, at one stage there were altogether 159 EfFT policies available for all members of the staff, which outlined basic guidelines concerning the running of the Academy. It is possible, of course, that there were even more aimed at senior leaders, which were not meant for wider circulation. However, already, the material available for all staff members sets out a tight framework within which the EfFT senior leadership teams were expected to operate.

In order to better describe the nature of senior leaders' work at Parkside, we will look closely at policy processes in Parkside. Put simply, this was the way in which the sponsor's policies were interpreted such that they became Academy-specific policies.

As the extract from the *EfFT Governance Policy* document below suggests, school leaders were expected to play a pivotal role in this process. Particular attention should be paid to the way in which the sponsor expects academy principals to operate within the overall policy framework:

> The principal is responsible for the leadership of the school. The principal is chief operating officer of the school and is responsible for the internal organisation, management and control of his or her school, the implement-ation of all policies approved by the [EfFT] Board and for the direction of teaching and the curriculum . . . the role requires him/her to guide the LGB in the formulation of school policy within the guidelines set out by EfFT as well as to ensure its implementation.
>
> EfFT Governance Policy, *p. 5*

As the extract suggests, the role of the principal was seen to be specifically in policy implementation, as opposed to formulation, indicating little, if any, involvement in the sponsor's centralised policy development. How policy implementation worked out in practice was through shared responsibilities between the principal, and the assistant principals. As explained in Chapter 6, in addition to the principal there were up to ten assistant principals (or senior leaders with other titles) covering different areas of responsibility, such as: teaching and learning, data, sixth form, etc. The responsibilities of each was to ensure that the academy policy within their remit was up to date and implemented accordingly.

In addition to implementing EfFT requirements, the senior leaders developed school-specific policies within their remit. In practice, for example, the assistant principal with responsibilities for teaching and learning was expected to ensure that the Parkside policy was in line with EfFT's, and that it was implemented in all subject departments. In addition, to ensure that the sponsor's strategies were in place, it was also the responsibility of school leaders to generate more specific teaching and learning policies which, as we saw earlier, covered areas such as marking students' workbooks, the colour of pens students may use in classes and the usage of traffic light cards. As such, senior leaders had the capacity to enforce Parkside policy, as long as it was in line with the EfFT guidelines. It is worth noting that it was this localised policy frame, developed by the senior leaders, to which the teaching staff mostly referred.

In addition to extensive and specific EfFT-level policy, national guidelines were seen to steer senior leaders' practices. For example, the school's policies concerning lesson observations were heavily influenced by Ofsted, with each observed lesson judged against the criteria used during inspections.

Interventions

In addition to hundreds of pages of policy, the modes of control constraining senior leaders' practice included various types of intervention from EfFT. Indeed, the senior leadership team was subject to such interventions on a regular basis throughout our involvement with the Academy.

As described in Chapter 6, some of the most direct interventions took place during the academic year 2010–2011, as the sponsor were seen to introduce into Parkside numerous additional representatives, as well as senior leaders from other EfFT academies. So far as we were able to detect, these new players, who took on a variety of senior leader roles, arrived without any consultation with, or without even prior information given to, the existing senior leadership team. We saw, for example, how staff from EfFT central office, a person from a private consultancy and two senior staff from other EfFT academies were all introduced into the Academy in spring 2011. They were positioned above the SLT in the organisational hierarchy, with significant capacity to intervene in decision making. The overall purpose of these introductions was articulated as to 'provide support' to the Academy leadership. However, this support could also be interpreted as a form of external intervention in leadership arrangements, one that narrowed the scope of action of existing senior staff members.

Changing roles

What complicates our analysis of the ways in which decisions regarding administrative matters were made was the poorly defined organisational roles of some of the key stakeholders, particularly during the 'turbulent' school year 2010–2011. Specifically, the blur in organisational roles between Academy senior leaders and

EfFT representatives made it problematic to distinguish which aspects of intervention were made at the EfFT level and which came from within the school.

One particularly influential intervention was, of course, the gradual change in the role of the Principal to EfFT Deputy Chief Executive. Although she remained as principal during that year, she was not physically present in the school, and in her absence other senior leaders were designated to cover her leadership duties. We therefore associated her more closely with the sponsor during that period, although this is not an entirely unproblematic approach to take in explaining what happened.

Another peculiar case of blurred organisational roles involved another person, who was introduced into the Academy as a representative of EfFT, with the title of regional executive. At the beginning of his involvement, in spring 2011, Parkside was one of the many schools in his region he was supporting, but gradually his involvement in the Academy grew stronger. Although a new principal was introduced into the Academy in October 2011, the Regional Executive remained a weekly presence, supporting the new principal for the whole of that academic year. Later, in the summer of 2012, when this principal resigned, the regional executive was himself named as the executive principal for the academic year, and this tied him even more closely to the Academy for the following period. Rather interestingly, these two roles, the regional executive's and the principal's, can be seen as being two sides of the same coin, as the Principal moved gradually from Parkside to EfFT, whereas the Regional Executive traversed from the sponsor to the Academy.

Giving the confusion around these changing roles, it is problematic at times to set boundaries between school-level and chain-level decision making. However, such a blur in organisational roles amongst the EfFT executive team and the Parkside senior leadership team is, in itself, a sign of a tightly-knit relationship between the Academy and its sponsor, and is indicative of heavy sponsor involvement. However, suggesting that EfFT policy was followed to the letter in Parkside would be an overly simplistic claim.

Although the Regional Executive, as well as other EfFT-assigned, short-term 'visiting leaders', were involved in the Academy and supporting the senior leadership team, the rapidity with which this external support was introduced, plus the lack of clarity in their roles, created inconsistent conditions for the senior leadership team to work in during spring and summer 2011. During these months of inconsistency – chaos even – policy implementation processes were disrupted, and the senior leadership team gradually became dysfunctional. Indeed, as we worked in the Academy throughout this period we witnessed times when it was not obvious who was leading the organisation.

At the same time, it was far from clear what the roles and relationships of the multiple leaders introduced into Parkside actually were. This confusion affected school policy processes, as staff were in a state of uncertainty regarding which senior leader instructions to follow, at what times. As such, we concluded that the consistency with which EfFT policy was implemented and enacted in Parkside was dynamic in nature, depending on who was leading at any particular time. It is worth adding by way of comment here that the absence of the sort of monitoring role traditionally provided by local authority officers was particularly noticeable through this period.

As a result of all of this, the capacity of senior leaders to experiment with alternative approaches in their roles was limited. Especially during the period of the principal changeover, the senior leadership team operated under the tight scrutiny of EfFT representatives, whose presence in the Academy significantly limited their capacity to experiment with alternative approaches. This meant that EfFT policy and intervention, in tandem with certain national guidelines, limited significantly the Academy senior leaders' managerial freedom and as such, restricted their capacity to experiment with alternative approaches. Rather, the changes in management arrangements that occurred were introduced by EfFT. These are analysed at a later stage in this chapter.

The role of governors

So far we have argued that the ways in which the Academy senior leaders' autonomy over administrative matters was constrained were rigorous and extensive. We have also showed that these constraints took the form of EfFT imposed *policies,* plus frequent and, at times, invasive EfFT *interventions.* In addition, national guidelines concerning examinations, as well as school inspections, further guided the work of senior leaders. All in all, this constrained environment in which the Academy senior leaders operated was not particularly fruitful ground for administrative and managerial innovations.

Moving on to another group of stakeholders with formal administrative functions, the local governing body, our account has revealed that their role was, to say the least, peculiar. Of all the EfFT policy documents available, there were two that discussed local governance arrangements: the *EfFT Memorandum and Articles of Association* and the *EfFT Governance Policy.* This limited body of otherwise extensive EfFT policy, framed rather explicitly the decision-making capacity of the local governing body. The *EfFT Governance Policy* in particular articulated that Parkside-related decision making would take place within the EfFT board and by its executive team. As we illustrated in the earlier chapters, the local governing body was excluded from these strategic and executive functions, leaving it with only a narrow remit within which to operate.

This is how the document describes the 'main responsibilities' of the local governing body:

- Providing advice on the future direction of the school.
- Monitoring the recruitment, deployment and performance management of staff and providing assistance when invited by the Principal to do so particularly with respect to the appointment and appraisal of senior staff.
- Monitoring the curriculum and educational programme of the school.
- Monitoring the academic achievement, behaviour and well-being of students.
- Monitoring the financial management of the school.

- Marketing the school and achieving pupil numbers.
- Implementing the EfFT Risk Assessment Register.
- Providing a body of appeal as set out in the relevant policies including, for example, Exclusions, Admissions, Disciplinary (The *EfFT Governance Policy*).

As this document suggests, the local governing body was seen, at best, as a minor player. Their tasks mostly included: monitoring the implementation of EfFT strategies at the local level; providing assistance when requested; and marketing. The evidence presented in Chapter 5 suggests that, in reality, the role of the local governing body in Parkside was even more peripheral, as the governors themselves were not quite sure how they actually could contribute to decision making in the Academy and over what matters.

All of this became particularly apparent through the appointment processes of the new chair of governors and Principal. As we saw in Chapters 5 and 6, decision making regarding both processes was carried out by the central governance of EfFT, excluding all other stakeholders. Although the Parkside Principal described the LGB as having a consultancy role, it became clear that local governors were not consulted in either of these recruitment processes. The process through which the chair of local governors was appointed was not made public and, indeed, details of the process remain unclear even as we write. However, as discussed earlier, the members of the local governing body were poorly informed about the process, their consultation was ignored and, as it seemed to them, the chair of local governors was chosen at the EfFT level and introduced to the rest of the local governing body after the appointment was made.

The dynamics of the appointment process of the new principal were similar, as governors reported that very little information regarding the process was shared with them. In the end, the appointment was made at the sponsor level, and the result was announced to the local governing body in a similar manner as to the rest of the academy community.

We see these as critical incidents which illustrate the relationship the EfFT central governance had established with the local governing body. Although the governors existed, they were marginalised from any decision making and excluded from information regarding actual decisions made at the sponsor level. As such, the EfFT's purposes for setting up and maintaining a local governing body, with minimal involvement in the Academy they 'locally govern', remained confused and, some might say, dubious.

The role of the sponsor

So far, our analysis has challenged the presumption embedded in academy-related policy rhetoric, and the views of the advocates of the academy movement, who claim that greater autonomy will lead to higher levels of local school-level decision making. By mapping and analysing the constraints which frame the autonomy of Parkside teachers, senior leaders and local governors, we have argued that rather than being autonomous, these actors were heavily constrained in their practice by EfFT and, to a lesser extent, school-level policies and interventions, which were mainly put in place to enhance the school's record in relation to examination results and inspections.

These patterns are in line with evidence from other research (Kulz, 2015; Bamfield, 2012; Exley & Ball, 2011; Goodman & Burton, 2012) which has challenged the notions of freedom that are supposed to be made available to local actors involved in 'autonomous' schools. Some of the constraints limiting Parkside teachers' autonomy in particular – such as pressures related to standards and inspections – are universal to the English education system and recognisable to teachers working in maintained sector schools. However, our analysis has also teased out some Parkside-specific constraints and conditions, specifically to do with the sponsor's involvement in decision making and relationships. In what follows we investigate more specifically the role of EfFT central governance in Parkside-related decision making.

Figure 7.4 considers the findings discussed so far in order to determine levels of influence over administrative matters. The horizontal lines stand for different areas of administration, which we have discussed in some detail previously in this chapter. The vertical columns stand for the different Parkside stakeholders: local governors, teachers, senior leaders and EfFT representatives. The vertical columns also display the nature of their autonomy: DA (developmental autonomy) referring to their capacity to influence agenda; and OA (operational autonomy) to their capacity to make decisions within the set agenda. The scale used in the table describes level of autonomy, summed up as being: *high*, indicating the groups capacity to overrule the decisions of others, where they consider it necessary; *some*, indicating decision-making capacity that may be intervened and overruled by others; and *none*, indicating a lack of involvement in the decision-making process.

As becomes apparent at a quick glance, administrative decision making was concentrated in the EfFT central governance, with little decision-making capacity distributed to other stakeholders.

The negotiation of employment contracts offers an illustrative example of centralised EfFT functions. As becomes apparent from the table, this area of administration was thoroughly centralised to the sponsor. That is to say, as far as we could

	Local governing body		Teachers		Parkside senior leaders		EfFT	
	DA	OA	DA	OA	DA	OA	DA	OA
Contracts	none	none	none	none	none	none	high	high
Recruitment	none	none	none	none	some	some	high	high
Timetables	none	none	none	none	some	some	high	high
Length of school days	none	none	none	none	some	some	high	high

FIGURE 7.4 Influence over administrative matters

determine, no other stakeholders had any influence over these issues, nor were their views consulted.

According to the accounts that were shared with us, reported in Chapter 5, contractual matters were all dealt with centrally within the EfFT, outside of the jurisdiction of other stakeholders. For example, all other groups were excluded from teachers' pay and conditions-related decision making, to such an extent that even staff whose pay and contracts were in question were not sufficiently informed about the basic terms of promotion and salary increases.

Similarly to pay and conditions, recruitment was also a matter that was heavily steered by the EfFT. However, senior school leaders were involved in teacher and certain other staff recruitment processes. On the other hand, we have reported two key recruitment processes that were managed centrally – the appointment of the chair of governors (Chapter 5) and that of the principal (Chapter 6) – which both highlight the nature of the sponsor's power over central decisions.

It seems, then, that the vacuum created by the lack of local authority involvement was filled by centralised EfFT decision making in regard to these processes. All of which is indicative of an organisation in which power is focused on a few within the sponsoring organisation, and in which other stakeholders are not only excluded from the decision making, but also from the consultation process, as well as from information regarding how these decisions were made.

Meanwhile, senior school leaders were able to use their judgement over matters that concerned the day-to-day running of the school. We have pointed to timetabling and determining the length of school day as examples. However, had the need arisen, we presume that EfFT could have overruled such locally made decisions through direct intervention or policy.

We have, of course, only provided a partial report concerning administration and management matters, as our access to these was limited. For example, details regarding finance were not revealed to us. Furthermore, the staff online area we had access to did not contain documentation regarding finances, and the senior leaders who could have cast some light regarding the issue denied us access to relevant information by either directly refusing to take part to an interview (the new principal and the business manager), or by not responding to an interview request (LGB chair of finances) or by expressing their lack of interest in discussing financial arrangements (the Principal and the Regional Executive).

Conclusion

This chapter has provided an analysis of our account of developments at Parkside, which was part of one of the first group of academies created in England during the early 2000s. The analysis was structured around a framework designed on the basis of a series of theoretical tools developed from international research literature. This led us to focus on the extent to which the various stakeholders had freedom to influence decision making regarding both educational and administrative matters.

Our analysis leads us to argue that although academies such as Parkside were legally freed from the national curriculum, which arguably gave them space to experiment with educational approaches and practices, this autonomy was largely theoretical. Based on our evidence, we conclude that because an academy's performance is measured against the same national performance indicators as other schools, in reality examinations and inspections set a tight frame for educational practice in these schools. The pressures this created led the sponsoring organisation to centralise much of the decision making.

As a result, Parkside's sponsor was seen to have a significant capacity to experiment with matters to do with the school's management, governance and administration, which it utilised actively. The alternative approaches introduced included: altering teaching pay and conditions; extending the school day; and shortening holidays for senior leaders in comparison to the maintained sector contracts. They also included alternative approaches to principal recruitment, as well as minimising the involvement of local governors.

The ways in which the sponsor actively used the freedoms it had under the legislation to experiment echo developments recently reported from other sponsored academies in England (see, for example, Kulz, 2015; Salokangas & Chapman, 2014; Stevenson, 2016). They are also in line with the views of one of the key architects of the early academies policy, Andrew Adonis, who was at that time Minister of State for Education. In his book *Education, Education, Education: Reforming England's Schools*, Adonis clarifies how the autonomy associated with academies should be understood:

> Academies are independent state schools but it is often stated, wrongly, that the magic academy ingredient is independence alone. Rather, it is strong, independent governance and leadership. To be effective, the governors – and the headteachers and management teams they appoint and sustain – need to be unambiguously in control of their schools without managerial interference from local and national bureaucracies. . . . It is crucial to understand that 'independence' and 'sponsorship' go together and cannot be separated.
>
> *(Adonis, 2012, pp. 123–124)*

In these senses, Parkside can be seen as an exemplary case of a sponsored academy.

In the next chapter we go on to relate our analysis of what happened at Parkside to subsequent developments in England, where the idea of school autonomy has come to be a central feature of national education policy. We also relate all of this to developments in certain other countries in order to review the extent to which greater school autonomy is fulfilling its promises of delivering: educational and managerial innovations; improvements in student attainment, particularly amongst learners from vulnerable groups; greater diversity of provision and, as a result, increased parental choice; and reductions in bureaucracy.

8

ANALYSING GLOBAL DEVELOPMENTS

Our analysis of developments at Parkside has led us to argue that much of the increased decision-making capacity associated with its academy status was centralised to its sponsoring organisation. In particular, the sponsor retained a significant capacity to make changes in the school's management, governance and administrative arrangements. Meanwhile, practitioners and school leaders were seen to have limited space to experiment with different practices, despite the fact that there was clearly untapped potential for improvement within the school. Similarly, there was limited involvement of the local community and few links with other schools in the local district.

In this chapter we relate this analysis to what has subsequently happened in England since the inception of the academies programme, and more globally in the autonomous school movement. This leads us to take a further look at developments in the three countries we considered in Chapter 1 (i.e. Australia, England and the USA), where the idea of school autonomy has, to varying degrees, become a major influence on national education policies. In particular, we analyse the extent to which these schools have delivered on their ambitious aspirations, as well as looking at their unintended outcomes.

The rationale

In Chapter 1 we explained how the independent state-funded schools that have emerged in various countries over the last 25 years or so seem to be based on a common overall rationale. Put simply, they all assume that giving schools greater freedom will enable them to educate all of their students more effectively, particularly those from economically disadvantaged and minority backgrounds. Using a medical analogy, we went on to explain how this new form of school has been introduced as a remedy for certain ills that are perceived to be evident in schools maintained by district-level administrations. In essence, these ills are seen by the advocates of autonomous schools as being mainly about the achievement gap that exists between students of different economic and cultural backgrounds.

Policy reforms based on this restructuring of schools are intended to achieve three types of outcome. First of all, it is anticipated that they will lead to *educational and managerial innovations* as a result of their autonomous status. In this way, it is assumed, the schools will be able to explore new ways of accelerating the progress of their students. It is assumed that this will be possible because they are freed from what is seen as the heavy bureaucracy and inefficient management that is associated with public administration.

Here, it is important to note moves towards the creation of various forms of school groups, some of which are sponsored by voluntary groups and others by profit-making companies, and the withdrawal of public administration from these schools. Related to this, some advocates intend that these developments will lead to the dissemination of new, more effective practices in order to stimulate system-wide change, whilst others argue that intensifying forms of competition between schools will motivate increased effort to bring about improvements.

Second, all of this is expected to result in *improvements in student attainment*, particularly amongst vulnerable groups of learners. This will be achieved, it is argued, because practitioners working in these schools are in better position to address the particular needs of their students due to their increased freedom to make decisions about educational practices. Here, it is significant that the school systems included in our analysis are all subject to high-stakes accountability mechanisms, such as state testing and examinations, and public ranking of schools based on their relative success in these assessments.

Third, it is anticipated that the introduction of independent state-funded schools will result in *greater diversity of provision* and, as a result, increased parental choice. In this more competitive context, the restructured schools are seen as having a chance to start afresh, especially in districts where there has been a legacy of underperformance and, therefore, less attractive local schools. In addition, some advocates argue that increased diversity of local schools will improve overall standards by further intensifying competition between schools. Meanwhile, others have argued that the schools will develop closer links with their communities, a factor that is seen to be necessary in order to improve educational outcomes for learners from disadvantaged backgrounds.

Keeping these complexities in mind, we go on to examine the extent to which the introduction of independent state schools has managed to deliver on their ambitious promises.

Impact of the reforms

In Chapter 1 we explained that the idea of independent state-funded schools has taken somewhat different forms in different countries. Indeed, within Australia and the USA this variation is also apparent in different parts of the country. In what follows we discuss the extent to which these reforms have delivered their ambitious promises in relation to increased innovation, improved educational attainment and greater diversity of provision.

Increased innovation

In discussing innovation across the three countries, we again draw on the theoretical frameworks we introduced in Chapter 1 and further elaborated in Chapter 7. First of all, we adopt Lubienski's (2003) two-dimensional conceptualisation of educational/ pedagogical and administrative/managerial innovations to analyse the impacts of autonomous schools. At the same time, we make use of the argument of Preston et al. (2012), who propose that charter school innovations should be seen in relative terms: that is, practices that are only possible within those schools, as opposed to other type of public sector schools.

Focusing first on the impacts of the English reforms, limited research evidence is available concerning pedagogical innovations in academies. However, the parallel developments of increased local autonomy and governmental grip on local actors through performance testing and targets has been noted by a number of researchers (Goodman & Burton, 2012; Exley & Ball, 2011; Kauko & Salokangas, 2015). Considering that students educated in these schools sit the same examinations as their peers in more traditionally managed schools, and because staff in these schools are subject to similar inspections concerning pedagogical practice as other schools, educational innovations that are only possible in academies and not in other types of publicly funded schools are, we suggest, less likely to occur.

Our study of developments at Parkside led us to conclude that there was considerable untapped potential within the school and its community that could be mobilised to improve the educational experiences of its students. We also reported the emphasis teachers in the school placed on collaboration and mutual support, a feature that is known to be a necessary condition for school improvement (Ainscow, 2016). Although this potential was drawn on to some extent, the overall emphasis on centralised decision making and top-down accountability measures tended to act as barriers to progress in this respect. Most significantly, the evidence we have presented confirms findings from elsewhere that factors within the school – shaped by pressures from outside to improve standards, as defined in tests – meant that teachers tended to be seen as delivers of policy, rather than as semi-autonomous professionals engaged in processes of knowledge creation.

On the other hand, we have seen how innovations associated with academies mainly relate to managerial and administrative matters. As we have explained, the hope of some of the early advocates of independent state schools was that greater autonomy would free schools from the burden of forms of administration that stifled creativity amongst practitioners. In particular, supporters of the movement have argued consistently that public administration is inefficient, slow and riddled with unnecessary bureaucracy which badly affects public education. Instead of focusing on fixing problems within the public administration, the autonomous school reform has allowed new actors to take over school administration and management. The hope is that this will lead to more efficient ways of working, reduce unnecessary bureaucracy and allow schools to become nimbler in responding to local challenges. In particular, leadership has been identified as a key for negotiating local decision making, with school leaders seen as being central figures in negotiating academisation efforts, by embracing and/or buffering conversion processes (Gunter & McGinity, 2014; Stevenson, 2016) and in running sponsored academies (Kulz, 2015; Salokangas & Chapman, 2014).

Meanwhile, there is a growing trend towards the formation of academy groups, originally known as chains but usually referred to nowadays as multi-academy trusts (MATs). Increasingly, these are led by schools defined as being outstanding, a development that the supporters of the academy movement have cherished (O'Shaughnessy, 2012; Husbands et al., 2013). As we have explained, the largest MAT in England now has 66 schools and national policy makers are trying to avoid groupings that are seen as being too small to be efficient in terms of use of resources (Mansell, 2016).

From a legal perspective, MATs are powerful new governance structures which hold considerable power over the academies they run. Referring to the Academies Act 2010, Wilkins (2016) reminds us that when subsumed within a MAT, a school is:

- "no longer managed by the bureau-professionalism of the local authority and its democratic mandate";
- "not a freestanding legal entity with powers to employ staff, enter into contracts and plan budget spending";
- "stripped of its assets and any legal entitlement to self-determination"; and
- "subject to the requirements and provisos of the MAT, specifically the board of directors or board of trustees who retain legal powers to shape key policy decisions for all the schools within the cluster or chain".

Concern has also been expressed about the fact that schools are not allowed to leave a MAT (House of Commons Education Committee, 2015).

Some observers see these newly emerging structures as opportunities to extend and deepen the tradition of school to school cooperation that has been a feature of English education for many years, following on from earlier initiatives such as the Education Action Zones, Excellence in Cities and City Challenge (Ainscow, 2015). However, as we saw in the case of Parkside, such collaboration may come at a price, particularly where the schools involved serve different parts of the country and are discouraged from collaborating with schools in their local districts. Nevertheless, it is encouraging to see the emergence of locally developed MATs which, despite the policy focus on attainment outcomes, are choosing to work within a framework of explicit values (Ainscow et al., 2016; Mansell, 2016).

As we have explained, an area in which English academies have clearly experimented is in relation to staff pay and conditions. In 2010, prior to the rapid expansion of the academies programme, the National Audit Office (cited in Morris, 2011) reported that most academies (79%) were still paying their teaching staff according to nationally agreed pay scales. It was also noted that the largest differences in salaries were between the senior staff working in more traditional schools and those in chains of academies. However, alongside the rapid expansion of the system, high salaries paid to senior academy staff have become a topic of heated public debate.

These developments have taken place mostly within groups of academies, where even higher salaries are often paid to executives, something that has also led to considerable media attention and controversy (Mansell, 2016). In fact, the financial management of trusts has been a topic of heated debate since the establishment of the early academies, and it has been argued that some have taken liberties in how they spend resources, with a series of financial irregularities hitting the national headlines (Beckett, 2007; Curtis, 2008; Adams, 2016). Unsurprisingly, the rapid expansion of academies has amplified this problem. Recently, for example, the National Audit Office (2016) released its second 'adverse warning', the most severe type of warning they issue, criticising the Department for Education's inability to handle academy trusts spending and calling for changes in the accounting of academy trusts:

> The Department's policy of autonomy for academies brings with it significant risks if the financial capability of the Department and academies are not strengthened; and the financial statements do not present a true and fair view and meet the accountability requirements of Parliament.

In her response, the then Shadow Education Secretary, Lucy Powell (cited in Sellgren, 2016) commented:

> This is a damning and very serious report, which highlights both the opaque financial arrangements within some academy chains as well as the almost impossible job the Department for Education has set itself in trying to directly run thousands of schools from Whitehall. . . . If this report was about a local authority, it would rightly be put in special measures and taken over.

Moving on to developments in the United States, charter school status has traditionally implied that the greater autonomy of these schools increases educational innovation and change (Wohlstetter et al., 1995). However, within-system diversity has proved problematic when examining national evidence on this issue. Nevertheless, some patterns have emerged.

As in England, the charter school innovations that have been identified by research are largely administrative and managerial rather than educational in nature. For example, Preston et al. (2012) argue that, on the whole, charter schools have most efficiently filled their promise of innovation and change in relation to teacher tenure. Indeed, research has identified patterns in charter school teaching pay and conditions and staff turnover.

Teachers working in charter schools, especially the ones run by MOs, tend to be hired under different styles of contracts than teachers in traditional public schools. For example, studies a decade ago indicated that teachers working in charter schools work longer hours, were paid less and received less job security than their colleagues working in traditional public schools (Malloy & Wohlstetter, 2003; Bulkley, 2005). It is also reported that teachers working in schools run by EMOs are paid less than their colleagues in other types of charter schools, and that in these schools staff turnover is higher (Hoxby, 2002; Ni, 2012; Roch & Sai, 2015). Teacher burnout – resulting from what has been described as a 'no excuses' culture evident in many MO-run charters – is said to be a contributing factor for teachers leaving these schools (Lake et al., 2010). In addition, it has become evident that prescriptive educational models in relation to classroom practice and student discipline that are in place in some MOs contribute to high staff turnover (Torres, 2014).

Already a decade ago, Finnigan (2007) argued that many constraints imposed upon charter schools, such as state laws, as well as school relationships with authorisers and partnerships with Management Organisations (MOs), had all impacted on the autonomy of school-level actors. When comparing teacher autonomy in charter schools and traditional public schools, teachers working in charter schools have reported greater autonomy than their colleagues working in traditional public schools (Oberfield, 2016; Ni, 2012; Renzulli et al., 2011). However, due to the great variety within the charter school system, teachers' perceptions of autonomy seems to differ from one charter school to another (Gawlik, 2007). Meanwhile, differences are also evident between different types of charter schools (i.e. stand alone, run by EMO or run by CMO), with the MOs tending to impose tighter control upon the schools they run (Johnson & Landman, 2000; Crawford, 2001).

More recently, Roch and Sai (2015) and Oberfield (2016) have shown that teachers working in charter schools run by MOs – especially the for-profit education management organisations (EMOs) – have lower levels of autonomy than their colleagues in other charter schools. This seems to be because classroom as well as school-level decision making tends to be tightly controlled by centralised decision making. As such, it has become evident that charter school autonomy is a complex phenomenon, where local actors' scope of action varies greatly from one school to another. In this respect it is worth noting that just 12% of charter schools are unionised, whereas some 60% of teachers nationally are members of a teacher union (Kahlenberg & Potter, 2014).

Looking at the impact of charter legislation on practice, Wohlstetter et al. (2013) conclude that 'more than 90% of the state charter laws included as one of the purposes behind the law to encourage school communities to use their autonomy in the classroom to experiment, innovate, and create new educational options for students' (p. 38). They concluded, however, that rather than create completely new innovative learning models, charter schools tend to adopt particular practices and serve specific student populations. Similarly, based on a review of literature, Lubienski (2003) found that although some charter schools were organisationally innovative, classroom practices tended toward the familiar. Although he found some evidence of innovative classroom practice – such as using technology to support instruction, cooperative learning and individualised instruction – he also noted the widespread use of these practices in traditional public schools.

As we have explained, the reforms in Australia are still in their infancy. It is, therefore, too early to report with any confidence on the effects they have had in the newly defined independent public schools (IPSs), nor on the system as a whole. The limited evidence that is available suggests that some managerial and administrative innovations have occurred. For example, an early evaluation of IPSs, commissioned by the Department of Education (2013), reported that the schools have more control over staffing issues. Conducted primarily from the perspectives of school leaders, the report suggests that they have embraced the autonomy associated with these schools.

However, Suggett (2015) summarises studies carried out in Western Australian schools which suggest that principals vary in their capacity for reasoned local decision making. The studies modelled factors affecting principals' perceptions of the regulatory framework and risk-taking in local decision making in 235 schools. This led Suggett to argue that tensions that arise between making local decisions and complying with centralised regulations is an unspoken and unaddressed feature of the difficulty of implementing school autonomy policies. He goes on to quote research by Betts and Tang (2011) who suggest that principals with a compliance view of governance are less likely to take reasoned risks and hence the benefits of school autonomy may not be fully realised. He concludes that this leaves open the question of how best to support principals in progressively expanding their decision-making capacity.

To summarise, then, the existing evidence across the three countries indicates that innovations in autonomous schools tend to be mainly focused on administrative and managerial matters. In particular, new developments have occurred in relation to teaching conditions and contracts as well as financial management. At the same time, a growing body of international research literature has raised questions related to the new actors involved in the administration of these schools, particularly the blurred lines between charitability and profitability of such groupings of schools (Olmedo, 2013) and how these entities bring together various stakeholders, including policymakers, education consultants, lobby groups and profit-making companies at both the national (Ball & Junemann, 2012) and global levels (Verger et al., 2016). Indeed, some of these have become considerable players in global education markets and powerful actors influencing national policy and practice.

In terms of educational practices, research in the three countries has not been able to trace much evidence of innovation. Rather, it has pointed out that teachers working in these schools are subject to similar, if not greater, control as their colleagues in other types of publicly funded schools, which greatly affects their practice. A worrying outcome of all of this is that school improvement becomes a search for one-size-fits-all teaching approaches that, it is assumed, will improve the attainments of all students, whatever their interests, preferences and backgrounds, provided they are implemented in a consistent way. This flies in the face of research evidence suggesting that increased student diversity requires teachers who are confident in adapting their lesson plans in response to the actions of the members of their classes during lessons (Ainscow et al., 2006; Bartolome, 1994; Hart et al., 2004). Initial teacher education, as well as school-based professional development is therefore a key factor in promoting the skills and confidence of teachers in carrying out this for demanding form of improvisation (Messiou & Ainscow, 2015). Related to this, in what follows we go on to discuss the extent to which independent state schools have been able to fulfil their promise of raising student attainment.

Improved attainment

By way of introduction to this theme it is important to acknowledge the difficulties involved in studying the impact of school autonomy on student progress. Hanushek, Link and Woessmann (2012) provide a helpful summary of the challenges involved. First of all, they suggest, there are the problems arising from the multifaceted nature of autonomy, with some schools having authority over certain kinds of decisions and others having authority over a different set, making it difficult to develop consistent measures. Second, they argue that account has to be taken of opportunistic and unpredictable behaviour by players at the school level. Third, there is the challenge of determining whether observed effects are as a result of autonomy. And, fourth, aspects of autonomy are often constrained by decisions at a higher level, for example, in those countries with national education standards, national assessments and accountability regimes.

Returning to our analysis of Parkside, the story is encouraging in respect of improvements in attainment, not least in the sense that the progress that occurred in the early years of its existence meant that students, many of whom were from poorer backgrounds, were offered a better deal. These improvements were reflected in rapid progress in the performance of its students in public examinations. And, as we have explained, this progress led to the school being designated as being outstanding by inspectors. However, if educational attainment is understood simply as student performance in standardised tests, this has considerable implications for education more widely, as we also saw at Parkside.

Looking to the wider impact of the introduction of the early sponsored academies in England, Mansell (2016) summarises evidence from the formal evaluation of the policy carried out during the period of the Labour government. This suggests that the first 24 sponsored academies (which, of course, included Parkside) had higher levels of student progress – as measured by comparing their national curriculum test results immediately prior to entering secondary academies aged 11 with their GCSE results aged 16 – than the national average. However, the evaluation still concluded that 'there is insufficient evidence to make a definitive judgement about the Academies as a model for school improvement' (PricewaterhouseCoopers, 2008, p. 19).

A more detailed and statistically robust study of Labour's early academies scheme was produced by Machin and Venoit (2011). This used a statistical model to compared the GCSE grade improvements of sponsored academies with those of other schools which would later go on to become academies. Their analysis found that results in the academies improved faster than those of the comparison group.

Furthermore, it also concluded that results in neighbouring schools gained a boost, suggesting that the academies policy was spurring on other secondary schools to achieve well through greater competition, as was hoped by some advocates.

Summarising evidence on the progress of these early sponsored academies, the report of the independent Commission argues that they had revitalised the system, including initiating what they saw as a 'shift in culture' (Husbands et al., 2013). Echoing our Parkside account, the Commission concluded that some of these schools had showed just how much could be achieved with high aspirations, determination that young people would achieve well and a rigorous and consistent approach to school improvement.

Looking to the subsequent expansion of the academies programme after the 2010 general election, when academy status was opened to all schools, the Commission report is much less sure of the impact. Noting that such schools typically contain lower proportions of disadvantaged pupils, the report explains that academies now have significantly fewer students eligible for free school meals and significantly better overall attainment at the GCSE level. There are, therefore, problems in looking to the academy programme before 2010 to learn lessons for the future. The Commission quotes Machin (2012) who warns:

> . . . it may be, in due course, that these new academies do deliver performance improvements. But we know nothing of this yet, and translating the evidence from the old programme over to the new, without appropriate reservations about whether the findings can be generalised, is, at the moment, a step too far.

It seems, then, that the core aim of the English academies programme to raise attainment amongst disadvantaged students has not, so far at least, been achieved, although there are examples of what seem to be effective practices. Nor, it seems, does academy status in itself guarantee better outcomes for students more generally (Gorard, 2014). Recently, for example, the education data company 'School Dash' suggested that academy status, as such, cannot be linked to improved educational outcomes (Dickens, 2016). On a more positive note, however, in sponsor-led academies like Parkside, which traditionally replaced schools experiencing significant difficulties, outcomes tend to have improved after three to four years. However, the report raises a warning that although improved results are both substantial and sustained, they should not be over-interpreted, as there might be other factors at play. The argument that chains of academies would lead to benefits of scale has also been contested and the capacity of some multi-academy sponsors to raise standards has been called into question (Mansell, 2016).

Keeping in mind our concern with unintended outcomes, it is also worth noting that recent statistics indicate that student exclusion rates per school are far higher in academies than government maintained schools (DfE, 2015). Linked to this, academies have been accused of manipulating student admission for their benefit, selecting those that are likely to deliver in examinations and, in so doing, discriminating against student that are more difficult to teach (Goddard, 2016).

Meanwhile, concern has recently been raised regarding so-called 60 'orphan' schools that, at least six months after a failed inspection, still have no certainty over who will be running them (*The Guardian*, 7 February 2017). In 12 cases, two years have passed since the inspection, without a sponsor being found. Commenting on this, the general secretary of the National Union of Teachers was reported as saying: 'In a marketised system, academy sponsors will refuse to take on schools which are in difficult circumstances. . . . It is a huge hole in the government's policy.'[1]

In terms of the American charter school developments, researchers have pointed out that, due to the diversity within the system, examining student outcomes is methodologically challenging (Hoxby & Murarka, 2008). In particular, the diverse nature of state laws framing charter schools, as well as differing funding regimes and local policy, lead to methodological difficulties in determining national effects on student achievement (Finn et al., 2000).

Meanwhile, evidence regarding the extent to which charter schools have delivered on their promise of raising student achievement, particularly amongst disadvantaged groups of learners, remains mixed. Raymond (2009) concludes that these differences in performance lie in the varying design of institutional structures for establishing and monitoring charter schools, such as systems enabling a choice of monitoring bodies, and schools 'gaming' the system. Charter schools have also been accused of manipulating test results through selective student enrolment practices (Albert Shanker Institute, 2016).

The evidence that is available suggests that, in general, charter school students do not outperform their peers in district schools in state standardised exams (CREDO, 2009; Berends, 2015; Hill et al., 2006). Some studies at the district level compare the results of charter and regular schools, such as a study of New York charter schools that found charter schools achieve higher results for some grades in reading and maths (e.g. Hoxby & Murarka, 2008). But the methodologies of these district studies are disputed on the grounds of weaknesses in the statistical models and for overstating the effects (Reardon, 2009; Raymond, 2009). One meta-analysis of five district based randomised controlled trials concluded their findings did not have validity outside their specific contexts and hence were not generalisable (Dynarski et al., 2010). More specifically, they could not identify what was common for success and whether being a charter school was the factor contributing to success or failure. Overall, then, the consensus appears to be that charter school performance is 'complex and difficult to measure' and that the results are 'sobering' (Raymond, 2009, p. 2).

This mixed picture leads Furgeson et al. (2012) to conclude that there is 'no consensus about whether, on average, charter schools are doing better or worse than conventional public schools at promoting the achievement of their students' (p. xxi). All of which suggests that charter schools, as a whole, have not succeeded in raising educational attainment of their students when compared to those in conventional public schools, although, as we saw in England, it is important to bear in mind that research has detected local effects on charter school student performance (Hoxby & Rockoff, 2004; Furgeson et al., 2012).

Moving on to Australia, what is significant about the reforms there is the fierce pace of change it has led to, particularly across the state of Western Australia.

Considering that 70% of public school students in that state attend this type of school prior to any credible evidence becoming available regarding student outcomes, it is hard to argue that that IPSs are an evidence-based reform. Furthermore, previous attempts to increase school autonomy in Australia, referred to as self-managing schools, are not encouraging, since they cannot be linked to improved student outcomes (Suggett, 2015).

Whilst there is great variance across Australia, the system as a whole does not yet seem to have delivered the promised improvements. For example, the Western Australian reforms were recently criticised by a parliamentary committee for creating a two-tier system that exacerbates inequality and does not improve student outcomes. This followed a review of the policy undertaken after concerns were raised by parents and teachers about how it impacted on students, particularly those with special needs (Parliament of Western Australia, 2016). Responding to the report in the media, the Minister of Education for Western Australia said:

> First of all the primary focus, in a general sense, was not to improve student outcomes. That will occur as a result of the process. . . . What we're dealing with in IPS is we're providing principals with the opportunity to select staff. And then you'll find with that improvement in teacher quality there'll be an improvement in student standards.
>
> *(ABC, 2016)*

To summarise, then, evidence of positive of school autonomy across the three countries is largely unconvincing. Caution is also needed when assessing progress using high-stakes testing systems as a positive indicator. So, for example, some American researchers suggest that systems with a strong emphasis on raising test scores may result in a narrowing of the educational experiences provided for students, as schools feel obliged to focus on preparation for the tests (e.g. Popham, 2001). There is also a related concern that this distracts attention away from culturally relevant curricula and teaching (e.g. Lipman, 2004; Valenzuela, 2005). Moreover, such high-stakes testing systems may result in schools offering limited opportunities for the development of critical thinking skills and creativity.

Although these studies focus on American schools, their findings seem to resonate with developments in other systems that have high-stakes testing systems. In so doing, they raise relevant questions concerning the nature of learning and pedagogy, as well as the taught content. Certainly, we saw evidence of this narrowing of the educational diet at Parkside, where teaching was heavily focused on exam preparation. We return to this theme in the final chapter.

Diversity of provision

The movement towards greater school autonomy clearly has implications for relationships with the wider community, particularly for families. Returning again to our account of Parkside, we have explained how it serves a remarkably diverse population by any standards. And, as its reputation in the community improved, the school was seen to be increasingly attractive amongst more aspirational families. Having said that, it is also true to say that the history of the school and its local district continued to put some families off and, of course, there were other schools within travelling distance that had better reputations. The implication is that market forces are, indeed, powerful in terms of their impact on parental choice. It will also be recalled that some local people were concerned that, as it became more successful, Parkside might become more selective in terms of its student intake, although we found no evidence of this trend.

Reflecting such worries, there are increasing concerns in England about the fragmentation of the education system, leading to increased segregation of students from varied socio-economic, cultural and religious home backgrounds (e.g. Ainscow et al., 2016; Mansell, 2016). Related to this, the Academies Commission argues that the reforms exacerbate inequities within the system by giving academies access to favourable funding arrangements and enabling them to manipulate admissions to their advantage (Husbands et al., 2013). Related to this, the National Audit Office (2013) questions the extent to which the introduction of free schools, another form of academy, represents the best use of limited resources for the benefit of the system as a whole.

Together, the English academy and free school programmes appear to channel funding in ways that are not driven by educational disadvantage, or any other measure of educational vulnerability (Ainscow et al., 2016). As a result, they reduce the level of funding that is available elsewhere in the education system and, in particular, divert it away from local authorities and the schools that remain within their control. Moreover, the manipulation of admissions alleged by the Academies Commission suggests that these initiatives may be contributing more directly to social segregation by effectively selecting 'easy-to-teach' students into favourably funded schools.

Similar patterns can also be detected in the USA. For example, Wohlstetter et al. (2016) report that researchers were sometimes surprised to learn that the early charter schools enrolled students in predominantly urban areas that had not been well-served by traditional public schools. However, the bad news was that charter schools, like other public schools across the United States, were often isolated by race. So, Wohlstetter and her colleagues are now conducting a study of 21 charter schools and charter networks that have an explicit commitment to diversity in their mission statements. Writing about their early findings, they note that, by definition, schools of choice located in urban neighbourhoods have the flexibility to enrol diverse students by drawing from different communities outside attendance areas that have high concentrations of poverty, an option not available to traditional public schools. This leads them to conclude that until all public schools have this option, 'the likelihood of achieving socioeconomic integration in urban schools seems very dim indeed'.

Summarising evidence about this issue as far as the USA in concerned, Kahlenberg and Potter (2014) describe how charter school advocates have increasingly targeted minority and low income groups. As a result, students from low-income families are far more likely to attend schools where the vast majority have similar backgrounds. The pattern also seems to be similar with regard to students from minority households. All of this suggests that the original intention to reduce segregation has been distorted by an overall policy strategy that sets schools against one another (Berends, 2015).

Here it is worth noting evidence from Sweden, another country that has gone down the route of school autonomy and parental choice. There, what are called free schools have struggled to deliver the promise of catering for students in most need. Instead, the evidence is clear that since the introduction of the reforms there is a considerable increase in segregation within the education system (Bunar, 2010; Wiborg, 2010b). Critiquing these market-driven policy reforms, Östh, Andersson and Malmberg (2013) argue that parents are increasingly choosing non-neighbourhood schools, especially in urban areas. They conclude that this has had a transformative effect on the education system overall, contributing to increased segregation between more and less privileged groups.

Returning to the recent report on developments in Western Australia, we read similar concerns about the wider impact of the independent public schools (Parliament of Western Australia, 2016). The report states: 'The IPS initiative has exacerbated existing inequalities in the public education system, both perceived and actual, reinforcing a "two-tiered system"'. It then goes on to suggest that 'more capable schools receive more benefits, and less capable schools fall further behind. Remote and hard-to-staff schools are particularly disadvantaged as a result'. It also found that while IPSs 'benefitted by being able to recruit the best teachers', this came at the expense of non-IPS, which were then forced to accept teachers 'rejected by independent schools who are less suitable for the school environment and have less experience'.

In summary, then, our review of international evidence points to worrying patterns regarding the impact of school autonomy developments on the dynamics of local school systems and, as a result, on the communities they serve. In particular, there are concerns about the tendency for them to create fragmentation and increased levels of segregation. Meanwhile, there is limited evidence to suggest progress in respect to the claim that the introduction of independent state-funded schools will result in greater parental choice. On the other hand, there are indications that, in some contexts at least, they may be impacting on overall standards by further intensifying competition between schools. However, this creates an additional concern that the progress of one school is being achieved at the expense of others within a local area.

Conclusion

In this chapter we have related our analysis of what happened at Parkside Academy to more recent international developments regarding the idea of independent state-funded schools. This has confirmed our view that they have been increasingly shaped by a belief that improvements in schools will be achieved by an intensification of market forces that increase competition. In this context, parental choice is seen to encourage schools to try harder in order to improve their performance within national testing systems, which are focused on a relatively narrow set of learning outcomes. As a result, the innovations taking place tend to mainly involve changes in governance, management and administrative arrangements, often within groupings of schools.

This market-based thinking contrasts with the views of some of the early school autonomy supporters, whose purpose was to provide greater space for school-level practitioners to explore ways of working that would best suit their particular students. In this way of thinking, independent state schools were seen as laboratories that are intended to generate new ways of working that can be shared with other schools in order to promote a kind of bottom-up system-wide change. Some advocates also stressed the importance of schools having strong links with their local communities and the other schools that serve them.

There are many individual examples, not least Parkside Academy, which show that greater autonomy can be effective in promoting rapid improvements in the attainment of students as measured by national testing systems, including those from disadvantaged and minority populations. However, the overall evidence from the countries we have considered is less convincing. There are also concerns that where progress has been achieved this has involved the use of standardised, one-size-fits-all responses, within an approach that involves a narrowing of the educational diet. However, the extent to which educational success and failure should be based on the narrow view of education that standardised testing implies is an important question which should be discussed and challenged.

Similarly, there is little evidence from the countries considered in this chapter to suggest that independent state schools are promoting greater social integration within school systems, another of the hopes of early advocates. Indeed, there are worrying trends suggesting movement in an opposite direction. In terms of overall improvements, this has to be a concern since there is increasing evidence that learner diversity can be a catalyst for bringing practitioners together in ways that stimulate professional learning. This is a theme we will return to in the next chapter.

Another trend is towards the idea of groupings of independent state schools, sometimes involving the involvement of profit-making organisations. On the other hand, there are also developments of school groups that are encouraging more participatory forms of school-to-school partnership with an emphasis on community involvement.

Related to all of this, the expectation that these reforms would lead to reductions in bureaucracy as a result of local authorities having little, if any, involvement in the management of schools is another important issue. The worry is that the efforts of the 'new' administrators to centralise policy decisions for their groups of schools have simply replaced one form of top-down control with another. Meanwhile, there are concerns that no one organisation has an overall coordinating role within a local district, such that existing inequities of provision could continue and, possibly, grow. This is another theme that is addressed in our final chapter.

Note

1 www.theguardian.com/2017/feb/07/failing-schools-academy-sponsor-ofsted

9

WHERE NEXT FOR AUTONOMOUS SCHOOLS?

In this book, we have examined the implications of a growing international trend that promotes greater school autonomy as the means of improving state education systems. As we have explained, the assumption is that this will allow space for innovations, leading to new organisational arrangements, practices and forms of management and leadership that will be more effective in promoting the learning of all students.

This global policy trend remains a matter of considerable debate and, as we have noted, there are varied views as to the extent to which it is leading to the desired outcomes. Meanwhile, there is limited evidence regarding what is actually happening within these schools in relation to decision making about policies and practice, and the extent to which this is leading to increased innovation and improved educational outcomes.

This book has begun the process of filling this vacuum, using evidence from our longitudinal study of one independent state-funded school in England and relating this to research findings about wider national and international developments. The analysis we have presented was guided by the following questions:

- What does autonomy mean for those involved in independent state-funded schools?
- To what extent have these schools delivered on their promises?
- What does this mean for thinking and practice in the field?

In addressing these questions, we have shown that the autonomous school movement reforms have resulted in what are mainly structural reforms that focus on organisation and management, rather than educational reforms that lead to the developments in pedagogical approaches. We have also shown that despite positive evidence from isolated cases, autonomous schools have struggled to deliver their ambitious promises, especially in relation to raising student attainment.

In this concluding chapter, we reflect on the implications of our analysis for thinking and practice in the field. In so doing, we adopt a pragmatic view that takes account of the fact that the movement towards greater autonomy is picking up speed across the world. In addressing this agenda, we recognise that there are no simple solutions to what are inherently complex problems. What we can do, however, is to reach out to reformers, and to local actors involved in negotiating reforms, in order to offer them signposts and critical thinking tools that can inform their future actions.

We begin by discussing tensions in the autonomous school debate, which, we argue, have blurred the clarity of purpose of these reforms, making it impossible for autonomous schools to fulfil their ambitious promises. We then go on to propose a way forward, one that is driven by a desire to promote more equitable and sustainable educational reforms.

Tensions at the core of autonomous school reforms

We have argued that, in the main, autonomous school reforms have not successfully delivered on their ambitious promises. A central reason for this is that there are have been contradicting forces at play, pulling the reforms in different directions. The coexistence of these forces has created tensions that have blurred the sense of purpose. In so doing, this has hindered autonomous schools from achieving what they were expected to achieve.

In what follows we summarise what we see as the three main contradictory forces.

Free market approaches vs. educational equity

As we have shown, the autonomous school movement is closely aligned with free market approaches in education, i.e. increased choice and competition, deregulation of provision and opening public school management and governance to new players, sometimes including private entities. The argument put forward to support these moves suggests that they will enhance educational opportunities for all children, since parents will be in a better position to choose what they see as the 'best' school. This, in turn, will enhance competition, so that standards in all schools will rise.

However, as we explained in Chapter 8, the reform has not delivered on its ambitious promises in this regard. Furthermore, if we look at evidence from different countries across the world, it becomes evident that market approaches in education more generally have not helped in achieving educational equity and social justice. For example, parental choice and competition between schools has widened the gap between desirable schools and less desirable schools in countries as varied as: Chile (Carrasco et al., 2015), Sweden (Wiborg, 2010a) and Finland (Kosunen, 2014). This evidence suggests that divisions between what are seen as 'good' and 'bad' schools contribute to social injustice in varied ways. What it also tells us, is that middle class, well educated and wealthier parents are much more capable at making preferable choices than parents from more disadvantaged backgrounds in competitive school markets (Ball, 2003; van Zanten, 2009; Waslander et al., 2010). In addition, where countries have a private fee-paying tier, these schools mainly serve better-off families.

These brief examples provide a flavour as to how market approaches in education, including autonomous school reforms, have failed to create more equitable school systems. They lead us to join the growing ranks of researchers contesting the argument that the education market will fix the system from within and, in so doing, reduce social inequalities to the particular advantage of learners from minority and economically disadvantaged backgrounds. Instead, we argue that if we truly want to see progress towards educational equity, some degree of central steering is needed in ensuring that the students in most need receive the support they require.

Innovation vs. the nature of work in schools

This second tension arises from the belief in innovation as a fix for many of the ills that are seen to exist in schools. In contrast, we argue that blind belief in innovations 'for innovation's sake' is incompatible with the nature of work taking place in schools. Let us illustrate what we mean.

Innovation has become a buzzword in recent years, which, as a term, carries great promise of a quick fix and a brighter future. However, it is not only education policy and public discourses that have been plagued with innovation hype, but public policy and governance more widely (Hodgson, 2012; Russell & Vinsel, 2016). This belief in the power of innovation as a solution to many ills can be traced back to technology industry discourses. Indeed, parallels have been drawn between autonomous school innovations and technological developments. So, for example, some promoters of disruptive innovation in education have claimed that charter schools should disrupt the education monopoly (Jacobs, 2015), following the direction taken by Uber in developing its taxi empire (Haeffele-Balch & Boettke, 2016).

Innovation holds a promise of something better than what was there before, simultaneously discrediting old practices as being poor. However, this kind of innovation hype is particularly problematic in relation to education, as it tends to ignore the unpredictable social nature of what takes place in schools, be it student learning, or staff efforts in academic, pastoral care or administrative work.

Take teachers' work as an example. In reality, their tasks involve: a mix of routine and creativity; careful planning and thinking on your feet; and tried and tested methods and experimenting with new ones, which sometimes work and sometimes do not. Anybody who has worked as a teacher knows that much of teaching can be repetitive drudgery, as with the learning of certain crucial skills and content – be it irregular verbs in second language, tables in maths or learning to swim – require considerable repetitive efforts from the learner to master. However, an experienced teacher also knows that teaching certain content and skills lend themselves to exploration, creativity, problem solving and Eureka-moments.

In relation to administrative and pastoral care work in schools, the term innovation tends to be an even worse fit, as both should safeguard and ensure the long-term well-being of all students. As Parkside has shown us, quick fix administrative innovations can, at worst, be risky for students, as they may destabilise the day-to-day work taking place.

The important thing here is to acknowledge this multifaceted and complex nature of work taking place in schools, and the fact that not all 'old, or tried and tested' practice is automatically poor. In line with the argument of Russell and Vinsel (2016), we suggest that instead of focusing on innovations, we should pay more attention to the maintenance of these complex systems and equip practitioners with the skills to improve the system 'from within'. That said, we acknowledge the importance of professional learning, creativity and the continuous development of new ways of working in schools. We also consider it a high priority to offer school staff opportunities to enhance their practices, learn, explore and try out new ways of working.

This is why, instead of blind belief in the power of innovations offering quick fix solutions for education, we call out for more sustainable long-term developments, in which teachers and other school staff have the capacity to explore and be creative in their ways of working. This means that we should focus on creating the organisational conditions in which a skilful workforce is able to use professional judgement in the complex social and pedagogical situations they face. It also means that practitioners must by supported by their schools and communities to do so, not least through appropriate professional development opportunities.

Autonomy vs. control

Finally, the third tension in the autonomous school reforms is the idea that local autonomy, especially teacher autonomy, and high-stakes accountability, can coexist. Whilst we have discussed this tension in some detail in Chapter 7, it is worthwhile to reiterate here that it is intellectually dishonest to claim that individuals who are subject to high-stakes accountability and control in their work environment are also autonomous in relation to their practice.

Bearing these tensions in mind, in what follows we make recommendations as to how the idea of school autonomy might be used to greater advantage as countries seek ways of promoting the learning of all of their children and young people. These suggestions take the form of a series of ideas that policy makers and practitioners might use as signposts and critical thinking tools to inform their future actions.

Towards more sustainable and realistic reforms

Due to the tensions that are at the core of the autonomous school movement, it has suffered from a lack of clarity of purpose and, as a result, has struggled in delivering its ambitious promises. This is not atypical of education reforms and initiatives more generally. Public education is a battleground, in which different interest groups' visions regarding what a good school looks like collides. In such contexts, as argued by Ainscow, Booth and Dyson (2006), one person's view of an improving school may be another's vision of educational hell.

This means that we cannot understand improvement in education without considering the values underlying the changes we would like to take place. As a result, reforms are often unsatisfying compromises of different interest groups' visions, expected to be implemented and bear fruit at unreasonably tight timelines, and lacking in consultation with the forces implementing these reforms: the teachers. Acknowledging tensions at the core of a reform is an important step in moving forward. However, there are other things to keep in mind when thinking about how to move towards more sustainable and realistic reforms.

It is, for example, common for education reforms not to achieve their early promises, or for them to produce outcomes that were not expected or anticipated. Research has offered other explanations for repeated reform failures. So, there is evidence suggesting that they tend to be ahistorical in the sense that they have a tendency to ignore or sideline social and historical contexts of education, and what Tyack and Cuban (1995) would call the grammar of education. Reforms are also often short-sighted in that they are too often planned within the life cycle of a government, rather than what may be needed from the perspective of educational practitioners, and introduced at such a fast pace that new reforms are introduced before the effects of previous ones can be assessed.

Bearing these concerns in mind, we argue that progress will require realistic expectations in terms of available resources. It also needs to be achievable within the particular social, economic, historical and political conditions that schools operate. Here, the age-old debate concerning the extent to which schools are able to change the society within which they operate is relevant. It reminds us that whilst schools can achieve great things with the students they teach, this is still limited by wider social factors (Kerr et al., 2014).

So, then, what does all of this mean for the idea of giving schools greater autonomy? In what follows we suggest five ideas that can help in minimising the potential dangers and maximising its potential for sustainable educational change. These focus on: clarity of purpose, school partnerships, links with local communities, research-based development and the rethinking of national policies.

1. Ensure clarity of purpose

We have shown how the autonomous school movement is torn by tensions that pull reforms in different directions. Moving on from this rather unsatisfying situation, we argue that autonomy for autonomy's sake, as it has been promoted in some countries, is not purposeful enough. Rather, the reform purposes should be grounded in values. In saying this, we have acknowledged education reforms to be a battleground loaded with multiple pressures directed from varied interest groups. However, without greater clarity of purpose, we will keep on engaging in unsatisfyingly compromised reforms which make ambitious promises, but lack the ability to deliver them.

As we have seen, the idea of school autonomy remains elusive: it can mean many things to different people. The version we want to encourage builds on the idea that schools are social communities, the members of which can all contribute to the creation of an environment that fosters the learning of everybody involved, provided this is encouraged (Barth, 2006). Therefore, in terms of the future of autonomous schools, we would like to see more genuine attempts in developing equitable education provision for all learners. The key question here is how autonomy, and what kind of autonomy, could assist in developing such school systems.

In this respect, the autonomous school system holds the potential to move from what we have described as a 'machine-like' approach, to a professionally driven system, where the decision-making capacity is held by education practitioners, who hold more collective and individual autonomy. This would place those who understand education in local contexts at the forefront of change, consulted and participating in reform efforts. Such an approach is in line with proposals suggesting that, in order for reforms to be successful, teachers and school leaders, who are at the frontline of reforms, need to understand, accept and be motivated to enact reforms on the ground (Simola, 2015).

2. Encourage schools to collaborate

The experiences described in this book lead us to propose a way forward that policy makers could use to ensure that the impetus that comes from greater school autonomy will lead to changes that benefit all children and young people. This is based on an assumption that education systems have further potential to change themselves, provided policy makers allow the space for practitioners to make use of their expertise and creativity. In these more professional systems, the aim should be to 'move knowledge around' and, we argue, one way to do this is through enabling greater collaboration between local schools (Ainscow, 2015).

Developments such as this have implications for the various key stakeholders within education systems. In particular, teachers, especially those in senior positions, have to see themselves as having a wider responsibility for all children and young people, not just those that attend their own schools. They also have to develop patterns of working that enable them to have the flexibility to cooperate with other schools and their wider communities.

Having said all of that, it is important to stress that it is often difficult for schools to cooperate, particularly in policy contexts within which competition remains as a major driver. In addition, robust evidence as to the impact on student progress of such strategies is still rather limited (Croft, 2015). Meanwhile, there are other difficulties that need to be addressed. For example: school partnerships can lead to non-productive time, as members of staff spend periods out of school; they might simply be a fad that goes well when led by skilled and enthusiastic advocates but then fades when spread more widely; schools involved in working collaboratively may collude with one another; and some school leaders may become 'empire builders', who deter others from getting involved (Ainscow, 2015). On the other hand, our research has pointed to the sorts of factors that make school partnerships effective (Ainscow, 2015; Ainscow & Howes, 2007). Therefore, it is crucial to create conditions in which cooperation stems from the needs of schools, rather than being imposed upon them from above as yet another expected performative exercise.

3. Reach out to local communities

A pattern that emerges from our analysis of international trends is the way in which greater autonomy is reducing connections between schools and their local communities. This is worrying in the light of research which indicates that in order to break the link between disadvantaged home backgrounds and poor educational outcomes, the work of schools with families and communities is vital (Dyson & Raffo, 2007). In this respect, we have seen important examples of what can happen when what schools do is aligned in a coherent strategy with the efforts of other local players – employers, community groups, universities and public services (Ainscow, 2015). This does not necessarily mean schools doing more, but it does imply partnerships beyond the school, where partners multiply the impacts of each other's efforts. It means ensuring that all children receive effective support from their families and communities, which in turn means ensuring that schools can build on the resources offered by schools and families, and support the extension of those resources.

With this argument in mind, our colleagues Kirstin Kerr and Alan Dyson have been promoting the development of 'children's communities'. These are area-based initiatives modelled partly on the Harlem Children's Zone in the USA, but also drawing on the long history of place-based initiatives in the United Kingdom (Dyson & Kerr, 2013; Dyson et al., 2012; Kerr et al., 2014). This work is attempting to improve outcomes for children and young people in areas of disadvantage through approaches that are characterised as being 'doubly holistic'. That is to say, they seek to develop coordinated efforts to tackle the factors that disadvantage children and enhance the factors that support them, across all aspects of their lives, and across their life spans, from conception through to adulthood.

In common with many other area initiatives, children's communities involve a wide range of partners working together in a coordinated manner. Schools are key to these partnerships and may be their principal drivers. The aim is to improve a wide range of outcomes for children and young people, including but not restricted to educational outcomes, much less, narrowly conceived attainment outcomes. Health and well-being, personal and social development, thriving in the early years, and employment outcomes are as important as how well children do in school. This arises not from a down-grading of attainment so much as from a recognition that all outcomes for children and young people are inter-related, and the factors which promote or inhibit one outcome are very likely to be the factors which promote or inhibit outcomes as a whole. As a result, the focus is on the population of a local area, rather than the population of schools per se, and they may be led by non-educational organisations, such as housing associations or regeneration partnerships. Moreover, in contrast to previous initiatives, they are envisaged as being long-term, thinking in terms of a ten-year time horizon, and they are committed to acting strategically, basing their actions of a deep analysis of the area's underlying problems and possibilities.

Children's communities are simply one of a range of initiatives that are emerging internationally to link schools and other agencies in area-based action. In the absence of coordination by central government, the idea of what is known in the USA as 'collective impact' (Kania & Kramer, 2011), is beginning to gain traction. In other words, the complex problems that beset schools in common with all public services in the context of diversity, inequality and disadvantage are seen as demanding multi-strand responses at local levels.

As the capacity of local education departments to provide such coordination declines, it is local institutions, such as schools, which have to take on wider roles and offer local leadership. Unfortunately, as we have shown, moves towards greater school autonomy within policy contexts dominated by high-stakes accountability regimes are tending to discourage schools from taking on such responsibilities.

4. Use processes of research

As we have explained, moves towards greater school autonomy sometimes can lead to unanticipated outcomes, some of which are a cause for concern. Using evidence in order to monitor progress and intervene where necessary is therefore vital. This is why research of various forms has an important contribution to make in the future development of autonomous school reforms.

Here it is important to stress that we mean independent research, rather than evidence collected by politically oriented lobby groups that drive their own agendas. In particular, we look forward to further research outputs which explore the genesis, evolution and routes of this travelling policy. A more comprehensive critical review of the international flows of the autonomous school policy would greatly contribute to our understanding of these reforms. In addition to work on policy flows, comparative empirical studies reporting from autonomous schools operating in different local and national contexts hold great potential in contributing to our understanding of what these developments mean for local actors. Comparative research on how autonomous schools have turned out in different national and local contexts, and especially what impacts these schools have had on equity and social justice in these settings, should therefore be a high priority for research.

A further important role for the research community is to engage with conceptual work concerning school and teacher autonomy and innovation. Our case study of Parkside has shown that school autonomy does not automatically mean teacher autonomy, which is why we have emphasised a clear distinction between the two. Existing conceptualisations of school autonomy are mostly system-specific, focusing on, for example, charter school autonomy (e.g. Finnigan, 2007; Lubienski, 2003), or academy autonomy (Glatter, 2012; West & Bailey, 2013). Further work is required in developing these conceptualisations and testing their applicability in different contexts. Furthermore, existing work on teacher autonomy tells us that we are dealing with a multidimensional, dynamic and context-specific phenomenon

(Frostenson, 2015; Wermke & Höstfält, 2014). As such, there is a need for conceptual work that will offer tools for examining school autonomy, teacher autonomy and their interdependence across varied international contexts.

Meanwhile, at a more local level, research can contribute more directly to school and teacher development. For example, collaborative approaches aimed at pedagogy and pastoral care have led to promising developments (Cochran-Smith & Lytle, 2009; Deppeler & Huggins, 2010). Research also shows that such developments can be stimulated through an engagement with the views of different stakeholders, bringing together the expertise of practitioners, the insights of students and families, and the knowledge of academic researchers in ways that challenge taken-for-granted assumptions, not least in respect to vulnerable groups of learners (Ainscow et al., 2012). This can also stimulate new thinking, encourage experimentation with alternative ways of working and promote ethical forms of leadership (Harris et al., 2017).

The evidence needed to create this stimulation can take many forms and involves a variety of techniques. What is common is the way it creates 'interruptions' in the busy day of teachers that lead to the sharing of practices and the generation of new ways of working (Ainscow et al., 2006). Much of our own work involves us in collaborating with teams of staff within schools in order to learn more about how to make this work within current policy contexts (Ainscow et al., 2016).

5. Formulate national policies that make this possible

All of this has significant implications for national policy makers. In order to make use of the potential of autonomy and minimise the potential risks involved, they need to foster greater flexibility at the local level in order that practitioners have the space to analyse their particular circumstances and determine priorities accordingly. This means that policy makers must recognise that the details of policy implementation are not amenable to central regulation. Rather, these should be dealt with by those who are close to and, therefore, in a better position to understand local contexts: teachers and principals. For example, in the English context it has been argued that educational leadership is directed centrally, and that schools are only left with tinkering around regarding how to best perform in examinations (Gunter, 2010). Empirical accounts from academies, including Parkside, support such a claim (Kulz, 2015; Salokangas & Chapman, 2014).

There is, therefore, a crucial role here for governments. They must provide a strong sense of direction regarding the principles that are intended to steer locally led developments. Linked to this, there is a need to ensure that national accountability systems reflect these principles. This involves a recognition that, within education systems, 'what gets measured gets done' (Ainscow, 2005). So, for example, the education systems discussed in this book now collect far more statistical data on schools than ever before in order to determine their effectiveness. As we witnessed at Parkside, this narrow view of education has led to significant pressures, as those guiding national policies in many countries have become preoccupied with comparing their progress with that of other countries through systems such as PISA (Programme for International Student Assessment).

This trend to measure learning through test scores is widely recognised as a double-edged sword precisely because it is such a potent lever for change. On the one hand, data are required in order to monitor the progress of learners, evaluate the teaching and learning, review policies and processes, plan new initiatives and so on. In these senses, data can, justifiably, be seen as the life-blood of educational decision making. On the other hand, if effectiveness is evaluated on the basis of narrow, even inappropriate, performance indicators, then the impact can be deeply damaging. While appearing to promote accountability and transparency, the use of data can, in practice: conceal more than it reveals; invite misinterpretations; and, worst of all, have a perverse effect on the behaviour of professionals to teach to the test, such that their efforts to include vulnerable children are not valued and recognised by schools and policy makers.

The challenge, therefore, is to focus on a broader range of data, where progress is determined not just in terms of scores on learning outcomes, but where information on progress regarding equity is incorporated into the analyses. This suggests that great care needs to be exercised in deciding what evidence is collected and, indeed, how it is analysed and used. In other words, we need to 'measure what we value' rather than is often the case, 'valuing what we can measure' (Ainscow, 2005).

Such thinking reflects the overall approach taken in Finland, a country which is often referred to as being successful in educating the vast majority of its young people. There, schools are given considerable space to determine how they work. In this context, teachers are seen as having a key role in developing policy and creating practices that will help to foster the progress of all of their students. In this respect, they hold considerable professional autonomy in comparison to their English and American colleagues.

While making such comparisons, we do realise the differences of status and emergence of professions between Northern European and Anglo-Saxon (Anglo-American) traditions (Svensson & Evetts, 2008). In the former, professionalisation was closely related to the state and its consolidation, with the result that professionals are autonomous in a classical sense, in terms of having more freedom of choice regarding their own professional means. Whereas, in the latter tradition, professions evolved in relation to state building, having been entrusted with the above-mentioned risk handling tasks by the state. Consequently, their autonomy is defined by the state, and professionals are expected to act responsibly towards their tasks within a given framework. It is the state that judges whether the profession acts according to defined expectations, and also secures professions. This backdrop offers an explanation to the current status quo, and the differences teachers and principals experience as they work in these different traditions.

All of this reminds us that education systems have to be viewed within the history, cultures and traditions of the countries they serve. It follows that notions of school autonomy have to be understood in relation to particular contexts.

Coda

Finally, it is sad for us to report that recent developments in the academy described in this book have led to a rapid decline in its progress. Following a further series of changes in leadership and staffing, the examination results for 2015 were by far the lowest since the school was opened and a subsequent inspection led it to be designated as 'requires improvement'.

This reminds us that in contexts where there are major challenges within the locality, educational progress is hard won and easily lost. The implication is that those who give their professional lives to achieving such improvements require respect, encouragement and support. We hope that the analysis we have provided in this book and the suggestions we have made will lead those who make policy decisions to bear this in mind.

APPENDIX

Notes on inquiry methods

In these notes, we each provide a short commentary on our roles within the study reported in this book and the ways in which the information we use was generated. This leads us to reflect on issues of stance, ethics and collaboration.

Maija's involvement

My status as a researcher at Parkside allowed me to observe from a close distance the daily life of the Academy. An agreement with the school to undertake the research provided me with privileged access, which has been reported as being specifically problematic for researchers studying sponsored academies to obtain (Woods & Woods, 2009).

Although I was given a member of staff status and a desk in a shared office, and remained a regular presence in the Academy, it took a long time to gain any sense of 'insiderness'. Clearly, the staff were not used to having a researcher based in the school and it took a while for them to figure out what to make of me.

Crucial to my insider/outsider negotiations was how I positioned myself in relation to the Academy community, as well as how the community positioned me. This was a dynamic process that was negotiated and contested throughout the research. Sharing an office with high-profile assistant principals and EfFT-level actors positioned me in the eyes of some staff closely with senior leaders.

As demonstrated elsewhere in this book, my impression was that the teaching staff were rather distant from the senior leadership team and, especially, EfFT representatives. Partly because of this, the teachers tended to remain distant to me during the first months of my involvement. However, as changes in the senior leadership began to take place (explained in more detail in Chapter 6), and my office desk was moved from the senior leader's office to an office in which the ICT technical staff worked, this undoubtedly brought me closer to the teaching staff, and to some extent helped in gaining their trust. The length of my involvement and frequent presence in the school corridors, staff room, school yard, staff meetings and assemblies allowed me to establish myself as a part of the school community, and build a presence from which relationships with staff in different roles could develop.

The first year of my involvement (2010–2011) was largely exploratory in nature. During this time, I got to know members of staff and their roles in the Academy, and also began to understand how it operated. I also conducted a small-scale pilot study that helped me to refine my research plans and rehearse data collection techniques. Various methods were used to obtain data, including staff questionnaires and interviews with teachers and senior leaders. Participant observations were also conducted, as I was invited to accompany teachers and students in some of the partnership activities and meetings with other EfFT academies. In these ways, this pilot study provided me with opportunities to meet members of staff working in a variety of roles in the school, as well as in EfFT, practice interview and observation techniques, and begin developing research relationships with members of staff across the Academy. I also communicated the early research findings to senior leaders and local governors through a presentation and research reports.

The intensive data collection period was between September 2011 and June 2012, during which time I conducted interviews and participant observations. At this stage, the staff had become accustomed to my presence in the school and I knew many of them quite well. I also spent more time in the school, conducting interviews and participant observations, but also engaging in office work in my Parkside shared office.

Altogether this book draws from 35 observed lessons across different departments. These observations were conducted in order to gain a better understanding of pedagogical practices, and to obtain data that would support and enrich the teacher interview data. All the teachers who were observed were also interviewed. This follow-up interview provided me with an opportunity to reflect on the observations, and to discuss teaching methods and materials I had seen in use, as well as to further inquire about planning and assessment practices.

Other stakeholders involved in the Academy were also identified for interview, including: senior leaders, local governors, EfFT representatives and support staff. Altogether the book draws from 31 interviews I conducted with participants, some of whom were interviewed on several occasions. These interviews took the form of informal conversations, which I began by introducing myself and describing the research project, before explaining why the participant was chosen for interview. Their length varied between 20 to 80 minutes. All interviews except two were recorded, as these two participants preferred me to take notes rather than having our conversations recorded. Of all the potential participants I approached, only three rejected my invitation, including one teacher, one senior leader, as well as the new Parkside principal who stepped into the role in autumn 2012. In addition, different types of documents were consulted.

To ensure that the study was conducted ethically, a contract between the researcher, the Academy and the university was signed to secure that each party were in a similar understanding of the terms and conditions of the research. The research also received ethical clearance from the University of Manchester. However, as typical for many conducting real world research, issues rose throughout the process that required additional ethical considerations, there and then.

The participants were all approached well in advance prior to the intended research activities (one to two weeks) to give them time to consider their participation. I approached participants via email or handed them a hardcopy of a letter of information, as well as a letter of consent. These procedures ensured that the participants were made aware of the content of the research, and that their anonymity was secured throughout the process. It was also made clear that data obtained may be used in publications and that the participants could withdraw at any stage if they so wished.

Protecting the anonymity of the participants and institution was a central consideration. In order to conceal the identity of participants, only their formal titles are used in the book. The Academy and its predecessor school, the sponsoring organisation, the area in which the Academy was located, as well as other schools mentioned, are all given pseudonyms in order to protect their anonymity. The descriptive accounts of people, places and institutions were conducted in a manner to conceal the true identity of participants, schools and organisations. At times, protecting anonymity led to compromises in using data. For example, photos from the Academy, which would have been useful in describing the school, or secondary sources such as newspaper articles regarding events in the Academy or members of the Academy or EfFT staff that would have potentially revealed too much of the real identity of the school or the participants were not used. Ofsted inspection reports are mentioned, but in order to protect the anonymity of the academy they are paraphrased rather than quoted directly. Also, the decision to associate direct quotes only to participants' formal roles, rather than pseudonyms, compromises the reporting a little, as it distances the individuals from their particular positions. However, after careful consideration and in line with advice from the publisher, it was considered important to take every possible step to conceal the participants' identities.

Maintaining anonymity was an issue I also had to negotiate with the Academy during the first year of my involvement. Expectations in the school were that I would be publicly associated with the Academy and the sponsor. This was rather confusing in the early stages, as, on the one hand, the Academy requested me to badge the Academy and the sponsor on my work, whilst, on the other hand, I wanted to ensure I was conducting ethically sound research by securing the anonymity of the organisation I was studying. An illustrative example of such negotiations was that I had to ask the Academy and the sponsor in several occasions to remove information identifying myself from the sponsor website.

An agreement was made that I would report research findings back to the Academy. However, as explained in more detail in Chapter 6, due to significant changes in the school's leadership, the ways in which my presence in the Academy was perceived altered dramatically. Parallel to Duggan's (2013) description of the changing nature of a researcher – transforming from 'a critical friend', to becoming 'a critical nephew' and, finally, to becoming a marginalised 'critical orphan' – my status/presence in Parkside was reduced as a result of changes in the senior leadership. For example, during my first year in the Academy, I was requested to report the results of my pilot study to the local governing body. In my second year, I approached senior leaders regarding the reporting of the development of my research, as per my agreement. However, I was told on two separate occasions that the timing was not quite right, and that I would be approached when there was a more appropriate time. This never materialised.

In order to check the accuracy, adequacy and fairness of observations, representations and interpretations of experience with those who they concern, member checking or respondent validation was conducted. Different strategies for checking the accuracy of obtained data were used. In particular, participants were asked to read their transcribed interviews, comment on field notes, as well as figures and graphs drafted from varied sources of data. Participants' comments and assistance in drafting and redrafting the graphs in Chapter 6, which display the changes in the Academy senior leadership team, encompasses the contribution of several members of staff.

In order to check the fairness and accuracy of interpretations, I also requested participants to reflect on reported findings. Throughout the research process some participants expressed their interest in reading and commenting on the work as it progressed, and as the first drafts of findings chapters were written, sections of them or full chapters were sent to participants for further respondent validation. However, as staff turnover was quite high, and changes in senior leadership team were considerable, not all participants were able to or interested in being included in the process.

Mel's involvement

When we decided to write this book I collected together materials, publications and notes that I had accumulated about developments at Parkside Academy over many years. My direct involvement had begun during the period when the school was being planned, when I was involved in discussions with representatives of the sponsoring organisation and the then newly appointed principal.

Subsequently, my involvement involved a range of both formal and informal activities, which saw me adopting different roles for different purposes. First and foremost, I became something of a critical friend to senior colleagues in the school, particularly the Principal, visiting occasionally to discuss developments and offer occasional advice.

These relationships led me to involve the school occasionally in research projects I carried out with other colleagues at the University of Manchester, all of which were carried out in accordance with the University's ethical guidelines. Of particular note was a study carried out during the period of Labour governments between 1997 and 2010, when extensive efforts were being made to develop coordinated area strategies to address the issue of poverty in general and its impact on schools in particular. Over a period of years, we monitored these developments in three local areas, one of which was the district served by Parkside. The study looked specifically at efforts to link school efforts to improve outcomes for learners from economically disadvantaged backgrounds with community action (see Ainscow et al., 2006, 2007, 2008 for more details).

A further study involving Parkside, carried out in 2007–2008, examined the extent to which alternative patterns of practice were emerging in response to the different school governance arrangements that were being introduced in England during that period, i.e. trusts, federations, academies and all-through schools. In carrying out this work we were guided by a set of questions designed to interrogate newly emerging leadership, management and governance practices across a group of schools that embraced a variety of these new structural arrangements (see Chapman et al., 2008; Ainscow, 2015).

And then, more recently, Parkside took part in a three-year programme of collaborative action research carried out by teams of teachers in eight secondary schools in three countries (i.e. England, Portugal and Spain), with support from university researchers (see Messiou & Ainscow, 2015; Messiou et al., 2016). This project was built, in part, upon lessons that emerged from the developments in the Parkside English department reported in Chapter 4. My involvement in these developments as a research partner provided many opportunities to observe classroom activities and professional development meetings. I also spent much time discussing all of this with the students and staff involved.

All of these relationships generated a plethora of notes, publications, videos and documents that we were able to draw on in building up our account of developments in the school. Given the nature of these varied involvements, the materials are but a partial record of what happened over a period of more than ten years. Knowing what I know now, I wish that I had been systematic in recording all that happened and done more probing in developing accounts based on the perceptions of more of those involved. Nevertheless, this accumulation of information proved to be invaluable, not least in providing a historical context for the more detailed, systematic research carried out by Maija over a 12-month period.

I should add that I am conscious of the ethical challenges to my reporting evidence accumulated through my involvement in the school, sometimes as a participant observer and, on other occasions, as an observer participant. In this sense, I have reported on action within which I was, on some occasions, very much part of that action.

With these concerns in mind, Maija and I have taken careful steps to protect the interests of those involved, not least by systematically avoiding the presentation of any material that could identify the context. We have also reminded readers a number of times that the account in this book is a partial one that is highly dependent upon our interpretations of the events we report. In this context, our partnership has proved to be crucial in testing these interpretations through challenging one another, not least because we each brought to this process different backgrounds, interests, professional expertise and theoretical perspectives.

REFERENCES

ABC (2016) Independent schools initiative 'exacerbates inequality', report finds, *ABC News*, 15 August. Available at: www.abc.net.au/news/2016-08-15/wa-independent-schools-initiative-entrenches-inequality-report/7735788 [accessed: 26/01/2017].

Academies Act (2010) Available at: www.legislation.gov.uk/ukpga/2010/32/contents/data.htm [accessed: 02/07/2013].

Adams, R. (2016) Lauded academy chain to be stripped of schools after finances inquiry, *The Guardian* 28 March 2016. Available at: www.theguardian.com/education/2016/mar/28/perry-beeches-academy-chain-stripped-schools-critical-finance-report?CMP=twt_a-education_b-gdnedu [accessed: 05/08/2016].

Adonis, A. (2012) *Education, Education, Education, Reforming England's Schools*. London: Biteback Publishing.

Ainscow, M. (2005) Developing inclusive education systems: What are the levers for change? *Journal of Educational Change* 6(2): 109–124.

Ainscow, M. (2015) *Towards Self-Improving School Systems: Lessons from a City Challenge*. London: Routledge.

Ainscow, M. (2016) Collaboration as a strategy for promoting equity in education: Possibilities and barriers. *Journal of Professional Capital and Community* 1(2): 159–172.

Ainscow, M. & Howes, A. (2007) Working together to improve urban secondary schools: A study of practice in one city, *School Leadership and Management* 27: 285–300.

Ainscow, M., Booth, T., Dyson, A., with Farrell, P., Frankham, J., Gallannaugh, F., Howes, A. & Smith, R. (2006) *Improving Schools, Developing Inclusion*. London: Routledge.

Ainscow, M., Dyson, A., Goldrick, S. & West, M. (2012) *Developing Equitable Education Systems*. London: Routledge.

Ainscow, M., Dyson, A., Hopwood, L. & Thomson, S. (2016) *Primary Schools Responding to Diversity: Barriers and Possibilities*. York: Cambridge Primary Review Trust.

Ainscow, M., Goldrick, S., Kerr, K. & Miles, S. (2008) *Equity in Education: Responding to Context*. Manchester: Centre for Equity in Education.

Ainscow, M., Crow, M., Dyson, A., Goldrick, S., Kerr, K., Lennie, C., Miles, S., Muijs, D. & Skyrme, J. (2007) *Equity in Education: New Directions: The Second Annual Report of the Centre for Equity in Education, University of Manchester*. Manchester: Centre for Equity in Education.

Albert Shanker Institute (2016) *Student Attrition And 'Backfilling' At Success Academy Charter Schools: What Student Enrollment Patterns Tell Us.* Available at: www.shankerinstitute.org/blog/student-attrition-and-backfilling-success-academy-charter-schools-what-student-enrollment [accessed: 12/08/2016].

Allen R. & Burgess, S. (2012) *How Should We Treat Under-Performing Schools? A Regression Discontinuity Analysis of School Inspections in England.* Bristol: The Centre for Market and Public Organisation.

Au, W. (2009) *Unequal by Design: High-Stakes Testing and the Standardization of Inequality.* London: Routledge.

Bailyn, L. (1985) Autonomy in the industrial R&D lab, *Human Resource Management,* 24(2): 129–146.

Ball, S.J. (2003) *Class Strategies and the Education Market.* London, UK: Routledge.

Ball, S.J. & Junemann, C. (2012) *Networks, New Governance and Education.* Bristol: Policy Press.

Bamfield, L. (2012) Setting schools free? Reflections on the freedom of autonomous schools, *Philosophy of Education,* 2012: 318–326.

Barth, R.S. (2006) Improving professional practice: Improving relationships within the schoolhouse, *Educational Leadership* 63(6): 8–13.

Bartolome, L.I. (1994) Beyond the methods fetish: Towards a humanising pedagogy, *Harvard Education Review* 54(2): 173–194.

Beck, J. (2009) Appropriating professionalism: Restructuring the official knowledge base of England's 'modernised' teaching profession, *British Journal of Sociology of Education,* 30(1): 3–14.

Beckett, F. (2007) *The Great City Academy Fraud.* London: Continuum.

Benn, M. (2012) *School Wars: The Battle for Britain's Education.* London: Verso.

Berends, M. (2015) Sociology and school choice: What we know after two decades of charter schools, *Annual Review of Sociology* 41: 159–180.

Betts, J.R. & Tang, Y.E. (2011) *The Effect of Charter Schools on Student Achievement: A Meta-Analysis of the Literature.* Seattle: Center on Reinventing Public Education, University of Washington.

Bidwell, C. (1965) The school as formal organisation, in March, J. (ed.) *Handbook of Organisations* (pp. 973–1002). Chicago, IL: Rand McNally.

Blackstone, B. (2000) Fresh Start Schools, House of Lords Hansard, 18 May. Available at: https://publications.parliament.uk/pa/ld199900/ldhansrd/vo000518/text/00518w03.htm#00518w03_spnew3 [accessed: 20/01/2016].

Blunkett, D. (1999) Excellence for the many: CBI President's reception address by the Rt. Hon. David Blunkett, 19 July 1999. London: DfEE.

Blunkett, D. (2000) *Blunkett sets out radical new agenda for inner city school diversity and improvement'.* Press notice, 15 March. London: DCSF. Available at: www.dcsf.gov.uk/pns/DisplayPN.cgi?pn_id=2000_0106 [accessed: 2/10/2009]

Braun, A., Maguire, M. & Ball, S.J. (2010) Policy enactments in the UK secondary school: Examining policy, practice and school positioning, *Journal of Education Policy,* 25(4): 547–560.

Braun, A., Ball, S., Maguire, M. & Hoskins, K. (2011) Taking context seriously: Towards explaining policy enactments in the secondary school, *Discourse: Studies in the Cultural Politics of Education,* 32(4): 585–596.

Buckley, J. & Schneider, M. (2007) *Charter Schools – Hope or Hype?* Princeton, NJ: Princeton University Press.

Bulkley, K.E. (2005) Losing voice? Educational management organizations and charter schools' educational programs, *Education and Urban Society* 37(2): 204–234.

Bunar, N. (2010) Choosing for quality or inequality – Current perspectives on the implementation of school choice policy in Sweden, *Journal of Education Policy*, 25(1): 1–18.

Caldwell, B.J. (2005) *School-Based Management*. No. 3 in the Education Policy Series of the International Academy of Education. Paris: International Institute of Educational Planning (IIEP), UNESCO.

Caldwell, B.J. (2016) Impact of school autonomy on student achievement: Cases from Australia, *International Journal of Educational Management*, 30(7): 1171–1187

Cameron, D. (2011) *Welcome to the Free Schools Conference*, speech delivered at free schools conference. Available at: www.education.gov.uk/schools/leadership/typesofschools/freeschools/conference/b0074146/speeches [accessed: 19/07/2016].

Carrasco, A., Falabella, A. & Mendoza, M. (2015) School choice in Chile as a soociocultural practice. In Seppänen, P., Carrasco, A., Kalalahti, M. Rinne, R. & Simola, H. (eds.) *Contrasting Dynamics in Education Politics of Extremes: School Choice in Finland and Chile* (pp. 245–266). Rotterdam, The Netherlands: Sense Publishers.

Chapman, C., Ainscow, M., Bragg, J., Gunter, H., Mongon, D., Muijs, D. & West, M. (2008) *New Models of School Leadership: Emerging Patterns of Practice*. Nottingham: National College of School Leadership.

Clark, L. (2012) The £320,000 superhead: State-funded academy chief's salary soars by 31%. . . and dozens more are also paid six figures, *The Daily Mail*, 8 December. Available at: www.dailymail.co.uk/news/article-2244916/The-320-000-superhead-State-funded-academy-chiefs-salary-soars-31---dozens-paid-figures.html [accessed: 04/05/2013].

Clifton J. & Cook, W. (2013) The achievement gap in context. In Clifton, J. (ed.) *Excellence and Equity: Tackling Educational Disadvantage in English Secondary Schools* (pp. 17–28). London: Institute for Public Policy Research.

Cochran-Smith, M. & Lytle, S.L. (2009) *Inquiry as Stance: Practitioner Research for the Next Generation*. New York: Teachers College Press.

The Conservative Party (2007) *Raising the Bar, Closing the Gap*. London: The Conservative Party.

The Conservative Party (2010) *Invitation to Join the Government of Britain: The Conservative Manifesto 2010*. London: The Conservative Party.

Courtney, S. (2015) Corporatised leadership in English schools, *Journal of Educational Administration and History*, 47(3): 214–231.

Crawford, J.R. (2001) Teacher autonomy and accountability in charter schools, *Education and Urban Society*, 33(2): 186–200.

CREDO (2009) *Multiple Choice: Charter School Performance in 16 States*. Stanford, CA: Center for Research on Education Outcomes.

Cribb, A. & Gewirtz, S. (2007) Unpacking autonomy and control in education: Some conceptual and normative groundwork for a comparative analysis, *European Educational Research Journal*, 6(3): 203–213.

Croft, J. (2015) *Collaborative Overreach: Why Collaboration Probably Isn't Key to the Next Phase of School Reform. Research Report 7*. London: Centre for the Study of Market Reform of Education.

Cuban, L. & Shipps, D. (2000) *Reconstructing the Common Good in Education: Coping with Intractable American Dilemmas*. Stanford, CA: Stanford University Press.

Curtis, A., Exley, S., Sasia, A., Tough, S. & Whitty, G. (2008) *The Academies Programme: Progress, Problems and Possibilities. A Report for the Sutton Trust*. London: The Sutton Trust.

Curtis, P. (2008) Government launches inquiry into academy funds allegations, *The Guardian*, 28 November, p. 11.

Dale, R. (1999) Specifying globalization effects on national policy: A focus on the mechanisms, *Journal of Education Policy*, 14(1): 1–17.

Department of Education, Western Australia (2013) *Evaluation of Independent Public Schools*. Available at: www.education.wa.edu.au/home/detcms/public-education/content/web-references/i/independent-public-schools--evaluation-of-the-ips-initiative.en?title=Independent+Public+Schools+-+Evaluation+of+the+IPS+initiative&skip=false&launch=true [accessed: 12/08/2016].

Department of Education, Western Australia (2016) *Independent Public Schools*. Available at: www.education.wa.edu.au/home/detcms/navigation/about-us/programs-and-initiatives/independent-public-schools/?page=2#toc2 [accessed: 12/08/2016].

Deppeler, J. & Huggins, D. (2010) Collaboration and equitable reform in Australian schools. In Slater, J.J. & Ravid, R. (eds.) *Collaboration in Education* (pp. 126–134). New York: Routledge.

DfE (2010) *The Importance of Teaching: The Schools White Paper*. Available at: www.gov.uk/government/uploads/system/uploads/attachment_data/file/175429/CM-7980.pdf [accessed 10/03/2015].

DfE (2015) *2010 To 2015 Government Policy: Education of Disadvantaged Children*. Available at: www.gov.uk/government/publications/2010-to-2015-government-policy-education-of-disadvantaged-children/2010-to-2015-government-policy-education-of-disadvantaged-children#appendix-2-pupil-premium [accessed 06/09/2015].

DfE (2016) *Schools Revenue Funding 2016 to 2017 Operational Guide Version 2*. Available at: www.gov.uk/government/publications [accessed: 10/12/2016].

DfEE (2001) *Schools: Building on Success: Raising Standards, Promoting Diversity, Achieving Results*. Government Green Paper. Available at: www.archive.official-documents.co.uk/document/cm50/5050/5050.pdf [accessed: 17/05/2013].

DfES (2002) *Investment for Reform*. Available at: www.education.gov.uk/publications/eOrderingDownload/Investment_for_Reform.pdf [accessed: 28/01/2017].

Dickens, J. (2016) The key findings: Do academies get better results than local authority schools?, *Schools Week*, 12 April 2016.

Dinham, S. (2015) The worst of both worlds: How the US and UK are influencing education in Australia, *Education Policy Analysis Archives*, 23(49): 1–15.

Duggan, J. (2013) *A Local Authority Initiative to Foster a Collaborative Culture between Organisations Working with Children and Young Persons*. PhD dissertation, School of Education, University of Manchester.

Duncan, G.J. & Murnane, R.J. (2011) The American dream, then and now [introduction]. In Duncan, G.J. & Murnane, R.J. (eds.) *Whither Opportunity? Rising Inequality, Schools, and Children's Life Chances* (pp. 3–26). New York: Russell Sage Foundation and the Spencer Foundation.

Dynarski, S.M., Kane, T.J., Pathak, P.A. & Walters, C.R. (2010) Inputs and impacts in charter schools: KIPP Lynn, *American Economic Review: Papers and Proceedings* 100(2): 239–243.

Dyson, A. & Kerr, K. (2013) *Developing Children's Zones for England: What's the Evidence?* London: Save the Children.

Dyson, A. & Raffo, C. (2007) Education and disadvantage: The role of community-oriented schools, *Oxford Review of Education*, 33(3): 297–314.

Dyson, A., Kerr, K., Raffo, C. & Wigelsworth, M. (2012) *Developing Children's Zones for England*. London: Save the Children.

Erixon-Arreman, I. & Holm, A. (2011) Schools as 'edu-business': Four 'serious players' in the Swedish upper secondary school market, *Education Inquiry*, 2(4): 637–657.

Exley, S. & Ball, S. (2011) Something old, something new . . . understanding conservative education policy. In Bochel, H. (ed.) *The Conservative Party and Social Policy* (pp. 97–118). Bristol: Policy Press.

Eyles, A. & Machin, S. (2015) *Academy Schools and Their Introduction to English Education*. London: Centre for Education Economics.

Finn, C., Manno, B. & Vanourek, G. (2000) *Charter Schools in Action: Renewing Public Education*. Princeton, NJ: Princeton University Press.

Finnigan, K.S. (2007) Charter school autonomy: The mismatch between theory and practice, *Educational Policy*, 21(3): 503–526.

Fischer, T. (2012) The American revolution in English schools, Available at: www.newstatesman.com/blogs/education/2012/06/americanrevolution-english-schools [accessed: 10/02/2015].

Frostenson, M. (2015) Three forms of professional autonomy: De-professionalisation of teachers in a new light, *Nordic Journal of Studies in Educational Policy*, 2: 20–29.

Furgeson, J., Gill, B., Haimson, J., Killewald, A., McCullough, M., Nichols-Barrer, I., Bing-ru, T. & Verbitsky-Savitz, N. (2012) *The National Study of Charter Management Organisation Effectiveness*. Washington, DC: Mathematica Policy Research.

Garner, R. (2013) Academy chain to break Government pay ceiling in bid to lure 'best teachers', *The Independent*, 18 August. Available at: www.independent.co.uk/news/education/education-news/academychain-to-break-government-pay-ceiling-in-bid-to-lure-best-teachers-8773443.html [accessed: 19/08/2013].

Gawlik, M.A. (2007) Beyond the charter schoolhouse door: Teacher-perceived autonomy, *Education and Urban Society*, 39(4): 524–553.

Geske, T., Davis, D. & Hingle, P. (1997) Charter schools: A viable public school choice option?, *Economics of Education Review*, 6(1): 15–23.

Gewirtz, S. & Cribb, A. (2009) *Understanding Education: A Sociological Perspective*. Cambridge, UK: Polity Press.

Glatter, R. (2012) Persistent preoccupations: The rise and rise of school autonomy and accountability in England, *Educational Management Administration & Leadership*, 40(5): 559–575.

Gobby, B. (2013) Principal self-government and subjectification: The exercise of principal autonomy in the Western Australian Independent public schools programme, *Critical Studies in Education*, 54(3): 273–285.

Goddard, V. (2016) Academies guilty of the most blatant gaming of all: A school place only for the brightest, *The Guardian,* 29 March. Available at: www.theguardian.com/education/2016/mar/29/academy-school-place-educating-essex-special-needs?CMP=share_btn_tw [accessed: 04/04/2016].

Goldring, E., Mavrogordato, M. (2011) International perspectives on academies: Lessons learned from charter schools and choice options around the globe. In Gunter, H (ed.) *The State and Education Policy: The Academies Programme* (pp. 185–198). London: Continuum.

Goodman, R. & Burton, D. (2012) The Academies Programme: An education revolution?, *Educational Futures*, 4(3): 58–78.

Gorard, S. (2014) The link between Academies in England, pupil outcomes and local patterns of socio-economic segregation between schools, *Research Papers in Education*, 29(3): 268–284.

Gove, M. (2012) Michael Gove speaks to the Schools Network, 11 January 2012, Available at: www.gov.uk/government/speeches/michael-gove-speaks-to-the-schools-network [accessed: 21/07/2015].

Gunter, H. (2011) Introduction: Contested education reform. In Gunter, H. (ed.) *The State and Education Policy: The Academies Programme* (pp. 1–18). London: Continuum.

Gunter, H. & McGinity, R. (2014) The politics of the Academies Programme: Natality and pluralism in education policy-making, *Research Papers in Education*, 29(3): 300–314.

Haeffele-Balch, S. & Boettke, P. (2016) Disrupt the education industry: Charter schools and private schools can do for education what Uber is doing for transportation. *US News*, 11 January. Available at: www.usnews.com/opinion/economic-intelligence/articles/2016-01-11/the-education-industry-needs-to-be-disrupted-by-an-uber [accessed: 02/02/2017].

Hammersley, M. (2013) *What is Qualitative Research?* London: Continuum/Bloomsbury.

Hanushek, E.A., Link, S. & Woessmann, L (2012) Does school autonomy make sense everywhere? Panel estimates from PISA, *Journal of Development Economics* 104(2013): 212–232.

Harris, J., Carrington, S. & Ainscow, M. with Comber, B, Ehrich, L., Klenowski, V., Smeed, J. & Spina, J. (2017) *Promoting Equity in Schools: Collaboration, Inquiry and Ethical Leadership.* London: Routledge, in press.

Hart, S., Dixon, A., Drummond, M.J. & McIntyre, D. (2004) *Learning Without Limits.* Maidenhead: Open University Press.

Hill, P.T., Angel, L. & Christensen, J. (2006) Charter school achievement studies, *Education,* 1(1): 139–150.

Hill, R. (2008) *Achieving More Together: Adding Value through Partnership.* Leicester: ASCL.

Hill, R. (2010) Chain reactions: A thinkpiece on the development of chains of schools in the English school system, national challenge. Available at: www.nationalcollege.org.uk/doc info?id=63281&filename=chainreactions.pdf [accessed: 20/03/2011].

Hill, R., Dunford, J., Parish, N., Rea, S. & Sandals, L. (2012) *The Growth of Academy Chains: Implications for Leaders and Leadership.* Nottingham: National College for School Leadership. Available at: www.thegovernor.org.uk/freedownloads/acadamies/the-growth-ofacademy-chains.pdf [accessed: 20/06/2013].

Hodgson, N. (2012) 'The only answer is innovation . . .' Europe, policy and the Big Society, *Journal of Philosophy of Education,* 46(4): 537–545.

House of Commons Education Committee (2015) *Academies and Free Schools: Fourth Report of Session 2014.* London: The Stationery Office Limited

Hoxby, C. & Murarka, S. (2008) Methods of assessing the achievement of students in charter schools. In Berends, M., Springer M. & Walberg H. (eds.) *Charter School Outcomes* (pp. 7–38). New York: Lawrence Erlbaum Associates.

Hoxby, C. & Rockoff, J. (2004) *The Impact of Charter Schools on Student Achievement: A Study of Students Who Attend Schools Chartered by the Chicago Charter School Foundation.* Working Paper, Harvard University. Available at: www0.gsb.columbia.edu/faculty/jrockoff/hoxbyrockoffcharters.pdf [accessed: 27/06/2011].

Hoxby, C.M. (2002) *The Cost of Accountability.* National Bureau of Economic Research Working Paper. Cambridge, MA: National Bureau of Economic Research. Available at: www.nber.org/papers/w8855 [accessed: 17/08/2016].

Husbands, C., Gilbert, C., Francis, B. & Wigdortz, B. (2013) *Unleashing Greatness: Getting the Best from an Academised System. The Report of the Academies Commission.* London: RSA/Pearson.

Ingersoll, R.M. (1996) Teachers' decision-making power and school conflict, *Sociology of Education* 69(2): 159–176.

Ingersoll, R.M. (2003) *Who Controls Teachers' Work? Power and Accountability in America's Schools.* Cambridge, MA: Harvard University Press.

Jacobs, J. (2015) Disrupting the education monopoly: A conversation with Reed Hastings, *Education Next* 15(1). Available at: http://educationnext.org/disrupting-the-education-monopoly-reed-hastings-interview/ [accessed: 02/02/2017].

Jha, T. & Buckingham, J. (2015) *Free to Choose Charter Schools: How Charter and For-Profit Schools can Boost Public Education.* St. Leonards, NSW: The Centre for Independent Studies.

Johnson, S.M. & Landman, J. (2000) 'Sometimes bureaucracy has its charms': The working conditions of teachers in deregulated schools, *Teachers College Record*, 102(1): 85–124.

Kahlenberg, R.D. & Potter, H. (2014) *A Smarter Charter: Finding What Works for Charter Schools and Public Education.* New York: Teachers College Press.

Kania, J. & Kramer, M. (2011) Collective impact, *Stanford Social Innovation Review* (Winter): 36–41.

Kauko, J. & Salokangas, M. (2015) The evaluation and steering of English academy schools through inspection and examinations: National visions and local practices, *British Educational Research Journal*, 41(6): 1108–1124.

Kenway, J. (2013) Challenging inequality in Australian schools: Gonski and beyond, *Discourse: Studies in the Cultural Politics of Education*, 34(2): 286–308.

Kerr, K., Dyson, A. & Raffo, C. (2014) *Education, Disadvantage and Place: Making the Local Matter.* Bristol: Policy Press.

Kosunen, S. (2014) Reputation and parental logics of action in local school choice space in Finland, *Journal of Education Policy* 29(4): 443–466.

Kulz, C. (2015) Heroic heads, mobility mythologies and the power of ambiguity, *British Journal of Sociology of Education* 38(2): 1–20.

Ladd, H.F. & Fiske, E.B. (2016) *England Confronts the Limits of School Autonomy.* Working Paper 232: National Center for the Study of Privatization in Education, Teachers College, Columbia University.

Lake, R., Dusseault, B., Bowen, M., Demeritt, A. & Hill, P. (2010) *The National Study of Charter Management Organization (CMO) Effectiveness: Report on Interim Findings.* Seattle, WA: Center on Reinventing Public Education.

Lawn, M. & Grek, S. (2012) *Europeanizing Education: Governing a New Policy Space.* Oxford: Symposium Books.

Lewis, C., Perry, R. & Murata, A. (2006) How should research contribute to instructional improvement? The case of lesson study, *Educational Researcher* 35(3): 3–14.

Lingard, B. & Lewis, S. (2016) Globalisation of the Anglo-American approach to topdown, test based educational accountability. In G.T.L. Brown & L.R. Harris (eds.) *Handbook of Human and Social Conditions in Assessment* (pp. 387–403). New York: Routledge.

Lipman, P. (2004) *High Stakes Education.* New York: Routledge.

Lortie, D. (1969) The balance of control and autonomy in elementary school teaching. In Etzioni, A. (ed.) *The Semi-Professions and their Organisations: Teachers, Nurses and Social Workers* (pp. 1–53). New York: Free Press

Lubienski, C. (2003) Innovation in education markets: Theory and evidence on the impact of competition and choice in Charter Schools, *American Education Research Journal*, 40(2): 395–443.

Lupton, R. (2003) *Neighbourhood Effects: Can We Measure Them and Does It Matter?* London: LSE.

Machin, S. (2012) Academies: Old research is being wrongly used to validate them, *The Guardian*, 9 April. Available at: https://www.theguardian.com/ education/2012/apr/09/ labour- academies-research-coalition- programme [accessed: 20/08/2016].

Machin, S. & Venoit, J. (2011) *Changing School Autonomy: Academy Schools and their Introduction to England's Education.* London: Centre for the Economics of Education, London School of Economics.

Malloy, C.L. & Wohlstetter, P. (2003) Working conditions in charter schools: What's the appeal for teachers? *Education and Urban Society*, 35(2): 219–241.

Manno, B.V., Chester E.F. & Vanourek, G. (2000) Charter School Accountability: Problems and Prospects, *Educational Policy,* 14(4): 473–493

Mansell, W. (2016) *Academies: Autonomy, Accountability, Quality and Evidence.* York: Cambridge Primary Review Trust.

Marklund, S. (1989) *Skolsverige 1950–1975*. Rullande reform. Stockholm: Utbildningsförlaget.

Messiou, K. & Ainscow, M. (2015) Engaging with the views of students: A catalyst for powerful teacher development? *Teacher and Teacher Education Teaching and Teacher Education* 51(2): 246–255.

Messiou, K., Ainscow, M., Echeita, G., Goldrick, S., Hope, M., Paes, I. et al. (2016) Learning from differences: A strategy for teacher development in respect to student diversity, *School Effectiveness and School Improvement*, 27(1): 45–61.

Meyland-Smith, D. & Evans, N. (2009) *A Guide to School Choice Reforms*. London: Policy Exchange.

Mills, P. (2013) Postal privatisation and the zero-hour workers' nightmare, *The Guardian*, 29 April. Available at: www.theguardian.com/commentisfree/2013/apr/29/postal-privatisationzero-hour-workers [accessed: 07/06/2013].

Mølstad, C.E. (2015) State-based curriculum-making: approaches to local curriculum work in Norway and Finland, *Journal of Curriculum Studies* 47(4): 441–461.

Morris, D. (2011) Building a big society: Will charity's creeping reach generate a new paradigm for state schools?, *Journal of Social Welfare and Family Law*, 33(3): 209–226.

Muijs, D. & Chapman, C. (2009) Accountability for improvement: Rhetoric or reality? In Chapman, C. & Gunter, H. (eds.) *Radical Reforms: Perspectives on an Era of Educational Change* (pp. 28–41). London: Routledge.

National Alliance for Public Charter Schools (2016) *Charter School Data Dashboard*. Available at: http://dashboard2.publiccharters.org/National/ (accessed: 10/08/2016)

National Audit Office (2013) *Establishing Free Schools*. London: National Audit Office.

National Audit Office (2016) *The Report of the Controller and Auditor General on the Department for Education's 2014–15 Financial Statements*. Available at: www.nao.org.uk/wp-content/uploads/2016/04/The-Report-of-the-Comptroller-and-Auditor-General-on-the-Department-for-Educations-2014-15-financial-statement.pdf [accessed: 04/08/2016].

Ni, Y. (2012) Teacher working conditions in charter schools and traditional public schools: A comparative study, *Teachers College Record* 14(3): 1–26.

Nicolaidou, M. & Ainscow, M. (2006) The experience of failure in urban primary schools. In Ainscow, M. & West, M. (eds.) *Improving Urban Schools: Leadership and Collaboration* (pp. 13–23). Maidenhead: Open University Press.

Northen, S. (2011) Too many senior staff in academies? *The Guardian*, 14 November. Available at: www.theguardian.com/education/2011/nov/14/academies-seniormanagement-salaries-taxpayers [accessed: 05/05/2013].

Oberfield, Z.W. (2016) A bargain half fulfilled: Teacher autonomy and accountability in traditional public schools and public charter schools, *American Educational Research Journal*, 53(2): 296–323.

OECD (2007) *No more failures: ten steps to equity in education*. Paris: OECD Publishing.

OECD (2012) *Equity and Quality in Education: Supporting Disadvantaged Students and Schools*. Paris: OECD Publishing.

Ofsted (2013) *The Report of Her Majesty's Chief Inspector of Education, Children's Services and Skills*. Available at: www.ofsted.gov.uk [accessed: 20/08/2017].

Olmedo, A. (2013) From England with love. . . ARK, heterarchies and global 'philanthropic governance', *Journal of Education Policy*, 29(5): 575–597.

O'Shaughnessy, J. (2012) *Competition Meets Collaboration: Helping School Chains Address England's Long Tail of Educational Failure*. London: Policy Exchange.

Östh, J., Andersson, E. & Malmberg B. (2013) School choice and increasing performance difference: A counterfactual approach, *Urban Studies* 50(2): 407–425.

Ozga, J. & Jones, R. (2006) Travelling and embedded policy: The case of knowledge transfer, *Journal of Education Policy*, 21(1): 1–17.

Parliament of Western Australia (2016) *IPS Report Card: The Report of the Inquiry into the Independent Public Schools Initiative*. Perth: Parliament of Western Australia.

Paton, G. (2012) Academy heads 'earning bigger salaries', NAO warns, *The Telegraph*, 22 November. Available at: www.telegraph.co.uk/education/educationnews/9694251/Academyheads-earning-bigger-salaries-NAO-warns.html [accessed: 05/05/2013].

Popham, W.J. (2001) *The Truth About Testing*. Alexander, VA: ASCD.

Preston, C., Goldring, E., Berends, M. & Cannata, M. (2012) School innovation in district context: Comparing traditional public schools and charter schools, *Economics of Education Review*, 31(2): 318–330.

PricewaterhouseCoopers (2008) *Academies Evaluation Fifth Annual Report*. Annesley: DCSF Publications.

Raymond, M. (2009) *Multiple Choice: Charter School Performance in 16 States*. Stanford, CA: Center for Research on Education Outcomes, Stanford University.

Reardon, S.F. (2009) Measures of ordinal segregation, *Research on Economic Inequality* 17: 129–155.

Reid, A. (2016) The use and abuse of research in the public domain, *The Australian Educational Researcher*, 43(1):75–91

Renzulli, L., Parrott, H. & Beattie, I. (2011) Racial mismatch and school type: Teacher satisfaction and retention in charter and traditional public schools, *Sociology of Education*, 84(1): 23–48.

Roch, C.H. & Sai, N. (2015) Nonprofit, for-profit, or stand-alone? How management organizations influence the working conditions in charter schools, *Social Science Quarterly*, 96(5): 1380–1395.

Rönnberg, L. (2015) Marketization on export: Representations of the Swedish free school model in English media, *European Educational Research Journal*, 14(6): 549–565.

Russell, A. & Vinsel, L. (2016) Hail the maintainers, *AEON*. Available at: https://aeon.co/essays/innovation-is-overvalued-maintenance-often-matters-more [accessed: 01/02/2017].

Sainsbury, D. (1996) *Gender, Equality and Welfare States*. Cambridge, UK: Cambridge University Press.

Salokangas, M. & Chapman, C. (2014) Exploring governance in two chains of academy schools: A comparative case study, *Educational Management Administration & Leadership*, 42(3): 372–386.

Salokangas, M., Chapman, C. & Beach, D. (2016) Independent state-funded schools and system change: Addressing educational equity? In Beach, D. & Dyson, A. (eds.) *Developing Equity in Cold Climates* (pp. 193–208). London: Tufnell Press.

Schildkamp, K., Ehren, M. & Lai, M.K. (2012) Editorial article for the special issue on data-based decision making around the world: From policy to practice to results, *School Effectiveness and School Improvement*, 23(2): 123–131.

Sellgren, K. (2016) Academy accounts 'uncertain', warns spending watchdog, *BBC*. Available at: www.bbc.com/news/education-36090672 [accessed: 05/08/2016].

Shepherd, J. (2010) Swedish-style 'free schools won't improve standards', *The Guardian*. Available at: www.theguardian.com/education/2010/feb/09/swedish-style-schools-wont-raise-standards [accessed: 30/08/2016].

Simola, H. (2015) *Koulutusihmeen paradoksit. Esseitä suomalaisesta koulutuspolitiikasta*. Tampere: Vastapaino.

Simola, H., Rinne, R., Varjo, J. & Kauko, J. (2013) The paradox of the education race: How to win the ranking game by sailing to headwind, *Journal of Education Policy*, 28(5): 612–633.

Skolverket (2010) Gymnasieskolan–Personal–Riksnivå. Table 4 A. Available at: www.skolverket.se/sb/d/1719/a/15474 [accessed: 12/01/2012].

Steiner-Khamsi, G. & Waldow, F. (eds.) (2012) *World Yearbook of Education 2012: Policy Borrowing and Lending in Education.* London: Routledge.

Stevenson, H. (2016) Challenging school reform from below: Is leadership the missing link in mobilization theory?, *Leadership and Policy in Schools*, 15(1): 67–90.

Storey, A. (2009) How fares the 'New Professionalism' in schools? Findings from the 'State of the Nation' project, *Curriculum Journal* 20(2): 121–138.

Suggett, D. (2015) School autonomy: Necessary but not sufficient, *Evidence Base*, 2015(1): 1–33.

Svensson, L.G. & Evetts, J. (2008) Introduction. In Svensson, L.G. & Evetts, J. (eds.) *Sociology of Professions. Continental and Anglo-Saxon Traditions* (pp. 9–32). Göteborg: Daidalos.

Tomlinson, S. (2005) Race, ethnicity and education under New Labour. *Oxford Review of Education* 31(1): 153–171.

Torres, A.C. (2014) Is this work sustainable? Teacher turnover and perceptions of workload in charter management organizations, *Urban Education* 51(8): 1–24.

Trimmer, K. (2013) Independent public schools: A move to increased autonomy and devolution of decision-making in Western Australian public schools, *Childhood Education*, 89(3): 178–184,

Tyack, D.B. & Cuban, L. (1995) *Tinkering toward Utopia: A Century of Public School Reform.* Cambridge, MA: Harvard University Press.

U.S. Department of Education, National Center for Education Statistics. (2006) The condition of education 2006 Indicator 5: Racial/ethnic distribution of public school students (NCES 2006–071). Washington, DC: U.S. Government Printing Office.

Valenzuela, A. (2005) *Leaving Children Behind: How 'Texas-style' Accountability Fails Latino Youth.* Albany: State University of New York.

van Zanten, A. (2009) Competitive arenas and schools' logics of action: A European comparison. *Compare: A Journal of Comparative and International Education* 39(1): 85–98.

Verger, A., Lubienski, C. & Steiner-Khamsi, G. (2016) The emergence and structuring of the global education industry: Towards an analytical framework. In Verger, A., Lubienski, C. & Steiner-Khamsi, G. (eds.) *World Yearbook of Education 2016: The Global Education Industry* (pp. 3–24). New York: Routledge.

Villegas-Reimers, E. (2003) *Teacher Professional Development: An International Review of the Literature.* UNESCO: Institute for Educational Planning.

Waslander, S., Pater, C. & van der Weide, M. (2010) Markets in education: An analytical review of empirical research on market mechanisms in education. *OECD Education Working Papers,* 52. Paris: OECD.

Wermke, W. & Höstfält, G. (2014) Contextualizing teacher autonomy in time and space: A model for comparing various forms of governing the teaching profession, *Journal of Curriculum Studies*, 46(1): 58–80.

West, A. (2014) Academies in England and independent schools (fristående skolor) in Sweden: Policy, privatisation, access and segregation, *Research Papers in Education*, 29(3): 330–350.

West, A. & Bailey, W. (2013) The development of the Academies Programme: 'Privatising' school-based education in England 1986–2013, *British Journal of Educational Studies,* 61(2): 137–159.

Whitty, G. (2007) Teacher professionalism in new times, *Journal of In-Service Education*, 26(2): 281–295.

Whitty, G. (2010) Marketization and post-marketization in education. In Hargreaves, A., Lieberman, A., Fullan, M. & Hopkins, D. (eds.) *Second International Handbook of Educational Change* (pp. 405–413). Dordrecht: Springer.

Wiborg, S. (2010a) Learning lessons from the Swedish model, *Forum*, 52(2): 279–284.

Wiborg, S. (2010b) The Swedish Free Schools. Do they work? *Lakes Research*, Report 18.

Wiborg, S. (2015) Privatizing education: Free school policy in Sweden and England, *Comparative Education Review*, 59(3): 473–497.

Wilches, J. (2007) Teacher autonomy: A critical review of the research and concept beyond applied linguistics, *Íkala, revista de lenguaje y cultura* 12(1), 245–275.

Wilkins, A. (2016) Rethinking Neoliberalism: Multi-academy Trusts and State-sanctioned Monopoly in British Education. Conference paper presented at the European Network of Neoliberal Education Policy, University of Roehampton 8–9 December 2016.

Wills, J.S. & Sandholtz, J.H. (2009) Constrained professionalism: Dilemmas of teaching in the face of test-based accountability, *Teachers College Record*, 111(4): 1065–1114.

Wermke W. & Salokangas, M. (in press) *Investigating Teacher Autonomy Empirically: Conceptual Considerations*.

Wohlstetter, P., Smith, J. and Farrell, C.C. (2013) *Choices and Challenges: Charter School Performance in Perspective*. Cambridge MA: Harvard Education Press.

Wohlstetter, P., Wenning, R. & Briggs, K. (1995) Charter schools in the United States: The question of autonomy, *Educational Policy*, 9: 331–358.

Wohlstetter, P., Smith, J. & Farrell, C.C. (2015). The choices and challenges of charter schools, revisited. *Journal of School Choice*, 9(1): 115–38.

Woods, G.J. & Woods, P.A. (2009) Editorial, *Management in Education* 23(3): 94–95.

INDEX

References to figures are shown in *italics*